DK

The Only Guides You'll Ever Need!

THIS SERIES IS YOUR TRUSTED GUIDE through all of life's stages and situations. Want to learn how to surf the Internet or care for your new dog? Or maybe you'd like to become a wine connoisseur or an expert gardener? The solution is simple: Just pick up a K.I.S.S. Guide and turn to the first page.

Expert authors will walk you through the subject from start to finish, using simple blocks of knowledge to build your skills one step at a time. Build upon these learning blocks and by the end of the book, you'll be an expert yourself! Or, if you are familiar with the topic but want to learn more, it's easy to dive in and pick up where you left off.

The K.I.S.S. Guides deliver what they promise: simple access to all the information you'll need on one subject. Other titles you might want to check out include: Playing Guitar, Living With a Dog, the Internet, Yoga, Sailing, Gambling, and many more.

GUIDE TO

Home Improvement

MARTIN PRESTON

Foreword by Amy Wynn Pastor
Cable Television's Favorite Carpenter

A Dorling Kindersley Book

LONDON, NEW YORK,
MUNICH, MELBOURNE, DELHI

DK Publishing Inc.
US Consultants Eve P. Steinberg, John T. Cunningham
Series Editor Jennifer Williams
Editorial Director Chuck Wills

Dorling Kindersley Limited
Project Editor Caroline Hunt
Managing Editor Maxine Lewis
Managing Art Editor Heather McCarry

Production Heather Hughes
Category Publisher Mary Thompson

Created and produced for Dorling Kindersley by
M-Press Publishing Ltd,
61-63, Churchfield Road, Acton, London W3 6AY

The M-Press team
Rob Bennett, Ieva Carroll, Jeff Carroll, Judy Fovargue,
Nicki Gault, Christine Heilman, Ed Herridge, Nich Hills,
Edward Horton, David Preston, Mike Trier,
Jerry Udall, and Darius Valoutis

First published in the United States by
DK Publishing, Inc.
375 Hudson Street
New York, NY 10014

Library of Congress Cataloging-in-Publication Data

Preston, Martin.
  K.I.S.S. guide to home improvement / author, Martin Preston.-- 1st American ed.
  p. cm. -- (Keep it simple series)
  Includes index.
  ISBN 0-7894-8397-1 (alk paper)
  1. Dwellings–Maintenance and repair–Amateurs' manuals. 2.
Dwellings--Remodeling--Amateurs' manuals. I. Title: KISS guide to home
improvement. II. Title. III. Series.

TH4817.3 .P74 2002
643'.7--dc21
                                                          2001055982

Color reproduction by ColourScan, Singapore
Printed and bound by MOHN media and Mohndruck GmbH, Germany

See our complete product line at
www.dk.com

Contents at a Glance

PART ONE

DIY Basics

Do You or Don't You?
Keeping it Simple
Don't Blame Your Tools!
Tricks of the Trade

PART TWO

Decorating

Painting Walls and Ceilings
Painting Woodwork
Wallpapering
Ceramic Tiling
Staining and Varnishing
Laying Floorcoverings

PART THREE

Indoor Improvements

Doors and Windows
Floors and Staircases
Shelves and Storage
Walls and Ceilings
Heating and Ventilation

PART FOUR

Outdoor Improvements

Fences and Gates
Paths and Patios
Walls and Roofs
Gutters and Drainage

PART FIVE

Plumbing and Electrics

Know Your Plumbing
Home Plumbing Jobs
Know Your Electrics
Home Electrical Jobs

CONTENTS

Foreword by Mike Lawrence   10

Introduction   12

What's Inside?   14

The Extras   15

PART ONE DIY Basics

CHAPTER 1   Do You or Don't You?   17

CHAPTER 2   Keeping it Simple   23

CHAPTER 3   Don't Blame Your Tools!   37

CHAPTER 4   Tricks of the Trade   47

PART TWO Decorating

CHAPTER 5	Painting Walls and Ceilings	65
CHAPTER 6	Painting Woodwork	85
CHAPTER 7	Wallpapering	97
CHAPTER 8	Ceramic Tiling	111
CHAPTER 9	Staining and Varnishing	127
CHAPTER 10	Laying Floorcoverings	137

PART THREE Indoor Improvements

CHAPTER 11	Doors and Windows	151
CHAPTER 12	Floors and Staircases	169
CHAPTER 13	Shelves and Storage	181
CHAPTER 14	Walls and Ceilings	195
CHAPTER 15	Heating and Ventilation	211

PART FOUR Outdoor Improvements

CHAPTER 16   *Fences and Gates*   223

CHAPTER 17   *Paths and Patios*   233

CHAPTER 18   *Walls and Roofs*   245

CHAPTER 19   *Gutters and Drainage*   255

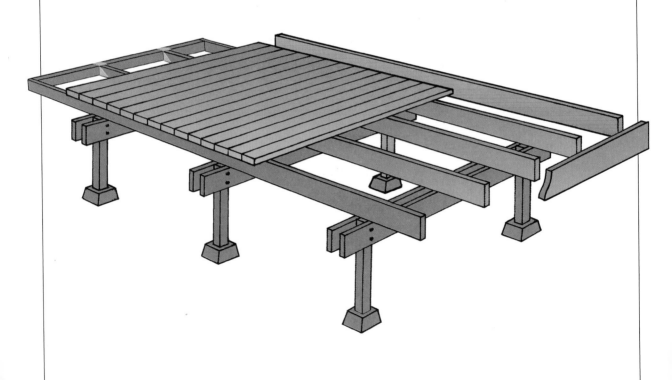

PART FIVE Plumbing and Electrical

CHAPTER 20   Know Your Plumbing   263

CHAPTER 21   Home Plumbing Jobs   275

CHAPTER 22   Know Your Electrical   293

CHAPTER 23   Home Electrical Jobs   303

APPENDICES

More Resources:

Professional organizations   322

Internet and Magazines   324

Books   325

Glossary   326

Index   330

Acknowledgments   335

Foreword

ONE OF THE BEAUTIES of a good DIY book is discovering which home-improvement and repair jobs can be safely tackled by the novice do-it-yourselfer, and which ones are best left to the professionals. Plastering, wiring, and roofing are three jobs you might want to consider farming out to the pros, but the number of jobs you can do on your own may surprise you. Whether you are doing this type of work for the fun and satisfaction of it, or to save yourself some money, all you need to do the job right is some time, the right tools, and plenty of advice from an experienced hand.

That's where this book comes in. Martin Preston is very knowledgeable about both materials and techniques of good home improvement. In my two years as a carpenter on The Learning Channel's Trading Spaces, I have tackled everything from installing new kitchen counter tops to hanging a swing in a child's bedroom. I have found plenty of useful information about home improvement in this guide — whether creating more closet space, putting down sub-flooring, repairing a porch, or hanging a door — it's all here.

I had no idea how capable I was of transforming the look of a home until I began working on Trading Spaces. I now get calls all the time from friends and family who are eager for me to help them with projects they want to do, but are afraid they can't handle. As much as I would love to help them all, my busy schedule and my own new apartment, on which I would like to work, prevent me from doing so. It's nice to know I can just hand them this book and expect they'll get the advice they need to do their projects without me.

Whether it's new or old, every house or apartment eventually requires minor repairs. My new apartment could use a bunch of work, including new tiling in the bathroom (Chapter 8), new cabinetry in the kitchen (Chapter 13), and more color every where (Chapter 5). Now an important thing to keep in mind is ownership. For those of you who are renting, like myself, you should think about what type of work will be worth doing to a place that you do not own. If you put down a new floor, you don't get to keep it when you leave, nor do you get any money for improving the worth of the space. However, if you build removable shelving units or window dressings, you can take them with you. What ever you choose to do there is a chapter in this book for you.

For those of you who wonder whether or not you have what it takes to handle even the most basic home repairs, don't be intimidated. I have learned that success in home improvement, as in all things, is never guaranteed, but if you have the help of a good book like this one, you certainly have a leg up. Half the battle is deciding when and where to start.

Good luck with all your future projects!

Amy Wynn Pastor

AMY WYNN PASTOR

Introduction

WELL DONE! Okay, so you haven't done very much yet. But you have opened this book, and that's a start. It's also a good investment, because the next time something goes wrong with your home, instead of reaching in a panic for the Yellow Pages, you'll be calmly picking up your tool box – and in all probability fixing the problem in less time than it takes a contractor to calculate the charges. Take that one bold step, and pretty soon you'll be walking tall. Shelves, kitchen cabinets, a new floor... easy; a new faucet, an extra socket, a sundeck... no problem. It's a wonderfully reassuring feeling to know you can do it. And now, that knowledge is within your grasp.

Not that it will all be easy, of course. I'd be less than honest if I tried to persuade you otherwise. When I first started fixing things, which admittedly was a very, very long time ago, I found myself breaking out in a cold sweat every time I so much as picked up a screwdriver. It felt like my first driving lesson. And then it dawned on me that like car drivers, every one of those people you see confidently cruising down the aisles of your local home supply store had to start somewhere. So don't worry if you're a little nervous – you've every right to be. It's your home, after all!

So, let's make some plans. First we'll go through the thorny question, "do you or don't you?" We'll be doing plenty, I promise, but there are some things that, as a relative newcomer to home improvement, you really would be better off leaving to the experts. Like pitched roofs, for example, where the safety risks simply don't justify attempting to save money. And plastering, which takes months, even years, of practice to get right.

Still with me? Great, then we'll move on to the basic skills that all self-respecting do-it-yourselfers need to have tucked under their belt. You'll be using or adapting the information in these chapters again and again, so please give it your best shot. Decorating comes next, and on the basis that people do it more than any other form of home improvement, I've really gone to town on this section.

The next two sections cover indoor and outdoor improvements – repair jobs and home-enhancing projects that won't stretch either your skills or your budget. Then, to round things off, we'll look at plumbing and electrical systems. In my experience, these split do-it-yourselfers neatly into two camps: those that do (and love it) and those who would just as soon take up brain surgery. But even if you're one of the latter, it will still pay off to know how these essential services work – and what to do in an emergency.

Finally, a couple points by way of explanation. First, I've tried to be non-product specific as much as possible. Do-it-yourself products and brands change faster than network TV's prime time lineups, and my sincere hope is that you'll find this book useful for many years to come. And lastly, apologies for not covering everything. Can I just say in my defense that if I had, this book would have gone on. And on. And on. Anyway, I've talked the talk, so now it's time to walk the walk. Don't worry – I'll be with you every step of the way. Oh yes, and good luck!

MARTIN PRESTON

What's Inside?

THE INFORMATION IN THE KISS Guide to DIY is arranged by the types of job you have to do, with early chapters getting you up-to-speed on some of the basic information and techniques you'll need to complete these tasks.

PART ONE

In Part One I'll teach you the basics that you should know before tackling any DIY project. You'll be introduced to the tools you need and to the basic techniques. I'll also advise on which jobs you can do yourself, and which are best left to the professionals.

PART TWO

Part Two will cover decorating your house. You'll learn about painting, wallpapering and tiling ceilings and walls, as well as preparing and painting wood. To finish off, I'll teach you about laying floor coverings.

PART THREE

In Part Three I'll teach show you how to improve the inside of your house. We'll cover doors and windows, floors and staircases, fitting and building shelving, walls, and and dealing with heating and ventilation.

PART FOUR

Part Four deals with outdoor improvements, covering the outside of your house as well as your garden. You'll find out about fencing, laying paths and patios, repairing and maintaining walls and roofs, as well as gutters and drainage.

PART FIVE

Part Five covers perhaps the most daunting areas of do-it-yourself – plumbing and electrical jobs. I'll teach you a bit of theory on both before covering the common jobs that a do-it-yourselfer should be able to tackle.

The Extras

THROUGHOUT THE BOOK, *you will notice a number of boxes and symbols. They are there to emphasize certain points I want you to pay special attention to, because they are important to your understanding and improvement. You'll find:*

Very Important Point

This symbol points out a topic I believe deserves careful attention. You really need to know this information before continuing.

Complete No-No

This is a warning, something I want to advise you not to do or to be aware of.

Getting Technical

When the information is about to get a bit technical, I'll let you know so that you can read carefully.

Inside Scoop

These are special suggestions and tips that come from my personal experience that I've found useful over the years.

You'll also find some little boxes that include information I think is important, useful, or just plain fun.

Trivia...

These are interesting DIY facts that will give you an extra appreciation for the history and background of some techniques.

DEFINITION

*Here I'll **define** words and terms for you in an easy-to-understand style. You'll also find a Glossary at the back of the book with DIY terms and phrases.*

INTERNET
www.dk.com

The Internet can be a useful resource for DIYers, so I've scouted out some web sites that will help source materials and give useful tips and advice.

PART ONE

Chapter 1
Do You or Don't You?

Chapter 2
Keeping It Simple

Chapter 3
Don't Blame Your Tools!

Chapter 4
Tricks of the Trade

START WITH THE BASICS

Chapter 1

Do You or Don't You?

SOME DO-IT-YOURSELF JOBS ARE EASY. Others aren't. Sometimes it's because they require a lot of expensive tools. More often, it's because they require practice – the kind of practice that comes from doing them day in, day out. As a beginner, it will pay you to know the difference, and to steer clear of the jobs that can land you in trouble. Rest assured, it's not defeatist; it's just plain common sense.

In this chapter...

✓ *Know your limitations*

✓ *Be prepared!*

✓ *Calling in the professionals*

Know your limitations

IT'S AMAZING how many do-it-yourselfers leap right in without really knowing what they're doing. You wouldn't attempt to do brain surgery without a little practice – and the same thing applies to some areas of home improvement!

Is it worth it?

Before you set out to do any project, ask yourself the following questions:

1 **Do I know what I'm doing?** This applies especially to changes or additions to plumbing and electrical systems, and to any kind of structural modification. If you're in doubt about the safety of a job, don't do it.

Some jobs are best left to the professionals, including anything to do with gas appliances, central air conditioning systems, and roof work. Remember, even if you're not scared of heights, working at a height is very different from simply being up high.

2 **Do I have enough practice?** Some home improvement skills, such as plastering, can't be learned out of books alone: you need to have a natural talent for them, and to practice – sometimes for years. If the job you're planning comes under this category, do the smart thing and call in a professional; otherwise you could spend twice as much time fixing your mistakes.

3 **Am I equipped?** Without the right equipment, your chances of carrying out certain jobs will be severely limited. Also, buying or renting what you need may well end up being more expensive than getting the job done professionally. The way to beat this trap is to build up a network of like-minded friends who will swap tools and equipment with you.

4 **Do I have the time?** As an enthusiastic amateur you'll almost certainly take longer to do things than an expert. This may not matter if you have time on your hands – but then again, you could be better off earning money doing something you're really good at and leaving the home improvements to a professional.

5 **Is it allowed?** In some cases you will need a building permit before you undertake a project. That means you will have to get approval of your plans from your local building department with regard, for example, to structural, electrical, ventilation, plumbing, and materials considerations.

Be prepared!

THERE'S A TIME and a place for everything, as they say – and that includes home improvements. Pick your time carefully, and be prepared for anything!

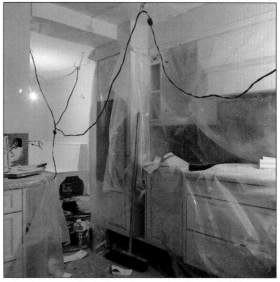

When to do it

Unless there's an emergency, it's a good idea to "store up" DIY jobs – particularly those in a single room or area – until you have enough of them to justify the time and trouble of preparing the house. And prepare the house you must, as even simple tasks can create clouds of plaster dust that get everywhere. Another great enemy of DIY is clutter, so organize things so that the area you're working in is as clear as possible.

■ **Clear up, cover up:** *it may be a chore, but time spent clearing away clutter, masking fixtures, and laying drop cloths will be rewarded.*

Old bedsheets make a far better dust protector than plastic disposable sheets, which tend to slip out of place and be slippery underfoot. Tape the sheets to baseboards, and run lengths of tape along the gaps around doors.

And some more points to remember...

● Those in the know do their DIY when the stores are open: no matter how well organized you are, there's bound to be something you've forgotten or need to rent in a hurry.

● Children and DIY don't mix. Kids have a fascination for tools, which could get them into a lot of trouble if they hang around while you're working.

● Keep the phone numbers of local professionals handy in case the worst does happen and you urgently need to get hold of an expert.

● Before you begin, make certain you know how and where to turn off services, such as water, gas, and electricity.

Calling in the professionals

IF YOU DO HAVE TO call in a professional, you want to be sure that he or she does a good job for a fair price. But as we all know, there are plenty of cowboys out there, just waiting to rope you in…

How to find contractors

By far the best way to hire a builder or other trade professional is by personal recommendation from someone you trust. In the absence of that, always get at least two quotes for the job. Choose firms that are licensed and insured and that provide you with a written quote on letterhead. If they seem reluctant to take on the job, go elsewhere.

■ **Someone has to do it!** *Contractors in the building trades are notoriously unreliable, but if you do your homework, you should be able to get one of the good guys.*

Be aware that you'll nearly always pay more for work done outside normal working hours. Even in an emergency, it may work out cheaper to make a stop-gap repair until you can get the job done properly during working hours.

Six steps to making a deal

1 Be sure both you and the contractor know the difference between an *estimate*, the price of which isn't binding, and a *quote*, which contains a guaranteed fixed price for the job. On larger jobs, if the contractor prepares a specification, any later deviation from it – for example, to fit better-grade windows – will be priced as an "extra." The same goes if you later insist on a specific brand on which the contractor is unable to get a trade discount.

2 Get contractors to explain what they propose to do and what problems they anticipate. If it doesn't make sense, go elsewhere; if it does, get it in writing.

> **DEFINITION**
>
> *An **estimate** is the contractor's opinion of what a job will cost, but it cannot be taken as binding. A **quote** is a written specification and price, and as long as the specification doesn't change, it is binding.*

③ Be realistic about timeframe. Good contractors tend to stay busy, so they may not be able to start immediately. Likewise, on jobs that must be done in good weather, both you and the contractor may be at the mercy of Mother Nature. Either way, don't be rushed into employing someone.

④ On bigger jobs, it's perfectly normal for the contractor to ask for an advance to cover the cost of materials, or even for a schedule of payments to be made at key stages of the job. But be sure to get a receipt, and don't pay more money if the job falls behind schedule. Oh, and never, ever, pay the entire cost of a job up front.

⑤ If you can't be at home, make sure your contractor takes security precautions and cleans up before leaving. It's also worth checking if the contractor is covered for site theft, which is becoming an increasingly common form of burglary.

⑥ Arrange a time and a place to discuss the job and to run through problems – but don't stand over people's shoulders nitpicking or you'll arouse resentment. Don't settle the final bill until all the "call-backs" have been dealt with! Having said all that, it is common sense to have a friendly, cooperative relationship with people who are doing any job for you.

Trivia...
In 1948, President Harry S. Truman decided to call in the professionals when he noticed that the bathtub was sinking into the floor of his White House bathroom. It soon became clear that the whole building needed extensive refurbishment – and the work took almost 4 years to complete.

A simple summary

✔ Be realistic about what you can and can't do, taking into account the time and equipment you have available. And don't attempt to work on plumbing and electrical systems or the structure of the house unless you're sure you know what you're doing.

✔ Save up small jobs until you have enough to justify clearing the area in which you intend to work and sending children out for the day.

✔ If you have to call in a contractor, try to get one through personal recommendation. Failing that, choose firms that belong to a reputable trade organization and get at least two quotations for the job.

Chapter 2

Keeping It Simple

WHERE DOING THINGS YOURSELF IS CONCERNED, the simpler the better. A simple job is less likely to go wrong, is more likely to yield significant savings, and stands a better chance of being finished. So put those attic conversion plans on hold and try some of the ideas in this chapter instead. They promise results – fast.

In this chapter...

✓ Indoor decorating

✓ Outdoor decorating

✓ Kitchen and bathroom facelifts

✓ Better storage

✓ Securing your home

✓ Selling your home

SIMPLE CHANGES CAN MAKE A BIG DIFFERENCE

Indoor decorating

THANKS TO THE USER-FRIENDLINESS *of modern decorating materials, you can accomplish in a weekend what once would have taken weeks of planning. So pick up your paintbrush and roller and try out some of the no-hassle facelifts described here.*

1 Stuck for a color scheme? Then start at the end! Go out and buy attractive blinds, curtain fabric, or bedspread and then pick out two or more colors from these. If a piece of packaging catches your eye, try combining the same colors, safe in the knowledge that they've been chosen by professionals! This is also the ideal time to take advantage of the paint-mixing services offered by many stores – just take a sample of the material with you and match it.

2 Not sure about that color you like? Buy a quart, paint a patch on a wall, and see how it looks under different lighting conditions. Paler colors, in particular blues, often look much more intense on the wall than they do on the paint card, and pale yellows can change dramatically depending on whether they're in sunlight or artificial light. Better to be safe than sorry!

3 Frustrated by those lumpy, uneven walls that show their worst side every time you switch on a light? If you don't want to go to the lengths of having them replastered, you can hide imperfections with one of the many textured wallpapers available on the market. Or you can try one of the specialized paints, such as those with sand or other texture mixed in. These are very easy to apply and can disguise very rough surface textures. An even easier option is to repaint the wall (see pp. 78–79 for paint effects). The broken colors will disguise any blemishes, as well as giving the room a fresh new look.

4 Good lighting will transform even the most tired room. Replace overhead hanging lights with recessed, low-voltage "high hats," spotlights hung from a tensioned wire, or wall lights. For even quicker results, try installing one or two free-standing floor lamps in the corners. Many come with their own dimmer switch, giving you even more control.

■ **These strikingly** *vivid curtains and cushions are perfectly set off by the cool beige tones that dominate the remainder of the room.*

Outdoor decorating

WHAT GOES FOR INDOORS goes for the outside, too, especially during the summer months when you don't want your spirits dampened by a tired looking house and garden. Aside from regular maintenance tasks, there are plenty of quick ways to brighten up your immediate surroundings.

1. Repaint your old wooden garden furniture in Mediterranean-style pastels or bright primary colors. Make cushions to match, with an inner waterproof lining and washable outer cover. Checks and stripes look good in the garden.

2. Use interesting containers for potted plants. This is one area where plastic imitations of classic designs and materials do just fine.

3. Give your plain concrete patio a new look. Cobblestones or bricks laid in a herringbone pattern is a low-cost option, as are wood decking "squares," available from large home centers. Alternatively, to "bring the inside out," consider continuing a terra cotta tile or slate floor out onto the patio; it may be expensive, but you'll find that in summer it turns the patio into an extra "room."

4. Replace old fencing or revive it with freshly painted trellis and plant bamboo in front of it to create a natural-looking screen.

5. Window boxes instantly brighten the outside of any home. For a clean, minimalist look, use plants or flowers all of one color. Terra cotta is the classic window box material, but wooden planters or plastic imitations of either of these are also very effective.

6. In a small garden, create the illusion of space and light by strategically placing a large mirror to catch the reflections from a brighter area. Carefully positioned, the mirror may even look like a doorway to another part of the garden.

7. If you don't want to go to the trouble of properly wired outdoor lighting, try illuminating the garden with candles on sticks, lanterns, or torches, all of which are generally available from garden centers.

■ **There is** *a huge variety of containers for pot plants that will brighten up a patio or terrace.*

Kitchen and bathroom facelifts

THE KITCHEN IS THE HEART of many homes, which often means it takes more of a battering than other parts of the house. The bathroom is likely to be a morning battleground for the entire family. In both cases, however, there's plenty you can do to give these rooms a new lease on life – short of a total refit.

Simple ideas for the kitchen

1 Kitchen cabinets can start to look dingy after a while, but if the cabinets themselves are structurally sound, consider replacing just the doors. Replacement door experts advertise in decorating magazines and on home improvement programs, and because most cabinets are modular, there's seldom any problem with matching sizes. You can buy just new doors and hardware to install yourself, or have the cabinet boxes refaced and new doors installed. Keep in mind that a small kitchen will look larger if cabinets and walls are the same color.

■ **Center-island** *worksurfaces (with pots and pans hung directly overhead) form the heart of this traditional-looking but high-tech kitchen.*

2 Bring a refrigerator back to life by scrubbing textured doors with steel wool and rust-removing cleanser. Replace the slide-out panels on dishwashers. Sand and repaint oven doors (take them off first) for a fresh look.

3 Fit a new worksurface. These days, the most popular countertops are laminates, which look nice but are vulnerable to damage, and acrylic or polyester resins in an amazing variety of surface effects. This may also be the time to think about installing a new oven or stove top.

4 Install a new floor. Popular materials include terra cotta tiles, vinyl or laminate tiles, or – simplest of all – sheet vinyl. Avoid hard ceramic tiles, as they tend to be cold and slippery underfoot and will show no mercy if you drop something on them.

5 Install or replace a tiled splashback. Old ones often consist of just a single row of plain tiles and accumulate layers of grime along the joint with the worktop.

Instead, consider carrying the new tiles up to the height of your wall cabinets, or finish them off with decorative border tiles.

6 Consider revising your cooking arrangements and fitting one of the latest generation "professional"-style freestanding ranges. These tend to be finished in stainless steel and come complete with matching exhaust hood and splashback. Prices are falling all the time, and you'll almost certainly recoup the cost when you sell your home.

Stainless steel refrigerators are popular now, and are stylish enough to be treated as pieces of furniture in their own right. It could be worth sacrificing a couple of kitchen cabinets to make the space, and then "cannibalizing" them to add storage space in the areas where the old appliances used to be.

Don't attempt to fit a new gas appliance yourself, even if the connections are already there. Quite apart from the safety aspect, modern gas ranges tend to be tricky and may need expert adjustment after installation.

7 Think about installing new faucets – and perhaps some matching accessories such as a utensil rack, towel rail, or wine rack.

8 Stop countertop clutter by installing perforated board. Hang utensils from butcher's hooks and hang wire baskets for odds and ends.

9 Take a long, hard look at the lighting – especially if you also eat your meals in the kitchen. Overhead lighting can be toned down by fitting low-voltage track lights operated with a dimmer switch. Use under-cabinet light fixtures for illuminating work surfaces and providing sidelighting. Simply screw them to the underside of your wall cabinets and connect to an outlet.

10 If your wall cabinets encroach too much on working space, consider replacing them with industrial-style, open, stainless steel shelving. Having perishable items on display is also a good way to avoid keeping supplies too long.

■ **Fluorescent downlighters** *softly illuminating natural materials like wood and brick can provide a kitchen with a warm, inviting atmosphere.*

Simple ideas for the bathroom

1. No matter how often – or how well – you clean tiled surfaces, the gaps between tiles will become grimy after a while. Clean the grouting using household bleach and an old toothbrush. Alternatively, you can buy a commercial grout whitener. If the grouting is beyond a facelift, scraping it out and regrouting is not a big job. At the same time, replace any worn sealant around the bathtub, sink, and so on. Gouge the old sealant out with a screwdriver and clean off any residue with paintbrush thinner, then reseal.

2. There's only so much that a bathmat can hide. If your bathroom carpet is worn or stained, a replacement will improve the look of the room instantly – look for cheap remnants in carpet stores. But first, is carpet really your best option? The inevitable spills of bathwater, toothpaste, toiletries, and talcum powder won't do a carpet any good. Sheet vinyl or resilient vinyl tiles are two economical, easily cleaned, and harder-wearing alternatives.

■ **Choose a new bathmat** *and a few matching accessories to give your bathroom an instant boost without spending a lot of money.*

3. Even though bathtub and basin faucets can be cleaned until they positively gleam, consider buying new faucets to give a fresh look to your bathroom without the expense of changing the entire suite. They are easy to replace, and give you the opportunity of upgrading to a more modern mechanism at the same time. Reinforce the effect with matching accessories.

■ **New faucets** *will brighten up your existing bathroom suite.*

4. Give the shower curtain a facelift. Shower curtains can be bleached and most are machine-washable; just hang them back up on the rail to dry. But a new shower curtain, perhaps with a new bathmat and matching towels, won't break the bank. A transparent plastic one with built-in pockets is a good buy. You can use the pockets for decorative items or to store everyday toiletries. Curtains are made in different thicknesses: the thin ones dry more quickly but may cling to your body when you are showering.

5 Getting rid of the clutter will make you feel better. If you can, keep toiletries in a cabinet. If you can't, buy a couple of matching baskets to store bottles and tubes. It'll make your life easier when it comes to cleaning, and even giving the bottles a clean will brighten things up.

6 Tired of that plastic bath paneling? Get modern and replace it with tongue-and-groove paneling. Continue the paneling around the walls up to chest height to give the room a unified feel. Use low-cost, pre-finished wainscot in a tongue-and-groove style.

If you decide to use unfinished tongue-and-groove paneling, it will need to be waterproofed. To prevent damage, paint the paneling and caulk it around the edges. Or apply a preservative wood stain or sealer.

7 If there are separate splashbacks around the bathtub and basin, consider unifying them with matching tiles up to chest height to give the room a smarter, more streamlined appearance. Finish the tiles off with a row of decorative border tiles or with painted or varnished quarter-round molding.

8 Give your bathroom window a new look. You could replace outdated patterned or textured glass with frosted glass. Consider replacing curtains with Venetian or slatted blinds.

9 Get rid of that old-fashioned lighting. Wall lights or recessed lighting will create a much cozier, more intimate atmosphere, or you can buy mirrors with integral lighting for a more subtle effect. (But make sure all lighting fixtures are UL-approved for use in bathrooms.)

10 Stained tubs, sinks, and tiles can spoil a makeover. Use a scale cleanser to give them a new lease on life. It will also add sparkle to taps, watermarked tiles, and mirrors.

■ **The soft glow** *of wall-mounted lights lends a warmer feel to a tiled bathroom. For extra calm and relaxation, light a few candles, too.*

Better storage

WHY DO OTHER PEOPLE'S HOMES *always seem to have more closet space? Perhaps they don't. They could be storing just the things they really need, or making better use of the space they've got.*

1 Before you reorganize your storage space, rationalize the things you are hoarding. Anything you haven't looked at, worn, or used in the past year can probably go, unless it is a valued memento. Check all foodstuffs for use-by dates and discard out-of-date spices and cans. Remember that make-up and toiletries have shelf-lives, too. Do you need to keep all your books and magazines? If you save magazines for inspiration, don't keep whole issues – just cut out the pictures you like and stick them in a scrapbook.

2 Items that you feel you must keep but which you're unlikely to use regularly, such as out-of-season clothes, holiday gear, decorations, and documents can be stored in less accessible places. Use boxes under beds, on tops of wardrobes, or in a cellar or attic.

3 Do you tend to throw things in an understairs closet, one layer upon another? You can store more under the stairs by building shelves. And lighting the area will help you find things more easily.

4 If you work at home, a simple box file unit – and a little self-discipline when it comes to using it – will enable you to keep on top of the paperwork.

5 Knowing what's in a closet or drawer helps. Label the doors or drawer fronts so you don't have to search through everything every time. Luggage labels with neat lettering look good. Or you could stick a Polaroid photo of a box's contents on the front.

6 Sub-divide spaces in closets and wardrobes with hanging fabric shelves or clear plastic boxes. Multiple hangers will help you arrange your clothes more easily, and they save acres of wardrobe space.

■ **A wooden box file** *unit, neatly stacked, can take the panic out of paperwork.*

7 Even when they are neatly arranged, you don't always want to look at your stored belongings. For an uncluttered look, hide walls of shelving behind louvered doors or narrow double doors. Where space is at a premium, roller blinds or simple muslin curtains are almost as effective.

8 Often the ideal solution is to use one room just for storage. Attic or cellar conversions are ideal, as are dark spare bedrooms; if you do it right, there's no reason why the room should look a mess. Line the walls with strong shelves and organize them by subject. Make sure the room is well lit and ventilated. Ensure that all of the shelving is accessible, or the room may quickly become a dumping ground that you don't dare enter.

■ **Floor-length curtains** *are a simple and elegant disguise for mismatched or inexpensive shelving and storage units.*

Craft shops are full of beautiful boxes in a wide variety of styles, colors, and materials. You're bound to find some that would look just right in your room. But if you're short on space, it's best to avoid gimmicky, over-specialized storage items: even if they look fantastic, they're usually expensive and take up too much room.

■ **A built-in storage space** *like the base of this window seat provides a spot to stash magazines and other clutter. For more flexibility, look for a coffee table with a hinged top.*

9 If space is tight consider that old favorite, the window seat, or items with unusual storage spaces, such as footstools and coffee tables with hinged lids and beds with drawers underneath.

10 For children's rooms, use open boxes. Place favorite toys on or near the floor for safety and ease of use. Label each box with a picture or a simple name and get your child into the habit of putting items away.

Securing your home

MOST BURGLARS ARE OPPORTUNISTS, on the look-out for a house or apartment that seems like an easy target. Don't let them choose your home. You can do a great deal to put off all but the most determined intruder by following the basic precautions described here.

1 Use lighting to fool a burglar into thinking that the house is occupied. Leave a light on in a living room or bedroom while you are out, preferably attached to a timer switch so lights aren't on at an unlikely time of the day or night. It's not a good idea to keep curtains and blinds drawn while you are away.

2 Don't bother installing a good lock to a weak door; someone trying to force an entry will only kick down the door. It's vital to replace a front or back door that has a hollow core with a solid hardwood door. The same applies to windows – it doesn't matter how many locks you install if the wood in your windows is rotten; a burglar will simply force the frame.

Don't leave windows and external doors open when you're not around to keep an eye on them. In about a quarter of all domestic break-ins, the burglar gains access through a window or door left open by careless householders who think it can't happen to them.

3 Choose the right lock for the job. Experts recommend the following:

- **Front door:** a heavy-duty deadbolt with a ¼ inch throw or longer, and a door lockset with deadlock.
- **Back door:** a mortise sash lock and mortise rack bolts or flush-mounted key locks.
- **Sliding glass doors:** install key-operated surface-mounted locks at the top and bottom, plus an anti-lift device to keep doors in their tracks.
- **Windows:** key-operated locks or sash stops.
- **French windows:** fit mortise rack bolts or security pressbolts at the top and bottom of each door.

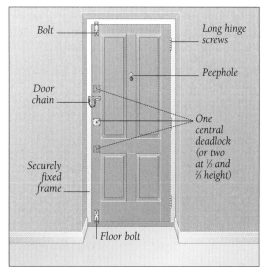

Bolt

Long hinge screws

Peephole

Door chain

One central deadlock (or two at ⅓ and ⅔ height)

Securely fixed frame

Floor bolt

■ **The front door** *is the point of entry for over a third of burglaries – make sure yours is secure.*

Spotlight illuminates passage to back garden

Windows accessible from roof securely locked

Alarm box visible from front and side of house

Low fence offers intruders minimal cover

Security light over front door

Ground floor windows securely locked

■ **Guard against intruders** *by checking each of the watchpoints listed above. Security lighting and an alarm system are useful deterrents, but there's no substitute for good locks on windows and external doors.*

4 Security lights fitted to the outside of the building make it difficult for a burglar to break in unseen at night. Passive infrared (PIR) units that work on body heat, rather than movement, will automatically operate lighting when anyone approaches your home. Key areas to spotlight are over the front door, garage, outbuildings, passages, and any other obvious entry point.

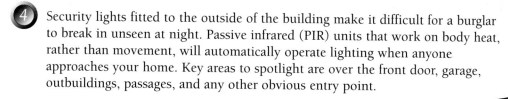

A break-in is not the only threat to your home – take the risk of fire just as seriously. Smoke detectors can be life-savers. Install ones that include automatic emergency lighting on hall and landing ceilings. Use a carbon monoxide detector as well, to quickly detect gas leaks in the home.

5 Lock away garden and DIY tools in a garage or shed; a burglar may use them to break into your house. For the same reason, never leave ladders lying around. If you don't have a shed or garage to put them in, lay them on their side and chain and padlock them to a secure fitting on the side of the house.

6 People living in homes fitted with burglar alarms make far fewer insurance claims than those without – in other words, housebreakers avoid them. A central station alarm system will be more expensive than a self-installed audible alarm, but will be more effective and reliable. It may also earn you a discount on your homeowner's insurance premium.

Selling your home

WHEN YOU'RE SELLING A HOME, *remember that appearances count for everything. Hide what can be hidden, clean what can be cleaned, and make your home as welcoming as you can. Fix what can be fixed. A home that looks well maintained will be more favorably viewed by potential buyers.*

Renew and replace

It could be worth replacing anything that is not up to scratch. A new carpet, a new fitted kitchen, or even a new bathroom won't be cheap, but the outlay will be worth it if it helps to sell your home – and is almost certain to be reflected in a higher asking price. There will be features that you cannot change, but make the most of what you do have. If a room is particularly small, make it look larger with some strategically positioned mirrors – they reflect what light there is back into the room, giving the illusion of increased space. If the house is fairly dark overall, arrange viewings for the morning when it will be looking its brightest.

Repair any holes or cracks – indoors and out. They may be only superficial, but they will raise worries in buyers' minds. Repair or replace any loose doorknobs, and make sure the lights work. Clean windows also make a house look cared-for.

First impressions

Make sure that your home looks like someplace where strangers might like to live. Updated bathrooms and large closets may help to sell it once prospects are inside, but if the garden is overgrown, then most buyers will switch off before they cross the

■ **If you have an open fire,** *light it – even in summer! There is no more welcoming sight.*

■ **Bathrooms sell houses,** *so consider making improvements and renew accessories.*

■ **Flowering plants** *placed in interesting containers will cheer up even the dullest backyard.*

threshold. Cut the grass, add some cheap props of flowering plants, and give the front door a fresh lick of paint. These will make the house look more inviting, and inspire would-be buyers to think of what they could do with the garden if it was their own. If there is any old junk in the yard, clear it away to make the area look more spacious. Although it is important that viewers feel they can make your home theirs, too many personal effects can work against a seller. Remove items such as family photographs, and if you own any pets (especially a barking dog), keep them out of the way until the appointment is over.

Keep them interested

Mess is a big turn-off, and once viewers are inside, make sure that they don't see any kitchen clutter or unmade beds. Tidy rooms also make a home seem bigger. Similarly, since buyers will want to feel their new home has plenty of storage, try to avoid bulging wardrobes and piles of paperwork. Bathrooms and kitchens sell houses, so fix any leaking taps and make sure that towels are fresh and clean. Use every good accessory you have. Dimmed lighting can make your living space look more cozy, but make sure that it isn't so dark that viewers think you've got something to hide. If you have to redecorate, choose a neutral color like white or beige, which gives viewers a blank canvas on which to visualize their new home. When you get them inside, bombard their senses with fresh flowers, jars of potpourri, and the smell of brewing coffee and freshly baked bread. Believe me, it works!

INTERNET

www.homes.com

This site covers a wide range of information about the legal and practical aspects of buying or selling a home, and also offers a searchable database of properties.

A simple summary

✓ Give the inside of your home a rejuvenating facelift.

✓ Brighten up the outside of the house to get the most from the garden in summer months.

✓ Kitchens and bathrooms are too important to life's comforts to simply take them for granted.

✓ Banish clutter by sorting out sensible storage.

✓ Give your home an immediate security survey and strengthen any weak points.

✓ When selling your home make sure it's clean, tidy, and welcoming to potential buyers.

Chapter 3

Don't Blame Your Tools!

THERE ARE VERY FEW JOBS YOU CAN DO YOURSELF without a decent set of tools. But that doesn't mean you have to spend a fortune on all the latest gadgets. The trick is to know what tools you'll use again and again, buy the best-quality ones you can afford, and then borrow or rent the rest. Oh, and you need to look after your tools, too. Blunt, rusty, or damaged tools are a liability – and if they cause things to go wrong, you really do have only yourself to blame!

In this chapter...
✓ Hand tools it pays to buy
✓ Acquiring power tools
✓ Somewhere to work
✓ Playing it safe

WELL-MAINTAINED TOOLS MAKE DIY JOBS EASIER

Hand tools it pays to buy

THE TOOLS LISTED HERE are all worth buying if you do-it-yourself on a regular basis. I can't guarantee that they'll cover you for everything, but they are almost certain to pay their way within a short space of time.

Hand tool buying do's and don'ts

- Buy the highest-quality cutting tools you can afford – and then look after them. At best, cheap cutting tools quickly deteriorate; at worst, they are dangerous to use.
- Don't skimp on sharpening tools for chisels and plane blades; blunt tools are dangerous! Have larger saws professionally sharpened. Stock up on replacement blades for coping saws, hacksaws, and so on.
- You can never have too many screwdrivers, drill bits, or clamps! Keep an eye out for "bargain" sets in stores.
- Ratchet or pump-action screwdrivers are costly, but they do save a lot of arm ache.

■ **Well-equipped –** *a carefully chosen set of hand tools will make any job easier. But the tools listed here should get you off to a flying start.*

A basic toolkit

The tools shown below are must-haves for anyone who owns a home. All have a variety of uses and at a pinch can often be used as substitutes when you don't have the correct tool for the job. So don't skimp: investing in a basic toolkit is a lot easier and cheaper than calling in a professional at emergency call-out rates!

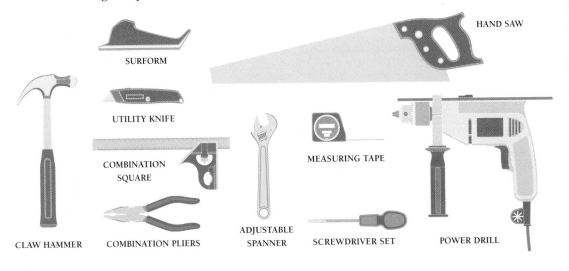

SURFORM

HAND SAW

UTILITY KNIFE

COMBINATION SQUARE

MEASURING TAPE

CLAW HAMMER

COMBINATION PLIERS

ADJUSTABLE SPANNER

SCREWDRIVER SET

POWER DRILL

GENERAL PURPOSE HAND TOOLS

Cutting and shaping

Hand saw	(crosscut blade) for general cutting of wood and boards.
Back saw	for moldings and joints; used with a **miter box**.
Compass saw	a saw blade with a handle on one end for cutting holes in boards.
Mini-hacksaw	for cutting pipes and other metal objects.
Utility knife	with replaceable blades.
Brickset	for cutting holes in solid plaster and masonry.
Set of wood chisels	for gaining hinges, joints, and mortises.
Block plane	for shaping and shaving wood and boards.
Surform	for shaping wood and filler.
Whetstone	for sharpening chisels and plane blades.
Sanding block	for general sanding.
Half-round metalwork file	for removing the burr from sawed metal.

Marking and measuring

Steel tape	for general measuring.
Steel ruler	for accurate measuring.
Combination square	for marking out wood at 90° and 45° (or buy a separate try square and sliding bevel).
Carpenter's level	for checking that something is level or plumb.
Bevel	used to copy and mark angles.

Drill and hammering

Scratch awl or gimlet	for making pilot holes for small screws.
Push drill	(with a selection of twist and wood bits) for drilling accurate holes in wood.
Countersink tool	for countersunk screws.
Claw hammer	for general nailing and removing nailheads.
Pin hammer	for fine nailing and tacking.
Mallet	for driving chisels.
Sledgehammer	heavyweight hammer for driving chisels.
Nail set	for sinking finishing nails beneath the surface.

Extracting and clamping

Tack claw	for lifting tacks and pins.
Flat pry bar	for lifting larger nails.
Crowbar	for general levering and prying jobs.
Pliers	for general gripping tasks.
Wire strippers	for cutting and stripping electrical cable.
Locking pliers	(visegrips) for general-purpose clamping.
Adjustable wrench	for tightening plumbing joints, nuts and bolts.
Set of C-clamps	for clamping woodworking joints and boards. A **pipe clamp** and **screw clamps** may also be useful if you do a lot of woodworking.
Portable workbench	(e.g. Workmate™) for clamping larger items and as a support for sawing.
Screwdrivers	buy sets of standard and phillips-head screwdrivers with various head sizes and blade lengths. Shorter sizes give good accessibility; larger handles give more turning force.

Acquiring power tools

SOME PEOPLE LOVE POWER TOOLS, *other people love giving them as presents! But before you rush out to buy a power tool, think about how often you'll use it: if the answer is every few months, you may well be better off renting a professional-quality model that's up to date.*

Power tool do's and don'ts

- With power tools, you generally get what you pay for. The better-quality tools are more powerful and more durable – but this may not matter if you rarely use them.
- Tempting as they are, drills with multiple attachments for sawing and sanding never work as well as their dedicated cousins; they are best avoided.
- It's worth paying extra for a secure case for each power tool that you buy.
- As with hand tools, blunt power saws are dangerous – only more so. Make sure you pick up a stock of replaceable blades when you buy.
- Check rented power tools carefully for damage, especially the power cords. Make sure you understand how to use them before leaving the store.
- Tie back long hair, avoid loose clothing, and wear appropriate safety gear.

Power tools to buy

An electric drill operated on household current (right) is indispensable if you plan to do DIY a kind of regular basis. Choose one with multiple speeds and a hammer action for drilling into masonry. If you do a lot of woodwork, consider buying a drill stand as well. Wire brush and circular sander attachments are inexpensive and useful for jobs such as removing rust – but a circular sander is no good for sanding wood.

You might also consider buying a cordless drill (right), which also doubles as a power screwdriver. Today's models hold their charge much better than older ones, and are powerful enough to cope with most indoor jobs. Once you get the knack of using them, the power screwdriver attachments are among the best labor-saving devices you can buy.

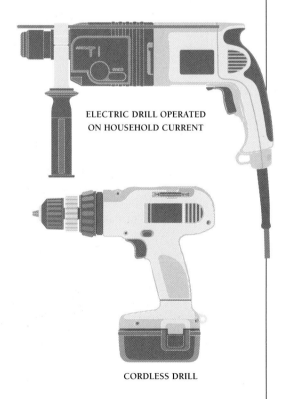

ELECTRIC DRILL OPERATED
ON HOUSEHOLD CURRENT

CORDLESS DRILL

POWER TOOLS TO BUY OR HIRE

It's great to own a power tool for every occasion, but consider how much you will actually use one before buying – you might be better off renting.

Circular saw

Makes short work of cutting all but the thickest wood and is the first choice for sheet materials such as particle board or plywood. Great for trimming indoors.
Even easier to use in conjunction with a saw table, for foolproof cutting of straight lines.

Jigsaw

Not as versatile or as powerful as a circular saw, but essential for cutting holes in panels – for example, when installing a sink or cutting surface in a countertop.

Band saw

Rented out with an integral saw table for cutting really heavy lumber such as floor joists or other structural members. Not really worth buying unless you're into heavy building work.

Power planer

A very easy and accurate way to plane planks of wood, but rarely needed for do-it-yourself work. A must-buy for keen woodworkers.

Router

A fantastically versatile power tool supplied with a set of different bits for making grooves, recesses, and mortises, or for turning and shaping moldings. The spring-loaded "plunge" type, in which the tool can be brought to the workpiece, is generally more useful than the bench-mounted type, which works the other way round. For general home improvements you can get by without one, but if you do a lot of woodworking, a router is a must-buy.

Sander

Orbital sanders are better at smoothing flat surfaces than circular drill attachments. For larger projects, consider hiring a belt sander or an in-line sander for gentle edge-work.

Angle grinder

Another superbly versatile power tool, capable of cutting thick ceramic tiles, metal bars and pipes, paving slabs, and roof tiles; also makes short work of cutting grooves or chases in masonry. Rarely worth buying, but a must-have for jobs involving any of the materials above. An angle grinder is potentially dangerous: be sure to read and follow the maker's safety instructions.

Somewhere to work

IF YOU DON'T HAVE THE LUXURY *of a garage or workshop in which to work and store your tools and materials, it pays to get organized before you tackle jobs of any size. There's nothing more frustrating than having to search for a can of paint, only to find it spilled in the back of some dark storage cabinet.*

A DIY home away from home

In the absence of somewhere permanent to work, you can't beat a portable folding workbench. The best types have a split work surface with a built-in vise and plastic inserts for holding larger pieces of wood and boards. They also double as a step stool, which is useful when wallpapering or working at ceiling height.

Fatigue brought about by working in discomfort is one of the most common causes of DIY accidents. Wherever you work, make sure it is warm and well ventilated. If you find yourself stretching or having to apply excessive force, stop and re-evaluate your working situation.

Even if space is at an absolute premium, allocate somewhere in the house where you can store your DIY tools and materials. Not being able to find what you need will inhibit you from doing anything at all. Home centers also do a big business replacing lost tools and materials that have been improperly stored. It may not seem much of an outlay compared with the cost of calling in a professional, but it all adds up.

■ **From holding boards steady** *while sawing, to providing a sturdy surface for measuring and marking, an adjustable workbench is an invaluable tool.*

STORING TOOLS AND MATERIALS

Keep your tools easily accessible and you'll overcome one of the biggest hurdles to starting a job. Put them away clean, sharp, and ready for use. Likewise, store left-over materials methodically and you'll be able to use them for future projects; for example, color-code the ends of cut lumber to show at a glance what useable lengths you have left. There are countless tool storage racks and hardware on the market, but the arrangements shown here can be custom-made to fit the space available and are likely to work out cheaper. Power tools are best stored in their cases and in a locked cabinet, especially if children might have access.

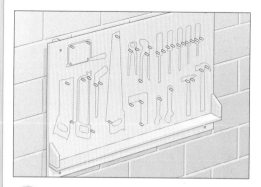

a **Tool storage board with outlines**

Mark the outlines of tools on a wall-mounted storage board so that you can see instantly where to replace them – or what's missing.

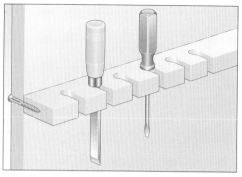

b **Batten with keyhole slots/clips**

Drill and cut keyhole slots in a 1 inch x 2 inch batten to store screwdrivers, chisels, and files. Alternatively, secure the handles in spring clips.

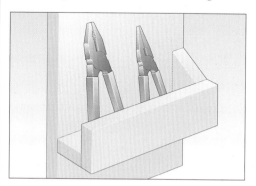

c **Shelf with front rail**

Screw together a batten shelf and front rail to store two-handled tools like pliers and cutters. Alternatively, hang them from screw-in hooks.

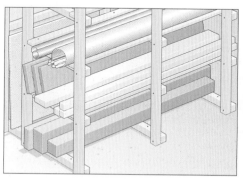

d **Storage rack for materials**

Store lumber, boards, and moldings on an open rack system. Lay lumber on edge, and fit dowels into pre-drilled holes to keep it from sliding.

Playing it safe

THE NUMBER OF ACCIDENTS in the home would surely be dramatically reduced if people were as cautious when carrying out DIY tasks as they are when, say, crossing the road. So make sure you wear the right protective gear and never take unnecessary risks.

Goggles with side air vents will cover glasses

Ear protection

Hard hat

Dust mask covering nose and mouth

Flame-retardant overalls will not melt like synthetic fibers

Workman's gloves made from leather and canvas

Knee pads protect knees and prevent fatigue

Heavy duty boots protect toes and feet

■ **Wear the right protective clothing** *for the task at hand.*

Personal safety and power tools

- Take care to remove any loose clothing or dangling jewelry when using a power tool.
- Keep the cord out of the path of a power tool, but be sure never to use the tool with the cord stretched tight.
- Never put a tool down while it's still running.
- Unplug tools before installing new attachments.
- Don't ever be tempted to remove a safety guard from a circular saw or angle grinder.
- Always plug your power tools into grounded receptacles only.
- Always uncurl power cords fully and, if you must use an extension cord with a power tool, be sure to use only a heavy-duty cord – never a lamp extension cord.

Treat flammable liquids with respect. Never use them near an open flame, or close to flammable materials such as paper or sawdust. Store them away from the floor – preferably on a high shelf – and in a cool, well-ventilated area.

Working with chemicals

- Keep the area you are working in well ventilated. If fumes are noxious, wear a NIOSH (National Institute of Safety and Health) -approved respirator.
- Wear rubber gloves when dealing with caustic fluids of any kind.
- Dispose of unused chemicals safely. Don't pour unwanted fluids down the drain.
- Have water close by to wash off any splashes.
- Always store chemicals in their original containers, and keep the labels readable.

Safety do's and don'ts

- Always switch off the main circuit breaker before working on an electrical circuit.
- Don't work in a poor light. Ensure your workspace is well lit, so that you can see exactly what you are doing.
- Don't trail power cords across your work area; someone (including you) could trip over them.
- Do keep tools sharp: less force is needed, resulting in greater accuracy and less chance of accidents.
- Do take care that pieces of work are securely clamped to a bench when cutting with a power saw.
- Don't place your free hand near a blade when sawing. When using a knife, keep to one side of the cutting line.

Never work at a height unless you are confident and your ladder is secure. Settle the base on firm, level ground and be sure the ladder extends four or five rungs above the stepping-off point. Pull the ladder out from the wall no more than one-quarter of its length.

A simple summary

✔ You can't hope to do any DIY without a reasonably complete set of tools. Buy the best-quality hand tools you can afford and look after them. Never work with blunt or rusty tools – they're dangerous.

✔ Power tools can save a great deal of hard work, but you won't recoup the cost unless you use them a lot. Before you buy, consider whether it might be better to rent them.

✔ Store tools and partly used DIY materials in an organized way so that you can find them easily the next time; not being able to find something will give you an excuse to put off the job.

✔ Take your safety and that of others very seriously. In particular, take steps to protect your eyes, hands, and ears when working with power tools, and keep leads and fingers out of the way of blades.

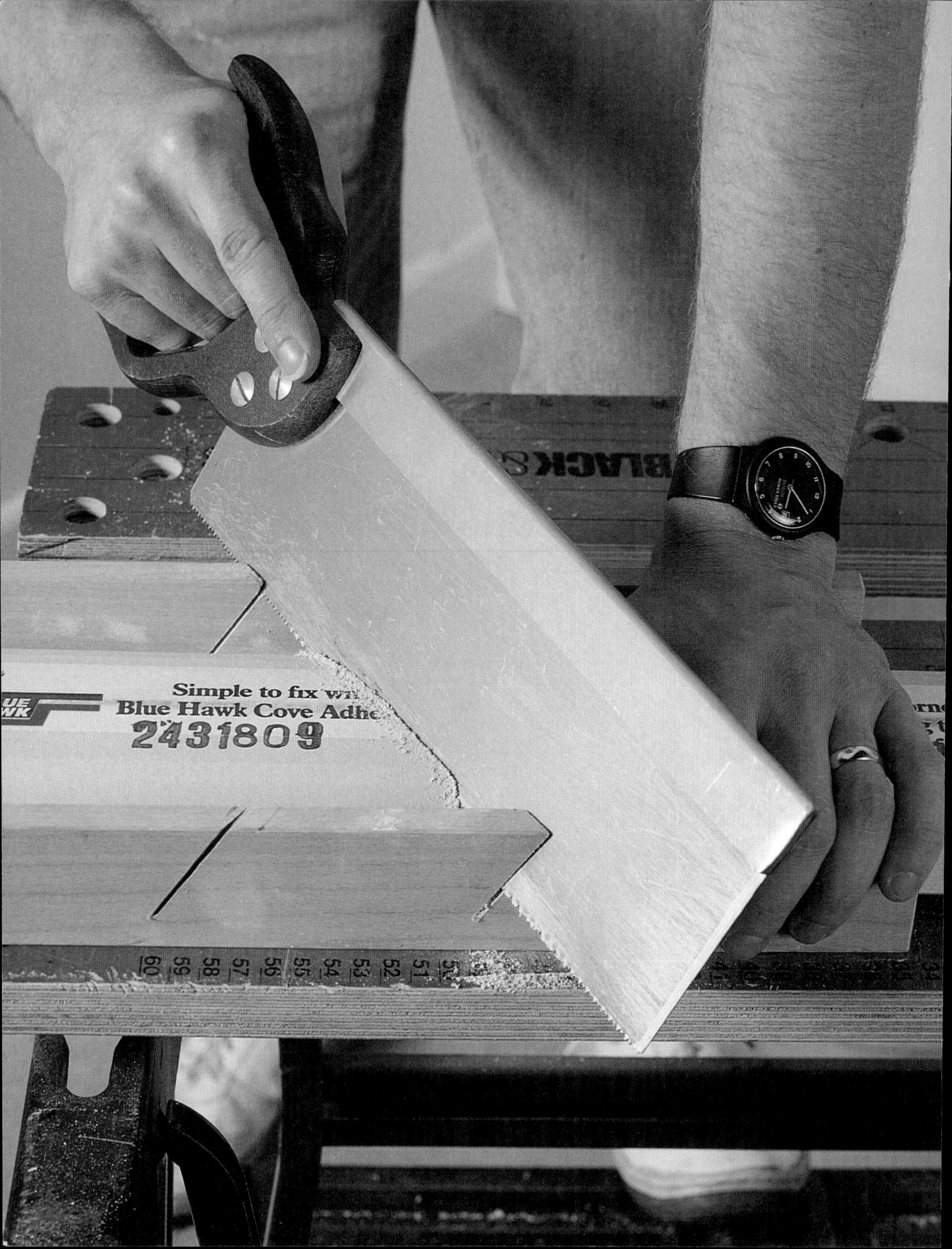
Simple to fix wi
Blue Hawk Cove Adhe
2431809

Chapter 4

Tricks of the Trade

THE BASIC SKILLS DESCRIBED IN THIS CHAPTER will cover you for a multitude of jobs, large and small. I won't pretend that they'll turn you into an expert overnight, but I guarantee they'll make things easier.

In this chapter...

✓ Measuring and marking

✓ Cutting wood and boards

✓ Gluing and joining

✓ Nailing, drilling, and screwing

✓ Fastening things to walls

✓ Curtains and pictures

✓ Concrete and mortar

✓ Working with drywall

EXPERT TECHNIQUES HELP CREATE PROFESSIONAL-LOOKING RESULTS

Measuring and marking

MEASURING AND MARKING *pieces of wood is a bit like boiling an egg: it's not as easy as it looks. Wood is a natural material, which means that your measuring and marking techniques have to account for variations in size between one piece and another. The golden rule is "measure twice; cut once."*

Marking out components

The big risk with measuring and marking wood is that you'll introduce cumulative errors by measuring from a side or edge that isn't straight, by forgetting to allow for the width of your saw cut, or simply by marking in the wrong place. So get into the habit of always applying the following rules:

- Never assume that a piece of wood or board is square.
- Allow a margin of waste at both ends of a piece of timber – the workpiece – and always cut to the waste side of the cutting line.
- For fine work, choose a face side and face edge for the workpiece – and, if needed, plane them flat (see below). Take all other measurements from here.

The best tip for measuring is: avoid it if at all possible. For example, when cutting components of the same size, measure one and then use this as a template to mark the rest. Similarly, if you can, mark individual components directly against the space they have to fit.

SQUARING UP TIMBER

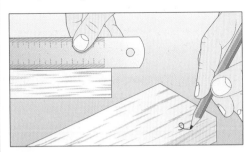

a **Choosing the face side**

Lay a ruler along the best-looking side of the workpiece to check for undulations and, if necessary, plane it flat. Mark it with a loop.

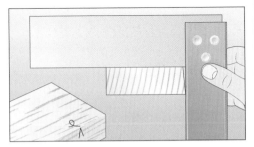

b **Choosing the face edge**

Lay the blade of a try square flat across the face side of the timber and sight along the edge. If necessary, plane it to 90° and mark it with a V.

TIPS FOR MEASURING AND MARKING

a Squaring the end of a workpiece

Take all length measurements from a mark squared across the end with a square. Draw a cross on the waste timber outside the mark.

b Measuring the length

Set the end of a ruler or measuring tape on the squared mark. At the dimension, mark an angled line each side of the point on the scale.

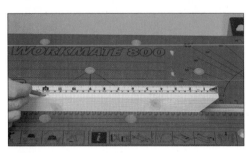

c Measuring a mitered component

Measure the outside length of the piece to be mitered (i.e., cut to 45°) and mark this distance on the face side and edge. Double-check it.

d Marking the mitered end

Set the handle of a combination square on the edge mark, with the blade sloping inward, and mark the miter on the face side.

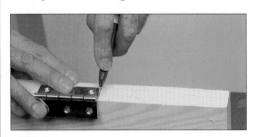

e Marking a hinge recess

Lay the hinge squarely on the edge of the door with the knuckle projecting. Mark around the hinge leaf with a sharp knife.

f Marking the hinge depth

Set a marking gauge to half the thickness of the closed hinge. Hold the gauge against the edge of the door and score the depth on the face.

Cutting wood and boards

THERE'S NOTHING MAGICAL *about sawing lumber straight, although it can be hard work unless you use power tools. Simply make sure that you use the right saw, that its blade is sharp, and that the workpiece is well supported.*

Sawing by hand

Cut lumber by hand with a hand saw, preferably one with a medium-toothed crosscut blade. Avoid cutting with the grain, as this tends to make the blade wander off-line. To saw across the grain, clamp the workpiece or support it against a firm edge with your free hand. Then, holding the saw at about 45°, position the blade to the waste side of the cutting line with your fingers, and lightly draw it back and forth to start the cut. Once the blade "bites" you can increase the length of your stroke – but don't force it; let it find its own way. To keep the saw on-line, sight down the length of the blade keeping the cutting line just visible. As you approach the end of the cut, increase the angle of the saw up to 90° to prevent tearing.

If a hand saw starts to stick, check how the workpiece is supported – it could be that the cut is closing up and pinching the blade. Failing that, remove the blade and rub it with an ordinary household candle. You should find it cuts more freely.

a **Sawing by hand with the grain**

If you have to saw with the grain, clamp the wood so that the waste hangs free. Use a ripsaw and saw at about 45°, sighting down the blade.

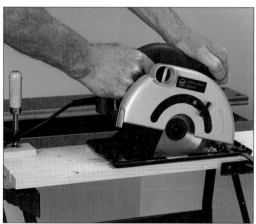

b **Power sawing with a circular saw**

Clamp a piece of wood parallel with the cutting line to act as a guide. Use the same technique to make straight cuts with a saber saw.

Power sawing

A circular saw is better for making straight cuts in large boards, but should always be used with a cutting guide, or the saw "fence" near the edges. Align the blade on the waste side or kerf of the cutting line, then clamp a straight piece of wood parallel to the line so that it just touches the soleplate of the saw. Double-check that the board is secure and that there's nothing underneath it to get in the way of the blade. Start the cut from the edge of the board, holding the saw against the guide as you go.

Fine cutting

To cut woodworking joints and to join lengths of molding in a 45° miter, use a back saw and a miter box (see below). Clamp the box in your bench, insert the workpiece, and place the saw in the slots so that the blade is just to the waste side of the cutting line. Then, guiding the saw with your fingers, draw it back and forth.

■ **Support a large board** *on pieces of wood and clamp it to a pair of sawhorses or low tables so that it doesn't slip or bow when you start sawing.*

CUTTING ACROSS THE GRAIN

a **Using a miter box**

Position the workpiece so the waste side of the cut aligns with the slot. Press the lumber against the back of the box when cutting.

b **Using a chop saw**

Set the saw to the required cutting angle and hold the workpiece against the backstop. Lower the saw slowly to make the cut.

Gluing and joining

TODAY, YOU CAN BUY ADHESIVES *to glue just about anything – and very efficient they are, too. But no adhesive will stick unless the surfaces are clean, dry, and free from grease. It's also vital to stop the parts from moving and to apply pressure while the adhesive dries, which may test your ingenuity.*

Holding and clamping

Most adhesives should be applied only in a very thin film – an excess will weaken the joint. Glued joints in wood can usually be held in place temporarily by nailing, and permanently by screwing or doweling. Otherwise, clamp the joint in your workbench or with individual C-clamps, which are sold in a range of sizes. Bind wood frame with a string or rope tourniquet, wrapped around a piece of wooden dowel. Wrap irregularly shaped objects with masking tape, or else bed them into a bowl of sand.

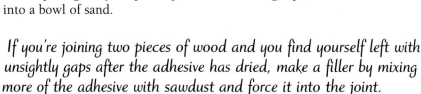

If you're joining two pieces of wood and you find yourself left with unsightly gaps after the adhesive has dried, make a filler by mixing more of the adhesive with sawdust and force it into the joint.

What glue to use where

Although there are many special-purpose adhesives, the following will cover you for most DIY jobs and are worth having in the home at all times.

- **Contact cement** is flexible and sticks leather, cloth, cork, and laminates. Apply it to both surfaces and allow it to dry before pressing them together.
- **White glue** is the first choice for wood, but it will also glue paper, canvas, and leather and is often used as a bonding additive in cement mortar. It comes in standard and waterproof, and will also bond ceramics. Apply to one surface, or to both if one of them is absorbent.
- **Contact adhesive** forms a very strong, immediate bond with sheet materials and laminates. Some types allow for adjustment. Coat both surfaces and allow to dry.
- **Epoxy resin** is a two-part resin/hardener adhesive. It is water- and heat-resistant and will also fill small gaps. Use it for metals, ceramics, and hard plastics.
- **Building adhesive** is gap-filling and is applied using a cartridge gun. Use it to bond sheet building materials and slab insulation to walls and floors.
- **Glass adhesive** bonds glass to glass and metal.
- **Superglue**, also known as cyanocrylate, gains full strength after 24 hours. It's ideal for an instant repair to most non-absorbent materials.

WAYS TO JOIN PIECES OF WOOD

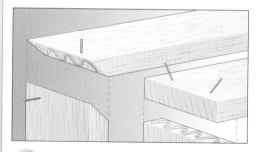

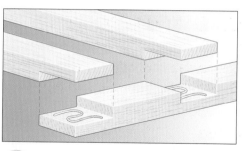

a Butt and miter joints

Use a glued butt joint, reinforced with nails or screws, for basic frames. Miter the joint for decorative frames and moldings.

b End and middle lap joints

For strong braces, a lap joint will resist distortion. Cut to a depth of half the thickness of the thinner piece of wood.

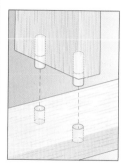

c Dowel joint

A strong joint with hidden reinforcement for frames. Use a dowel jig to drill the holes accurately. The dowels should have grooves to let excess adhesive escape.

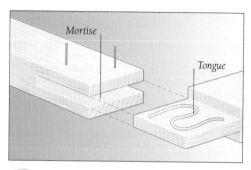

d Open mortise-and-tenon joint

Open mortise-and-tenon joints are stronger than lap joints. Cut the tongue to one-third the of wood's thickness, then cut the mortise to accept it.

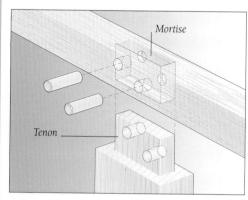

e Hidden mortise-and-tenon joint

A strong joint for furniture and structural frames. Cut the tenon, then mark the mortise from it. Drill and chisel out the mortise.

f Dado joint

Mechanically very strong for vertical loadbearing. Cut the housing to a maximum of half the wood thickness. Can be reinforced by nailing or screwing.

Nailing, drilling, and screwing

NAILS AND SCREWS *come in all shapes and sizes, and many are designed for specific purposes. Get to know what these are, and you'll always have the right hardware for the job at hand.*

Nails

Common nails are the all-purpose option for general, heavier carpentry and joining. Finishing nails can be punched in and concealed. Among the special purpose nails you may come across are spiral shank nails, which have a ridges for extra grip when fixing boards, and floor brads, which should be aligned with the grain to stop floorboards from splitting. Drywall nails have a jagged shank for extra grip; drive the head flush with the surface of the board. Use finishing nails for cabinet work, for nailing wooden molding, and for reinforcing glued joints. Choose double-head nails to secure temporary construction (the second head allows them to be removed later), and tacks to fasten carpet, tarpaper, or fabric to wood.

Drive nails in at opposing angles – called "toe-nailing" – for extra strength. Tap small nails in with the back of a tack hammer. To save your thumb, hold small nails in a strip of cardboard or pliers.

Drilling and screwing

Drilling successfully is 90 percent about choosing the right drill for the material and the right diameter for the screw or wallplug. When screwing into wood, you're supposed to drill at least twice – a pilot hole for the thread and a larger clearance hole for the plain shank, plus a countersink, too, if the head is countersunk. In practice, though, you can

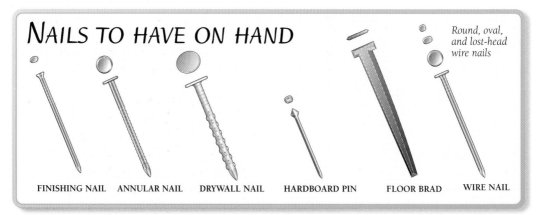

NAILS TO HAVE ON HAND

Round, oval, and lost-head wire nails

FINISHING NAIL	ANNULAR NAIL	DRYWALL NAIL	HARDBOARD PIN	FLOOR BRAD	WIRE NAIL

get away with just a pilot hole for screws No. 6 gauge or under. In ordinary softwood, you can do this quickly by hand, using an awl or gimlet. For masonry and ceramics, set your drill to slow, with the hammer action on for masonry and off for ceramics. Use the size of drill recommended for the work.

Safety do's and don'ts

- Always screw thin to thick. For maximum strength, the screw length should be around three times the thickness of the thinner piece of wood.
- Use the handle grip supplied with an electric drill for greater control. Fix a scrap of tape over the marked hole if the drill bit slips on the surface.
- Always try to match the tip of your screwdriver to the slot size of the screw, or it may slip and hurt you. If using brass or chrome screws, drive in an equivalent-size steel one first to avoid chewing up the vulnerable heads.
- Keep hammers clean and smooth to stop them from skidding off nails.

■ **Basic drill set:** (1) countersink; (2) hole saw; (3) spade bit; (4) twist bit; (5) twist bit for metal; (6) and masonry bit.

SCREW SENSE

Knowing at a glance what type and size of screw to use is a key skill to master for any do-it-yourselfer. The descriptions below refer to items from left to right and top to bottom.

■ **Screw head profiles** *Countersunk head sits flush with surface; raised head is for architectural fittings; round head sits above surface; pan head is found on machine and self-tapping screws.*

■ **Screw head recesses** *Slotted head is mainly for driving by hand; phillips head is found mainly on machine screws; square socket is good for use with power drivers, as is hexagonal recess.*

■ **Screw shanks** *Woodscrew; machine screw; cabinet screw (grips in end grain and minimizes splitting); twin-thread screw (reduces driving time and effort in timber and boards).*

■ **Screw sizes** *Common screws; the gauges (and clearance hole diameters) are: No.4 (⁹⁄₆₄ inch); No.6 (⁵⁄₃₂ inch); No.8 (³⁄₁₆ inch); No.10 (⅛ inch); No.12 (⁷⁄₃₂ inch); and No.14 (⁵⁄₃₂ inch).*

■ **Screw materials** *Steel for general work; brass for cabinet work; zinc-plated and galvanized to resist corrosion; japanned for black iron fittings. Use stainless steel screws (not shown) in oak.*

Fastening things to walls

THERE ARE SEVERAL GOLDEN RULES *for fastening to walls.*
Always choose a fastener substantial enough for the load it's taking is one;
always use the recommended size screw is another; and always check that the
wall is sound before you attach anything to it is a third. In drywall, it's wise to
screw anything heavy directly into a stud. On masonry walls, try to avoid
driving fasteners into the mortar joints between the bricks or blocks and keep
heavy-duty fasteners well away from the ends of walls.

FASTENERS FOR SOLID AND HOLLOW WALLS

Wall fasteners come in all shapes and sizes,
but are sure to fall into one of the
categories shown here.

KEY

 Wall material: solid masonry;
concrete block; frame wall.

 Vertical load supported: light;
medium; heavy.

 Insertion tool: drill; hammer;
screwdriver; wrench.

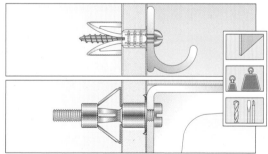

a   **Masonry nail and screw**

These easy-to-use wall fasteners are mainly
suitable for temporary and light vertical loads.

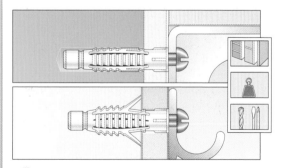

d   **Universal wall anchor**

A general-purpose anchor for use in both solid and
frame walls. The fins give the fixing strength.

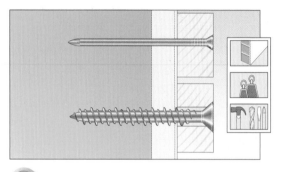

e   **Hollow wall anchors ("mollies")**

Plastic wall plugs (top) can't take much weight; the
metal expansion anchor (bottom) is more robust.

The right stuff

Remember that whatever the load-carrying capacity of a wall fastener, it will only be as strong as the material around it. Avoid fastening heavy things to drywall, and repair crumbling masonry before attaching anything to it. If you suspect there may be pipes or cables in the wall (e.g., above or around fixtures and fittings), or you're trying to locate frame studs, an ultrasonic stud finder is a good buy, although not 100 percent reliable.

■ **Install heavy-duty fasteners,** *like this anchor, into the bricks, not the mortar joints between, and keep away from the end of a wall.*

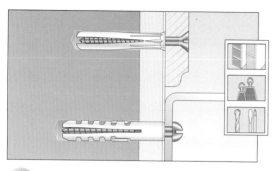

b **Solid-wall anchors**

General-purpose (top) and nylon (bottom) plugs. Use only nylon plugs in concrete block.

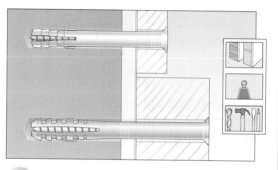

c **Frame fasteners**

Hammer-in (top) and screw-in (bottom) frame fasteners. Only use the screw-in type in masonry.

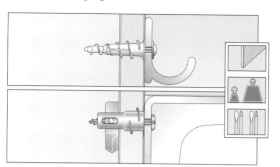

f **Drive-in hollow wall fasteners**

Drive-in fasteners require no pre-drilling. Gravity toggle types (bottom) can take heavier loads.

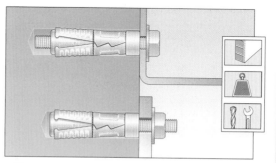

g **Masonry bolts**

These heavy-duty fasteners create great pressure. Don't use more than one per brick or block.

Curtains and pictures

ALWAYS CONSIDER THE IMPLICATIONS
when hanging things on your walls. Curtains and pictures can be quite heavy and need to be properly attached if you don't want your world to start falling down around you.

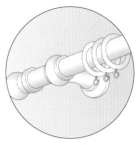

WOODEN POLE

Curtain poles, rods, and tracks

You can screw a curtain rod to the wall, to the joists, or to the window frame. Both poles and tracks can be hung from the ceiling joists above, either directly or on a supporting batten. For fastening either side of a lintel, poles can be screwed directly to the wall, while tracks need a batten to support the intermediate brackets. Tracks can also be fitted to the wood frame of the window. If the curtains are to be hung from the sides of the window reveal, choose a pole. Both tracks and poles can be fixed to the face of the lintel, but only tracks should be used for hanging from the underside.

PLASTIC TRACK

Plastic curtain rods can be bent to fit a bay window. The rod will bend more easily if it is warm. You'll need more brackets than you would with a straight window edge.

TRACK ON BATTEN
WITH PELMET

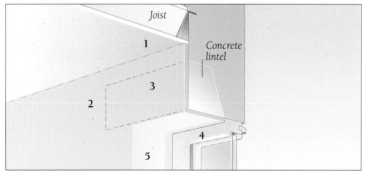

Joist

1

Concrete
lintel

2

3

4

5

■ **Fixing options:** *(1) to the joists, directly or on a batten; (2) to each side of the lintel; (3) to the face or underside of the lintel; (4) to the wood window frame; (5) to the sides of window recess.*

CURTAIN CORDSET

Pictures and mirrors

There's a right and a wrong way to hang framed mirrors and pictures. It doesn't pay to experiment!

Don't improvise when you hang mirrors and pictures. A wire nail and a piece of string may be out of sight, but they certainly won't be out of mind when the nail pops out, bringing a chunk of the wall with it and smashing the picture frame in the process. Use the hooks and hanging hardware made for the job, and you can be sure your pictures will stay up. Always use wallplugs or "mollies" for very heavy items.

Think about artificial and natural light when you position pictures and mirrors. Reflections and glare on a picture may make it difficult to see. But remember that with mirrors, reflected light is an advantage. Carefully positioned mirrors brighten a dark corner with "borrowed light" and can be used to make a small room seem bigger.

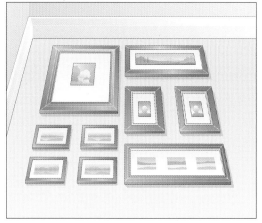

■ **Trial run:** *test out how an arrangement of pictures will look by laying them out on the floor before you hang them on the wall.*

PICTURE FIXINGS

Picture pins/hooks
Molding hanger
Frame hangers
Hanging wire

a **Hardware for hanging**

Self-nailing hooks are for light loads only. Always drive in nails at a downward angle.

b **Molding hangers**

When hung from a picture rail, these will support heavier weights than standard hooks.

c **Attaching hanger wire**

Thread a length of picture wire through the ring, loop it back over itself, and feed the end through the loop.

Concrete and mortar

PORTLAND CEMENT, SAND, and gravel are the three dry constituents of concrete and mortar. You'll find it more convenient to buy them pre-mixed in bags labeled "general purpose concrete" or "bricklaying mortar" for most small masonry jobs around the home. Only if you're tackling a patio or driveway will you need to order them separately from a builders' supplier.

Know your materials

Buy the ingredients you need for your concrete or mortar from a lumber yard or quarry and use this recipe for general projects such as walkways: mix 1 part cement, 2.5 parts mason's sand, and 3 parts gravel with water. See below for simple instructions on how to mix concrete by hand.

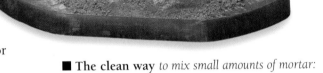

■ **The clean way** to mix small amounts of mortar: on a special tray or a trash can lid.

MIXING BY HAND

1 **Create a cavity**

Mix the sand and cement thoroughly. Form the pile into a "volcano" with the shovel.

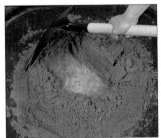

2 **Add water**

Pour water into the "crater" you have made and gradually turn in the sides.

3 **Cut and test**

Chop the mixture through. It is ready to use when it slips easily off the shovel.

Working with drywall

FOR MANY YEARS *the most popular way to surface walls and ceilings has been sheetrock, since it is easy to cut and provides a flat, smooth surface.*

Know your drywall

Standard drywall has a grey paper covering on one side and an ivory-colored surface, suitable for decorating, on the other. Drywall is made in several thicknesses. All-purpose drywall – for lining walls and ceilings – comes in 8 x 4 foot sheets and is easily cut and installed. Particleboard is made of resin and wood particles, and certain grades are used for walls. It is harder to work with than standard drywall and may not fasten as securely. Greenboard is moisture-resistant drywall used for bathroom walls and other high-moisture areas. It is used just like standard drywall, and its surface is suitable for tiling. For a totally waterproof surface such as untiled shower walls, you should consider using concrete backerboard. Although it is harder to work with than other types of drywall, it is waterproof.

SHEETROCK

Drywall is surprisingly heavy, so don't attempt to carry more than one sheet by yourself.

PARTICLEBOARD

When moving drywall, always carry sheets vertically so that they won't crack or snap. Cut them in half if handling them is too difficult.

CONCRETE BACKERBOARD

PAPER TAPE

WEBBED TAPE

■ **Materials:** *to cover joints between boards with webbed or paper tape (above) and compound. Hang drywall sheets with drywall nails (far right), or, preferably, with drywall screws (right).*

DRYWALL SCREWS   **DRYWALL NAILS**

Hanging drywall

When installing drywall – for example, on a partition wall with a wood frame – start in one corner and work across the wall to the other end. Using full sheets, nail or screw the edges of the board at 7-inch intervals; the rest of the sheet can be nailed at 12-inch intervals. After you've covered as large an area as possible with full sheets, measure and cut smaller pieces to fit the gaps. Nails or screws can be used on a wooden frame, but always use screws for fixing to metal laths.

Position drywall panels vertically on walls 8 feet or less; position them horizontally on walls higher than 8 feet.

HANGING AND TAPING DRYWALL

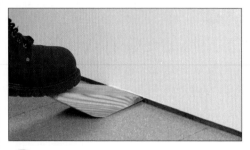

1 Wedge the sheet into position

To free your hands while you fasten the sheet, use a wooden foot lever – made from an offcut of wood – to hold the sheet in place.

2 Apply self-adhesive joint tape

After installing the sheets, apply self-adhesive, mesh joint tape to cover the gaps between them. Press the tape firmly along the gap.

3 Cover tape with joint compound

Apply compound over the tape to mask the joints and any indentations. Use a joint knife or spatula and repeat if necessary.

4 Feather the edges

To disguise the joints, "feather" the edges of the compound while still wet by wiping with a sponge. Any other imperfections can be sanded.

Joining at corners

Coat internal corners with a thin layer of filler, then press a length of joint tape into the corner. Cover the tape with more filler, doing one wall first and then the other. Strengthen external corners with metal corner beads nailed at 6-inch intervals. Fill one side, scraping the filler downwards towards the corner. Then repeat this process on the other side.

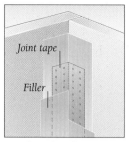

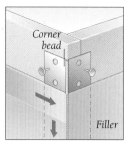

INTERNAL CORNER   **EXTERNAL CORNER**

1 **Cutting drywall**

Mark the cutting line in pencil, then cut with a utility knife held against a metal straightedge.

2 **Snapping boards**

After cutting, turn the sheet on edge and snap it against your knee.

A simple summary

✔ Don't forget the golden rule: "measure twice; cut once".

✔ When sawing, use the right saw and support the workpiece.

✔ Surfaces to be glued should be clean, dry, and grease-free.

✔ Know which nails or screws you should use for a particular job.

✔ Check a wall is sound before fixing anything to it.

✔ There's more than one way to hang a curtain.

✔ Concrete and mortar can be bought ready-mixed.

✔ Drywall is easy to work with and gives a smooth surface.

Part Two

Chapter 5
Painting Walls and Ceilings

Chapter 6
Painting Woodwork

Chapter 7
Wallpapering

Chapter 8
CeramicTiling

Chapter 9
Staining and Varnishing

Chapter 10
Laying Floorcoverings

Chapter 5

Painting Walls and Ceilings

FOR FAST RESULTS, PAINT IS STILL THE number one choice – and modern paints are easier to use than ever. But no paint will disguise a substandard or poorly prepared surface; you get out what you put in.

In this chapter...

✓ *Paint for walls and ceilings*

✓ *Before you start*

✓ *Using rollers and pads*

✓ *Spray painting*

✓ *Texturing and stenciling*

✓ *Creating paint effects*

✓ *Access to awkward areas*

✓ *Outdoor decorating*

Paint for walls and ceilings

NOT SURE WHAT TYPE of paint to buy? Your choice depends mainly on what surface you're covering, the finish – gloss or flat? smooth or textured? – and on how much wear and tear the newly painted surface will have to endure.

Paints for inside the house

For interiors, water-based latex paint is by far the easiest and most popular option. Think twice before painting walls in oil-based alkyd paint, as it is harder to paint over next time around and far more difficult to deal with; if you want the high gloss of oil-based paint, consider using a gloss or semi-gloss latex instead.

1 **Latex paint:** the most common type of paint. Made with vinyl or acrylic binders, latex paints come in flat, satin (eggshell), semi-gloss, and gloss finishes. Paint quality – how well it will cover and how evenly it will spread – varies, but price is generally an indicator of quality. Dozens of colors are readily available, and most paint stores and home centers will custom blend from a color swatch such as a piece of fabric.

As a rough guide to estimating quantities, measure the area of the surface to be covered (width x height). Generally, a gallon will cover 300 to 350 square feet, though this varies depending on the number of windows, the darkness of the underlying paint, and other factors.

2 **Primers:** thinner types of water- or oil-based paints. They seal the underlying surface and provide a good bond for the top coats, helping them adhere to the surface better. Flat latex white can be used as a primer for water-base paints.

3 **Surface technique paints:** these are growing in popularity. They include such effects as denim texture, crackle finishes, and "aging" paint.

4 **Climate-specific paints:** these are offered by many manufacturers. They include paints with fungicides (mold inhibitors) for humid southern states.

5 **Ceiling paint:** a flat, white latex or oil paint that is glare and crack resistant and offers a very uniform sheen. It can be tinted to match wall paint, and also as textured paint to hide imperfections. Dripless types are cleaner to use.

6 **Textured paints:** these can add a unique look to a room, and are also excellent choices for walls with imperfections that you want to conceal.

Paints for outside the house

1 **Exterior paints**: these come as water-based or oil-based formulas, in four basic sheens: flat, satin enamel, semi-gloss enamel, and hi-gloss enamel. They are formulated to cover most exterior surfaces, although the different sheens are normally used on different surfaces. Flat or satin enamels are usually used on wood siding, vinyl or aluminum surfaces, and brick, masonry, or stucco. Semi-gloss and hi-gloss are usually reserved for doors, windows, and shutters.

2 **Stucco paint**: specially formulated to be more flexible, with a much more durable coating, resisting the cracks that are common on this surface. Some stucco paints will even coat and seal hairline cracks, helping protect the surface from water.

3 **Porch and floor paints**: durable gloss paints that saturate and protect exterior porch floors and decks.

4 **Concrete paint**: sometimes called "garage floor paint." This is used for those areas and other smooth concrete surfaces such as some foundation walls. These paints seal the surface and protect against staining.

5 **Rust-preventative paint**: this helps protect metal areas, such as railings and exterior junction boxes. It is most commonly offered in gloss black or gloss white.

INTERNET

www.diyonline.com

This site offers an excellent paint calculator that estimates how much paint and primer you need. It even allows for doors, windows, and other room features.

■ **Once you have** *selected a paint type, you must decide on your color scheme. Do you want the paint on the walls to create a strong visual impact or form a neutral backdrop? Get it right and the result can be breathtaking.*

Before you start

A PROFESSIONAL-LOOKING PAINT JOB starts with thorough planning. An empty room is far easier to paint than one full of furniture, and if you can clear the room completely, all the better.

Pointers for getting the room ready

- Take down all mirrors, pictures, curtains, and blinds, and remove them from the room. Clear the room of everything else that is portable.
- Cover the floor with drop cloths, taped to each other and to the baseboards. Use canvas if possible because it won't slip. If you want to use inexpensive plastic drop cloths, use only a single layer, and cover with newspaper.
- Move heavy furniture away from the walls and cover with plastic sheets.
- Wrap light fixtures in plastic bags secured with twist ties. Remove switch plates, outlet covers, doorknobs, and other fixtures; if you can't, mask them.

When working around light fixtures, light switches, and electrical outlets it's wise to turn off the power to the room at the breaker box or by removing fuses. Leave a sign on the box so that nobody turns the power back on.

Masking fittings

Professionals don't bother with masking tape – often to the chagrin of the people employing them! But unless you're extra-confident of your ability to paint a straight line, it's worth masking any fixtures and fittings that you can't remove. When applying blue painter's tape or regular masking tape, smooth down the paint-side edge and leave the other edge unstuck. This will make it easier to remove the tape, which you should do as soon as the paint is dry to the touch. If you leave the tape on any longer, it may not come away cleanly.

Suggestions for lighting and ventilation

- Arrange for some portable lighting so that you don't overlook drips and runs or miss any areas. If you are working on a wall, bounce the light off the ceiling to throw as even a light as possible onto the surface, and vice versa.
- Before doing any sanding or scraping that will raise a lot of dust, seal doorways with plastic sheeting taped around the outside.
- Use a window fan and a cartridge respirator when using oil base paints or solvents. A fan is useful to create a cross breeze when using latex paints.

Preparing surfaces

Surfaces for painting should be as smooth and blemish-free as you can make them. They need to be clean, too. Bear in mind that textured wallpaper may be hiding a multitude of sins in the plaster beneath. Look out for flaking paint. Scrape it back to a sound edge with a paint scraper. If the paint is gloss, sand it lightly with a medium grit sanding sponge to provide a good bonding surface for the new paint.

Strip that wallpaper

It's not a good idea to paint over wallpaper. Even if the seams look stuck down, they will almost certainly curl after painting – and you'll never get them to stay stuck down. Painted-over wallpaper is also very difficult to strip. Below are two methods of stripping wallpaper

1 **Soaking and stripping by hand:** This is usually the best way to remove wallpaper. Score the paper before soaking. If the paper doesn't scrape off easily, score and soak again. Remove any remaining paste with clean, warm water.

2 **Steam stripping:** This method is best for heavy or textured paper, and essential for painted-over paper of any description. Score the paper before you start.
  - Fill the machine with water and let it heat up. Put on gloves and overalls.
  - When steam starts seeping from the plate, apply it to the wall in short bursts until the paper starts to loosen. Ideally, you should have someone following you with a scraper before the paper dries out. Again, clean off any residue with warm water and fine-grade steel wool.

STRIPPING OLD WALLPAPER

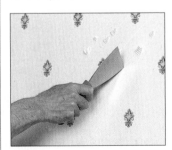

1 **Score**

Score paper with the edge of a scraper, but be careful not to dig into surface beneath.

2 **Soak**

Use a sponge to soak the paper with water. Leave for about 15 minutes before scraping.

3 **Scrape**

Scrape away the paper, keeping the scraper at a shallow angle to avoid damaging the surface.

Repair those cracks and holes

Inspect the surface and circle any dents, cracks, peeling paint, bumps, or nail holes in pencil so that you don't miss them. Also look out for tobacco and mildew stains and old water stains – especially on ceilings. Now assess your repair strategy.

To cover up a wall with lots of small blemishes, consider lining the walls with lining paper if you are going to hang wallpaper. Hang the lining paper horizontally to avoid seams matching with the wallpaper seams. Follow the manufacturer's directions for type of adhesive. If you plan on painting the walls, smooth the surface by skim coating – applying an even layer all over – with joint compound or plaster. You'll find that joint compound is much easier to use. Coat the wall evenly using a drywall knife and then sand the surface smooth with a sanding sponge. You may need to apply and sand more than one coat.

Patch general wear and tear with spackle. For holes more than about ¼ inch deep, apply the spackle in layers and let each one dry before applying the next. This may seem time-consuming, but it's worth it in the long run. It's also worth the effort to repair all minor cracks and chips, because even the smallest flaw will show through your finished work. In particular, look out for nail holes. Force spackle into the nail hole with the edge of a narrow putty knife or the end of your finger. Then smooth over with the knife and sand smooth and level once the spackle is dry. Use the same procedure for dents.

To fill a hole in a plaster wall, first clean the hole, dampen the surface, then patch it a layer at a time using patching plaster. Score each layer when dry, then apply another

FILLING CRACKS

1 **Cracks in plaster**

Rake out the loose material with the corner of a putty knife, then brush out the dust with a paintbrush.

2 **Fill with spackle**

Press the spackle into the crack with the knife, leaving it smooth, but slightly above the surface.

3 **Sand**

When dry, sand the repair until it's smooth and level, using a sanding block and fine-grade sandpaper.

layer. Sand to make an even surface. If the wooden laths are broken, staple a piece of wire mesh across them to act as a base for the repair. Patch small holes in drywall with the patch shown below. Cut larger holes back to the nearest studs using a utility knife and straightedge, then cut a drywall patch to match and screw it in place using drywall screws. Tape, compound, and sand the seams of the patch.

Fill the gaps around moldings, window frames and sills, and other woodwork with silicone caulk, which comes in tubes that are loaded into an inexpensive caulking gun. Lay down an even bead of caulk, with steady pressure on the trigger, and smooth afterward with a moistened fingertip.

Dealing with stains and cleaning

Mold and mildew occur anywhere ventilation is poor, and often point to condensation problems. Wash with a mild bleach solution, then wash with a TSP solution and allow to dry completely before painting. Cover old water stains with white shellac. For very badly stained areas use stain-blocking primer to stop stains from coming back through after you've repainted. Having said all that, it is best to sort out the cause of the mold and mildew before dealing with its symptoms.

Whatever the surface, even on sound painted walls, wash the entire surface with a TSP cleanser, sand lightly, and wipe off remaining dust. TSP (trisodium phospate) products are available at home centers and hardware stores.

FILLING SMALL HOLES

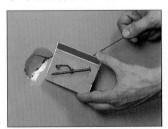

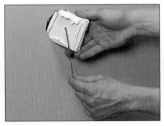

1 **Measure hole**

Cut a drywall patch that is big enough to fit behind the hole. Attach string to the patch with a nail.

2 **Coat with compound**

Spread wall compound around the edges, feed the patch through the hole, and pull back until it sticks.

3 **Hide the repair**

Cut the string before filling the recess with wall compound, then sand the repair level with the surface.

Using rollers and pads

ROLLERS ARE THE BEST CHOICE *for painting large areas of wall or ceiling – although you still have to cut in around the edges with a brush. Not so with the paint pads. These are an increasingly popular alternative to rollers, and are especially good for dealing with awkward areas. They come in a range of different sizes and special shapes.*

Types of paint rollers

Standard paint roller frames are 9 inches wide, as are the roller covers or sleeves that go on them. Choose a roller with a wire frame and a handle threaded for an extension pole. It is also handy to have a smaller roller with a long handle for reaching down behind radiators and other awkward areas. Specialty rollers include cones, doughnut-shaped, and 3-inch trim rollers.

Before filling a roller tray, line it with a plastic tray liner so that you don't have to clean the tray when changing colors. Tray liners are sold in bulk or singly at home centers and paint stores, but buy at the same time as the tray, to ensure the sizes match.

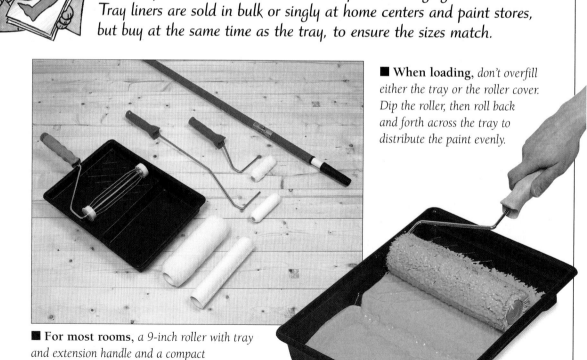

■ **When loading,** *don't overfill either the tray or the roller cover. Dip the roller, then roll back and forth across the tray to distribute the paint evenly.*

■ **For most rooms,** *a 9-inch roller with tray and extension handle and a compact mini-roller are all you need.*

Picking the right roller cover

The three basic types of roller cover materials are synthetic, natural fibers such as lamb's wool or mohair, and foam. Synthetics are used for water-based paint, although many are acceptable for oil-based paint and stains as well. Natural fibers should be used only with oil-based paints. Foam is used with oil-based or high-gloss latex paints. You also need to choose a nap, or fiber length. For most surfaces, ⅜ inch is ideal. Extremely smooth surfaces, such as metal door frames, call for a thin nap, such as 3/16 or ¼ inch. Rough, textured surfaces require a ¾-inch nap or thicker.

Do not lift the roller off the surface between strokes. If you do, it may spin and spray paint in all directions. Guard against patchy painting by monitoring how evenly the paint is going on, adjusting pressure on the roller accordingly.

ROLLING A WALL

Ironically, the secret of successful rolling is knowing how to cut in with a brush to leave a clean line along adjoining surfaces. Use a 3- or 4-inch sash brush, not too heavily loaded with paint. Hold it on edge, apply just enough pressure to get some spring in the bristles so that they fan out, and draw the brush along in a single, smooth stroke. Paint from the dry area back into wet to avoid lap marks, and paint slowly to avoid mistakes.

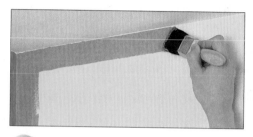

1 **Cut in with a brush around edges**

Successful cutting in comes with practice. If you make a mistake, clean off the paint mark and continue.

2 **Lay on the paint**

Begin rolling about the middle of the wall, rolling with even pressure toward the ceiling and down again in shape of a "W."

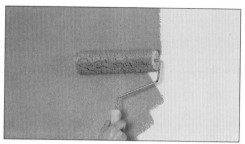

3 **Smooth out the paint**

Even out the paint with horizontal or vertical strokes, blending into the wet edges. Double-check you haven't missed any spots.

Using paint pads

Often overlooked, paint pads are a handy alternative to rollers for difficult areas, smooth surfaces, and areas that are susceptible to drips. The pads themselves come in a variety of shapes and sizes, with special shapes for painting moldings, muntins, and even corners.

Paint pad techniques

Larger pads tend to be limited in their use. They hold less paint than a roller, so they take longer, and on large areas it can be tricky to get an even coverage of paint. Paint pads really come into their own when working on edges, where they can be used instead of cutting in with a brush, and in special circumstances such as corners which can be tricky with a roller.

You can apply the paint from an ordinary roller tray, but a paint pad tray with a wheel is a better bet because it avoids overloading. Work the pad steadily across the surface and blend wet edges in much the same way as you would with a roller.

■ **A basic paint-pad kit,** *with a selection of pads and a loading tray, would be a good starting point for any painting project.*

APPLYING PAINT WITH A PAINT PAD

1 **Loading paint**

Load the pad from the wheel of its paint tray, scraping off the excess as you go to avoid drips.

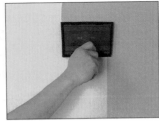

2 **Using a pad**

Grasp the handle firmly and draw the pad in a single direction with smooth strokes.

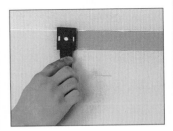

3 **Edging**

Use a small pad to paint edges instead of cutting in with a paintbrush.

Spray painting

IF YOU'RE DECORATING *a number of rooms at once or a large open space, renting or buying a paint sprayer may be a worthwhile option. As you have to mask everything first, using a roller is probably quicker for smaller jobs. You'll need the correct filters for the type of paint you are using. Protect floors and other surfaces from overspray and take safety precautions such as wearing a respirator.*

Using a spray gun

Always wear a respirator when using a spray gun and keep the room well ventilated. For best results, move the gun gently from side to side as you spray, keeping the nozzle perpendicular to the surface. Start in the middle of the wall so that you can get used to the spray range. You can cut down on overspray by adjusting the nozzle, but it's wiser to protect the surrounding woodwork even if you're going to paint over it afterwards. Be aware that a cross breeze might also blow the paint spray where it's not wanted.

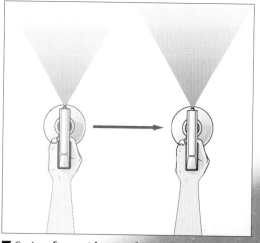

■ **Swing from side to side** *as you spray, but keep the nozzle perpendicular to the surface. Avoid spraying in an arc.*

Texturing and stenciling

IT ISN'T TO EVERYONE'S TASTE, *but there's no easier way to disguise a poor quality wall or ceiling surface than with texture paint. Stenciling is a fun and easy way to brighten up plain walls.*

Using texture paint

There are three basic types of texture paint: ceiling texture paint, which can be used on drywall or acoustic tiles; sand texture paints; and smooth-wall texture paint, which is a thicker bodied version of latex paint. All of these are offered either pre-mixed or in a powder form that is mixed with water and blended to a thick consistency. Powdered mixes generally allow for thicker texturing. Regardless of the type you choose, create a variety of textures by using a patterned roller, whisk broom, comb, or other tool – even your fingers!

■ **Texture paint** *can be satisfying to apply on inferior wall surfaces, but the only way to get rid of it is to replaster the area.*

TEXTURE PAINTING

a **Random swirls**

Twist a damp sponge to make overlapping swirls.

b **Graceful arcs**

Lightly pass a paint comb over the surface in graceful arcs.

c **Regular patterns**

A textured roller creates a finer, more regular texture.

Stenciling

Stenciling decorative patterns on painted walls is a quick, inexpensive way to add a personal touch to your decorative scheme. You can use it to pick out interesting features in a room, or for your own custom border design. And unlike most decorating, it's fun!

Getting in shape

You can buy many different types and styles of stencils in large home centers, paint stores, and art shops. These range from simple teddy bears for a child's room to intricate floral designs for borders. Some stencils are adhesive backed, but others must be stuck to the wall with stencil tape, which won't damage the surface underneath. Although you can use spray paint or latex, you'll find it easier to get good

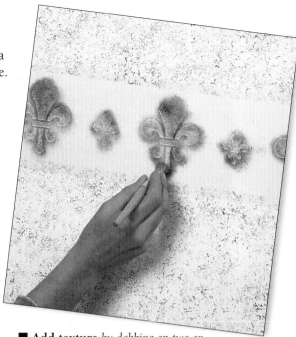

■ **Add texture** *by dabbing on two or three colors with a short-bristled stencil brush.*

results with stencil paint, a creamy, almost dry paint made specifically for working with stencils. Apply the paint with a stiff stenciling brush or sponge for best control. Load the brush lightly with paint and dab onto scrap paper until you have the color density you want.

STENCILING A DECORATIVE BORDER

1 Paint base color

Apply the first color by dabbing the brush, keeping it perpendicular to the surface.

2 Add details

Apply a second color when the first is dry, to give a more three-dimensional effect.

3 Finish

Gently peel off the stencil as soon as the paint is touch-dry to avoid smudging.

Creating paint effects

PERSONALIZE YOUR WALLS *or disguise blemishes with a multi-color specialized paint finish. Generally this involves painting on a base coat of solid color – usually eggshell finish – then applying a textured coat of paint or a glaze over the top.*

Rag rolling

This is done by rolling a rag over a second color that has been applied over a base coat, or by soaking the rag in the second color and rolling over the base coat. The top coat paint is usually mixed with a glaze to make it more translucent, though you can just dilute the top coat paint. To begin, roll a rag into a cylinder and roll it down the wall; overlap adjoining rows slightly. For a slightly different effect, you can dab with a crumpled rag in a method called "ragging." Make sure your rags are lint-free cotton or linen, and change them often, before they become over-saturated with paint. Use only one type of fabric for the entire project.

■ **Rolling with a cloth soaked in paint:** *twist the rag into a cylinder, coat with paint (inset), and apply, varying the direction for a random effect.*

Sponging

Sponging, as its name implies, involves dabbing irregular patches of paint onto a dry base coat with a sponge. For best results, use a natural sponge about 10 inches across. Soak the sponge in water until it swells to its full size, then wring it out again before dipping it in the paint. Dab the paint on with a light, twisting jerk of the hand, ensuring each dab merges with the last. When the first coat is dry, repeat the process with a second color. Alternatively for a deeper, more

■ **Set out your colors** *for sponging in a paint tray – there's no reason to limit yourself to two. But don't apply the first color too densely and be careful not to overload the sponge.*

subtle effect, sponge on a second coat of a lighter version of the first color. You can achieve an entirely different, much denser sponging effect by dabbing a damp sponge into the base coat while it is still wet. It's best to practice first on an unobtrusive area of wall, inside a closet, or on a spare sheet of plywood.

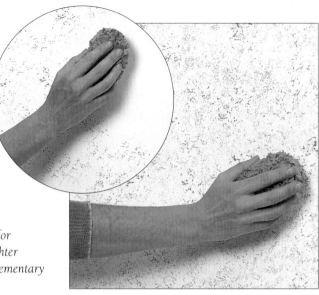

■ **Two colors are better than one** *for sponging. Make the second color a lighter version of the first, or choose a complementary color for a brighter effect.*

Colorwashing

Colorwashing allows you to create a range of effects from a marbled surface to a water effect, and is a great way to cover an inferior wall surface. The technique involves applying streaks of concentrated second color over a lightly painted underlying color so that inconsistencies – and the brushstrokes – show through. You can enhance the effect with a third color. The base and topcoats can be paint on paint, or more commonly, a special glaze available at paint stores and home centers. Apply both with a wide soft wall brush.

APPLYING A COLORWASH

1 Base coat

Neutral eggshell paint makes a good base coat. Brush the paint on and allow to dry.

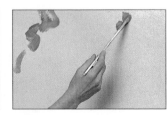

2 Second color

The second color can be much stronger. Dab on and brush out over the surface quickly.

3 Brush out

Finally, sweep the brush lightly over the topcoat at random so that the brushstrokes show.

Access to awkward areas

FALLING FROM A HEIGHT can be fatal, so if you have any doubts at all about working above ground level from a ladder or platform – don't: call in a professional. If you do decide to go ahead, take care to use the right equipment and follow the safety precautions outlined here.

Building a platform for a stairwell

Gaining access to the upper reaches of a stairwell takes thought and planning. Rent scaffold platform boards to make a platform and make sure that the supporting ladders can't slip by blocking the feet with sandbags or other heavy bracing.

- Make sure the ladder is not placed at too steep an angle.
- The platform ends should overlap ladder rungs by 2 feet or more.
- Use C-clamps to attach the boards to the ladders and to each other. Or tie them together with rope wrapped around nails part-hammered into the boards.
- Check the braces on stepladders regularly to ensure they are locked and tight.

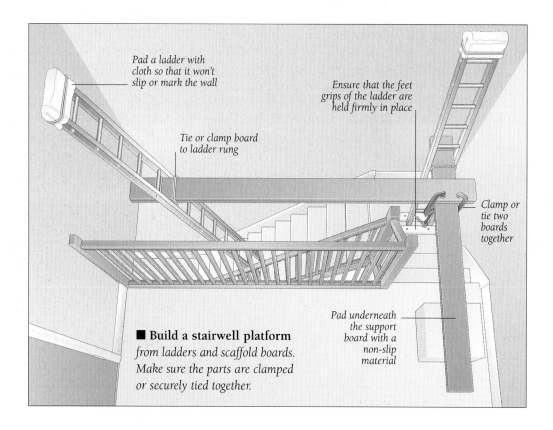

Pad a ladder with cloth so that it won't slip or mark the wall

Ensure that the feet grips of the ladder are held firmly in place

Tie or clamp board to ladder rung

Clamp or tie two boards together

■ **Build a stairwell platform** *from ladders and scaffold boards. Make sure the parts are clamped or securely tied together.*

Pad underneath the support board with a non-slip material

Ladder safety

Falls from ladders and stepladders are the most common cause of DIY accidents, so be careful. For outdoor work up high, consider renting a steel scaffold tower instead. These are built up in sections on adjustable feet and are much more stable. Remember the following safety rules:

● Always place a ladder on a firm, level base. If it has to go on an uneven surface, build a stable platform for it to stand on – it's much safer than propping up one leg.

● When climbing a ladder, keep your hands free to grasp both sides. Carry tools in a bag or tool belt and keep one hand on the ladder at all times.

● If you stand higher than the third rung from the top, your chances of losing your balance are greatly increased. Likewise, "walking" a ladder along a wall is asking for a fall. Never be tempted to over-reach – the easiest way to make a ladder tip over.

● Don't stand on the top step of a stepladder – it is only designed to take the weight of tools.

Never attempt to repair a ladder. You should replace it with a new one if it seems even slightly unstable or unsafe.

● Try not to position a ladder in front of a closed door. If you must, be sure it can't be opened by unwary passers-by.

● If the top of a ladder has to rest against a window, lash a stud across the ladder so that the stud can straddle the width of the opening.

● Wear shoes with non-slip soles.

■ **A rented scaffold tower** *can be built up in sections. Always lock the wheels and climb up the inside or use a separate ladder for access.*

Outdoor decorating

KEEP ALL EXTERIOR PAINTED SURFACES *in top condition by sticking to a 4-year repair and repainting cycle. You can begin with woodwork in year one, then tackle metal surfaces the following year, masonry the year after that, and fences and wooden garden structures in the fourth year.*

Exterior woodwork

Exterior woodwork is vulnerable to the effects of weather, especially on the side getting the most sun. So make a point of checking for deterioration at least once a year and patch it up quickly, before it gets any worse. Cut out and replace any rotten wood. Scrape away any flaking paint, then sand the surface and brush away the dust. Coat any new or bare wood with primer and patch cracks in the wood itself with an exterior-grade wood filler. Give the patch one or two coats of undercoat, then a coat of exterior gloss paint. Fill any gaps between woodwork and masonry using a caulking gun.

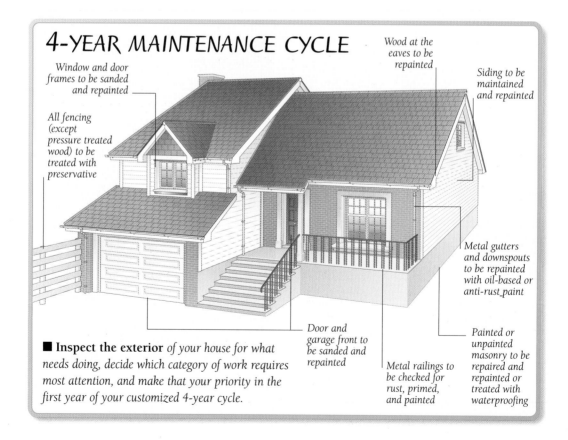

4-YEAR MAINTENANCE CYCLE

Wood at the eaves to be repainted

Window and door frames to be sanded and repainted

Siding to be maintained and repainted

All fencing (except pressure treated wood) to be treated with preservative

Metal gutters and downspouts to be repainted with oil-based or anti-rust paint

■ **Inspect the exterior** *of your house for what needs doing, decide which category of work requires most attention, and make that your priority in the first year of your customized 4-year cycle.*

Door and garage front to be sanded and repainted

Metal railings to be checked for rust, primed, and painted

Painted or unpainted masonry to be repaired and repainted or treated with waterproofing

Metalwork

Metal begins to rust as soon as its protective layer of paint cracks. In most cases, it can be retouched with oil-based paint. Gutters and downspouts are often protected with metal paint, so the same type of paint must be used. Coat bare metal with metal primer or anti-rust paint. Then apply two or more topcoats.

Masonry and fencing

Follow the following pointers for painting masonry and fences:

- Re-point crumbling mortar joints with new mortar.
- Remove crumbling bits of concrete or stucco and repair with a patch of new concrete or stucco over a wire bed. Seal foundation cracks with exterior-grade filler.
- Treat mold and mildew stains with fungicide solution.
- Use a short-nap roller to apply paint to smooth surfaces, and a thick-nap roller on textures.
- Fences decks, sheds, and any other exposed wood should be re-coated every 4 years with a waterproof sealer. Apply it generously, working it into the vulnerable crevices. Add the second coat where weather conditions are severe.

A simple summary

✔ Select paint not just on the basis of color, but on the punishment it's going to take.

✔ The more time you spend on preparation, the better the result will be. At the very least, make surfaces sound and clean.

✔ The fastest way to paint walls and ceilings is with a roller, plus a brush or selection of paint pads for the corners and edges.

✔ Spray painting can be a very fast way to paint.

✔ Stenciling is a quick and easy way to add a personal touch to your room's decor.

✔ Special paint effects can disguise blemishes on your walls.

✔ Most DIY accidents involve falls from ladders. Take extreme care whenever you're working off the ground.

✔ Try and keep the outside of your house looking its best by following a 4-year repair and repainting cycle.

Chapter 6

Painting Woodwork

L ET'S FACE IT: PAINTING WOODWORK is a chore. But it has to be done, so the least you can do is make life easy for yourself next time by preparing the surface properly. If you don't, the paint will flake off and you'll be right back where you started. It's important to paint doors and windows in the right order, too.

In this chapter...

✓ Paints and tools
  for woodwork

✓ Preparing painted wood

✓ Preparing bare wood

✓ Painting molding
  and doors

✓ Painting windows

PAINTING WOODWORK FREEHAND TAKES PRACTICE: IT'S OFTEN EASIER TO MASK AREAS WITH TAPE

Paints and tools for woodwork

THERE ARE PLENTY OF PAINTING *tools, but you don't need many for woodwork. The same goes for paint: basically the choice is between oil-based, which tends to be more durable, and water-based, which is easier to use.*

Choosing the right equipment

Invest in some quality basics. Three sizes of paintbrush should cover you: a 2-inch brush for tackling window muntins, raised moldings, and the edges of baseboards; a 3-inch brush for painting door and window frames and rails; and a 4-inch brush for covering large, flat areas like door panels and flat doors. For applying water-based gloss paint, which is on the thin side, consider using paint pads to combat drips and runs. Specially shaped paint pads are also very good for complex moldings where runs are a problem. Use a plastic paint shield to protect adjacent surfaces – it's much quicker than masking with tape.

One specialized piece of equipment that is worth buying is a sash brush for cutting in. This has its bristles shaped at an angle, so that they fan out to a much finer line when pressure is applied. It takes practice, but cutting in is definitely the fastest way to paint woodwork.

FINISHES FOR WOODWORK

	Oil-based paint	Water-based paint	Wood stain	Polyurethane	Varnish	Oil	Shellac
Suitable for:							
Softwoods	Yes	Yes	Yes	Yes	Yes	Yes	No
Hardwoods	Yes	Yes	Yes	Yes	Yes	Yes	Yes
Interior use	Yes	Yes	Yes	Yes	Yes	Yes	Yes
Exterior use	Yes	Yes	No	Yes	Yes	Yes	No
Apply with:							
Brush	Yes	Yes	Yes	Yes	Yes	Yes	Yes
Paint pad	Yes	Yes	Yes	No	No	No	No
Cloth pad	No	No	Yes	No	Yes	Yes	Yes
Spray gun	Yes	Yes	No	Yes	Yes	No	No

Coverage guide for 1 pint:
primer 50–60 sq ft; undercoat 80 sq ft; gloss 75 sq ft; one-coat gloss 50 sq ft

Plastic paint shields

Paint buckets

4-inch brush

3-inch brush

Sandpapers of different grits

2-inch brush

1-inch brush

Angled sash brush

Paint scraper

Sanding block

Hook scrapers

Putty knives

Preparing painted wood

AS LONG AS THE OLD PAINT is stuck to the woodwork, there should be no need to strip it. But use your judgment: on windows especially, there comes a time when the accumulated layers of paint make surfaces look lumpy and cause edges to lose their sharpness. If you experience problems with sticking as well, it might be time to get out the heat stripper…

Deciding what to do

Paint simply needs to be washed with a mild detergent to remove any dirt and grease. The dirtiest areas will be those that get touched, such as around handles. First, check for any blemishes. Fill shallow scratches with glazing compound and deeper holes with wood filler. Sand smooth, and remove the dust with a damp cloth or tack cloth before painting.

Sanding painted woodwork with sandpaper can generate a surprising amount of heat, so take care not to burn your fingers. As a rule it's best not to use power tools, as they can burn the paint.

Old, damp paintwork may show a green or brown growth of mildew, which will ruin the new finish if it is not removed before you start painting. Wash down with a dilute solution of household bleach, let it dry, then wash again with TSP solution and rinse thoroughly. Remember to work from the top downward, to avoid dribbles of dirty water.

Any flaking paint should be scraped off. If this leaves you with bare wood, you must prime the area before repainting. If you find yourself left with shallow gouges, fill with wood filler and then sand smooth.

Keep an eye out for knots that have swelled. These should be sanded and primed. If a knot is "live" and is bleeding resin, make sure that you treat the area with a sealer primer.

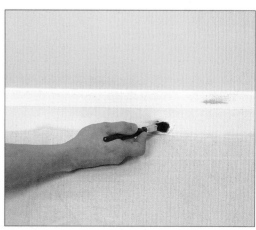

■ **Prevent the top coat** *of paint from sinking into any patches of bare wood by applying primer. This will hold the paint on the surface.*

PREPARATION PROCEDURE

1 Fill any chips

Use wood filler to cover blemishes in the existing woodwork. Use the corner of a small putty knife to fill hard-to-reach places.

2 Sand

Sand down the filler with sandpaper wrapped around a wood sanding block. In tight corners, fold the paper into a pad and use the edge.

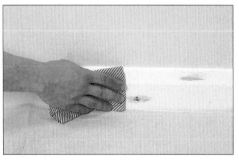

3 Wipe away dust

Remove dust from intricate moldings with a cloth dampened with rubbing alcohol. Leave the surface to dry before painting.

4 Wash down

Finally, wash the paintwork down with a detergent solution to remove grease and to prepare the surface for the new paint.

Fill any gaps around the woodwork with silicone caulk using a caulking gun. You should use paintable silicone caulk around the outside of doors and windows, then paint over the caulk as normal when you come to paint the frames, to provide a totally watertight seal.

Crumbling putty on window panes can be scraped out and filled with glazing compound – unless the pane is loose, in which case you'd be well advised to reglaze it entirely before you start painting. It's not a difficult job and well worth doing. Be sure to deal with any mold growth before painting, which may be a problem if the old paint seal has been broken.

Preparing bare wood

FOR ALL ITS VERSATILITY AND BEAUTY, *bare wood has its drawbacks. The softwood used for general carpentry is often peppered with knots, cracks, and other blemishes that will stick out like sore thumbs if you simply paint over them.*

Choosing a primer

Primer seals the wood and provides a bonding surface for further coats. Which type you use depends on your choice of topcoat: use water-based primer under water-based paints, but you may need to sand before painting the top coat because water-based primers tend to raise the grain of the wood. You can use oil-based primers under both water- and oil-based paints, but they are best used with oil-based top coats. If using an oil-based primer, wait at least 24 hours for it to dry.

If, for some reason, you choose to paint hardwoods such as teak, you need to use special primers that absorb into the denser grain structure of those woods.

PREPARING BARE WOOD FOR PAINT

1 **Seal knots and fill any blemishes**

Sand dead knots and fill. Seal any resinous knots with shellac-base primer. Using a putty knife, fill any gaps with flexible wood filler or glazing compound.

2 **Prime**

Very open-grained wood can be smoothed with a thinned coat of wood filler. Once the surface is smooth and level, paint with general primer, making sure it is well worked into any joints.

Better left bare?

With wood that's going to have a natural finish, you have to take a little more care about how you treat any gaps and blemishes. Home centers and paint stores offer a range of wood putty and fillers stained in various wood shades. If you are going to stain the wood, use a stainable putty. On outdoor woodwork, be sure to use a *wood filler* made for exterior use. Fill and sand any gaps with adjoining surfaces before finishing the woodwork.

If you have a problem matching the color of your wood, improvise a filler by mixing sawdust from the same wood with wood glue.

If the wood to be painted has a very open grain, sand it with a medium grade steel wool or a very fine grade sandpaper. Brush or wipe away the dust, then seal the surface with a sanding sealer.

There's no need to treat resinous knots before applying varnish or polyurethane, but it's worth checking that any dead knots won't fall out: if any are loose, simply secure them in place with wood glue and sand when dry. As a final precaution against dust, wipe the entire surface down with a tack cloth, and leave to dry before finishing. Pay particular attention to corners and crevices, where dust may have accumulated over the years.

PREPARING BARE WOOD FOR VARNISH

1 Fill holes and cracks

Fill blemishes with wood filler or putty, smoothing it with the putty knife so that it is just above the surface.

2 Fill gaps

Use your finger or the edge of a putty knife to force the filler or putty into the tight corners around the molding.

3 Sand

Leave the filler to dry completely, then sand it level with the surface using a sanding block and fine grade sandpaper.

Painting molding and doors

CLEANLY PAINTED WOODWORK *with crisp, firm lines puts a finishing touch to your interior decor. Your biggest enemies are drips, runs, stray lines, and the fuzz from carpets.*

Painting baseboards and molding

Unless you're really confident of your ability to paint with a steady hand, masking molding and baseboards will save you time in the long run. Masking is also virtually essential for the joint between baseboard and a carpeted floor – not only to protect the carpet, but also to stop stray fibers from working their way into the wet paint. If you're pressed for time, use a plastic paint shield instead – but make sure that you force it hard into the joint and wipe it frequently to avoid drips. When painting narrow molding, use a narrow brush size, to avoid splashing paint. If your paint is oil-based, it's better to apply the first coat thinly, let it dry, then apply another coat, rather than risk a lot of drips and runs.

Always paint along the grain of the wood. Paint the raised parts of decorative molding first, so that any runs can be caught when you come to paint the wider parts.

PAINTING ALONG ADJOINING SURFACES

a Mask with tape

Masking tape guarantees a clean line along baseboards. Peel off before the paint dries.

b Edging

An angled sash brush gives a reasonably clean line – but only if your hand is steady.

c Shielding lines

Move a paint shield as you paint and wipe frequently to prevent seepage behind it.

Painting doors

There are as many ways of painting a door as there are door types, but in all cases your aim is to paint from the top down to avoid runs. Before you start painting, remove as much of the door hardware as possible and wedge or prop the door open. If you're working outside, choose a windless day to avoid the risk of dust or insects getting caught in the paint.

Speed is of the essence on doors, and you should aim to complete one side in a single session. Apply the paint in sections, starting with any panels, followed by the frame, and then the

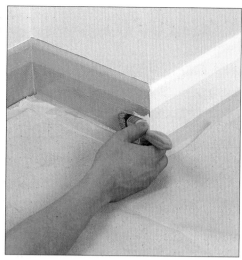

■ **Brush away from corners** *and edges to prevent paint buildup.*

edges. Finish each section with light, vertical strokes and blend the wet edges into the adjoining sections. Flat-faced doors should be brush painted top to bottom, left to right. Alternatively, paint them with a roller, starting in the middle, and smoothing the finish with a brush.

Glazed doors

Paint French windows and glazed doors in roughly the same order as paneled doors, first masking the panes. Mask just slightly in from the edge of the glass so that the paint forms a seal over the muntins and putty.

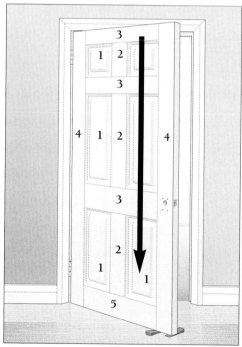

■ **The order for painting** *a paneled door is as follows: inner panels (**1**) first, followed by the inner stiles (**2**), rails (**3**), outer stiles (**4**), and bottom rail (**5**), and then edges. Work from top to bottom between sections to avoid runs.*

Unless you catch them right away, leave stray bristles in the paint to dry, then sand smooth.
Likewise, leave drips on the glass to dry, then scrape off with a blade.

Painting windows

KEEP THE EDGES *of window frames sharp and unstuck by painting them in sequence. This will stop pools of paint from gathering in the crevices and will leave you with enough dry edges to be able to close the window that night.*

Keeping unstuck

As with doors, paint window frames from top to bottom to avoid runs and take care not to let paint build up along the edges. Remove any hardware first. Mask inside the muntins ⅛ inch or so in from the edge of the glass so that the paint forms a watertight seal against the weather or condensation. You may also use a paint shield to achieve the same effect.

On double-hung windows, apply the paint as thinly as possible and don't allow it to gather in the recesses. Keep it away from the sash cords, too, or they will become brittle and snap. Open casement windows are vulnerable to dust and flying insects, so choose a calm day for painting. Watch the lower edge of the bottom rail for paint build-up that could cause the window to stick.

Don't leave open windows and doors unattended while the paint dries. Make sure you're around to keep an eye on them. Burglars are opportunists and may view an open window or door as an opportunity to break into your home.

KEEPING PAINT OFF THE GLASS

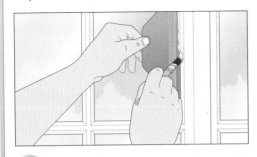

a **Use a paint shield**

Paint against a plastic shield – but wipe the shield frequently to avoid accidental drips.

b **Remove paint spatters**

Leave stray flicks of paint on the glass. Remove when dry with a razor blade or scraper

Order of painting

Follow the procedure described below to make painting windows easier.

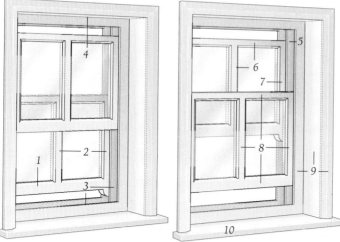
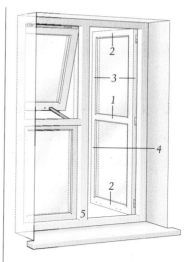
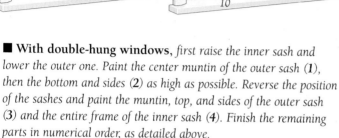

■ **With double-hung windows,** *first raise the inner sash and lower the outer one. Paint the center muntin of the outer sash (**1**), then the bottom and sides (**2**) as high as possible. Reverse the position of the sashes and paint the muntin, top, and sides of the outer sash (**3**) and the entire frame of the inner sash (**4**). Finish the remaining parts in numerical order, as detailed above.*

■ **With casement windows** *paint the muntins and inner frame edges (**1**), then the frame edges (**2** and **3**). Finish with the opening edges (**4**), and finally the rails, stiles, stool, and apron (**5**).*

A simple summary

✔ A basic set of good quality brushes and the correct primer and top coat is essential when painting woodwork.

✔ If the existing paint is sound and smooth, there's no need to strip it before painting – simply wash down with detergent to remove dirt and grease.

✔ Fix knots, cracks, and other blemishes before painting.

✔ Unless you are good at painting straight lines, you'll save time by masking wood molding.

✔ Painting windows in the right sequence will make the job a whole lot easier.

Chapter 7

Wallpapering

NOTHING BRIGHTENS UP A ROOM more than a fresh covering of wallpaper. More decorative than painting and generally cheaper than tiling, hanging wallpaper is also within the capabilities of even the most inexperienced do-it-yourselfer. So long as you prepare correctly and hang the first length of paper properly, you will find the job becomes easier and easier as you go on.

In this chapter...

✓ Preparing and lining walls

✓ Choosing wallpaper

✓ Wallpapering equipment

✓ How to hang wallpaper

✓ Papering problem areas

✓ Wallpaper borders

DECORATING WITH TODAY'S WALLPAPERING MATERIALS IS NEARLY AS EASY AS PAINTING

Preparing and lining walls

BEFORE HANGING WALLPAPER, *you'll need to strip off any old paper or textured lining paper and make sure that the underlying surface is reasonably smooth. Some wallpaper manufacturers recommend that you line the walls, too. Ideally, repaint the ceiling and any woodwork before papering.*

Off with the old

Soak and scrape off old wallpaper by hand – or rent a steam stripper if the paper is thick and/or painted-over. Many modern wallcoverings are "strippable" meaning that you can just peel them off before repapering. However, it's generally safer in the long run to strip the backing off completely before hanging the new paper. Repair any large cracks and holes before continuing.

Lining walls with paper

Lining paper comes in various forms for covering up less-than-perfect walls. It dries rigid, and sturdier types can safely span cracks as large as ¼ inch wide.

Ordinary lining paper is sold in rolls that are usually 36 inches wide – wider than wallpaper rolls – and comes in both heavy and light weight. Lighter weight liners are good for covering walls with minor imperfections; heavier weight liners can create a

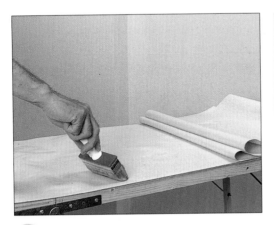

1 **Brush and fold**

To give liners a better bond, carefully brush on an adhesive activator. Then "book" the row of paper, folding pasted sides together.

2 **Lining up for corners**

Hang the lining paper with an ⅛-inch gap at corners so that the wallpaper can be pushed fully into the corners later.

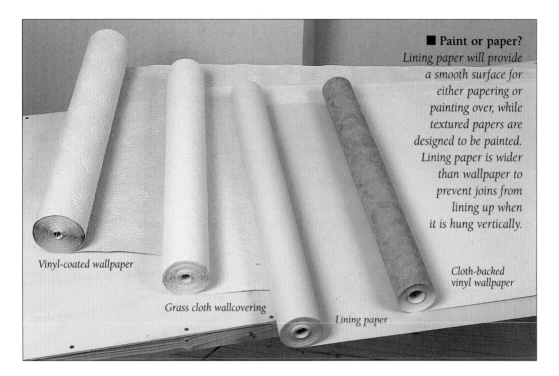

■ **Paint or paper?**
Lining paper will provide a smooth surface for either papering or painting over, while textured papers are designed to be painted. Lining paper is wider than wallpaper to prevent joins from lining up when it is hung vertically.

Vinyl-coated wallpaper

Grass cloth wallcovering

Lining paper

Cloth-backed vinyl wallpaper

smooth surface over plaster, concrete block, and even paneling. Liner paper can also be used on ceilings. Hang lining paper horizontally to prevent the seams from lining up with your wallpaper seams. When hanging, butt strips together. Leave for 24 hours before papering over.

Most liner papers are prepasted – coated with their own adhesive – and just need to be run through a tray of water before hanging. However, for extra adhesive strength, use a paste activator that eliminates the need for water. Just brush it on.

Textured lining papers

Aside from ordinary lining paper, there are heavier textured and embossed papers that can be hung for their decorative effect or – more cynically – because the plaster underneath is falling apart. Many of these have attractive surfaces all on their own, although most are just white.

Embossed papers are extremely tough and come in a range of surface treatments, including stucco, plaster, and even tin plate that can provide a unique look to an inferior ceiling. They are hung in the usual way, but may require sticking with their own special adhesive.

Choosing wallpaper

STEP INTO ANY HOME CENTER, and a quick glance at the mountains of swatch books on display will give you some idea of the vast choice of wallcoverings around.

I'd like to buy some wallpaper, please!

Most modern vinyl wallpapers are prepasted and are just soaked in water to hang.

- **Self-adhesive papers** are simply hung by peeling the backing and sticking the paper. Finer papers are dryback, and must be pasted for hanging. You can also choose strippable paper, which is made to come off the wall easily, and peelable paper that peels off it's backing when it's time for redecorating
- **Solid vinyl papers** are the most common and are durable, washable, and easy to hang. Vinyl-coated papers are somewhat less rugged, but are good for areas such as a living room or dining room.
- **Embossed paper** has a raised pattern backed by another layer of paper. The two are bonded together to form one sheet. This type of paper is easy to hang.
- **Flocked paper** has a velvet texture and is one of the most expensive wallcoverings.
- **Grasscloth** is made of natural fibers and is excellent for covering a damaged wall.
- **Foil paper** is reflective and can brighten up a small, dingy room. Although expensive and harder to work with than other papers, this type is stunning. It requires a smooth surface underneath.
- **Fabric** is an elegant paper that is made from woven textiles with no pattern to match. Difficult to hang, this paper does not clean well either.

ESTIMATING HOW MUCH YOU'LL NEED

Estimating your wallcovering needs is a fairly basic process, but one that should be done very carefully so that you avoid buying too many rolls or – heaven forbid – too few! Follow this formula and measure twice to ensure accuracy.

1. Measure the wall area to be covered (height x width).

2. Measure the areas of baseboards, molding, windows, and doors. Subtract this from the total area.

3. Add 15% to this number (multiply the number by 1.15), for waste.

4. Divide this number by the square footage rating for the paper you choose, and round up. This will be the number of rolls you need.

ORDER OF WORK

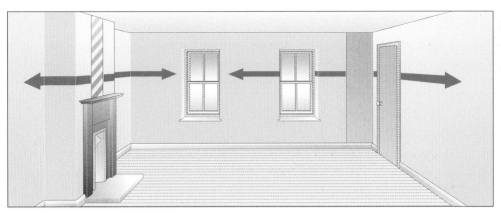

Where you start papering is largely a matter of preference, although starting from a focal point is a good idea. It's best to work clockwise around the room if you are right-handed and counterclockwise if you are left-handed. By working away from the window, any less-than-perfect joints will not be emphasized by casting shadows. With a large-patterned paper, center the first length (or lengths) on a dominant feature, such as a chimney breast, and paper outwards from there (above left).

Add a little extra

Use the formula opposite to work out how many rolls you need. Add on a couple of extra rolls if you are using a complex "step-and-repeat" pattern that's difficult to match. Most suppliers don't mind if you over-order so long as you take unused rolls back undamaged and before too long. It also makes sense to have some spare paper in case you need to make repairs in the future.

If you're hanging paper with a step-and-repeat pattern, there will be far less waste if you cut alternate strips from two different rolls. It makes the job easier, too

Wallpaper labels have dye lot numbers that identify the particular lot the paper is from. Due to quirks in the production process, paper that seems identical can look disturbingly different once it is on the wall if it comes from different lots. Check when you buy. At the same time, don't forget to buy the paste if you need it. Today's wallcovering adhesives come in both powder (which requires mixing with water) and liquid forms, although the liquid forms are far more common. You might also find it handy to buy a seam adhesive, sold in syringes, to secure seams that curl up after the paper has dried out.

Wallpapering equipment

THERE'S NO SENSE IN SKIMPING *on wallpapering tools. None of them cost very much and they make the job a great deal easier. If you're only covering a small area, consider postponing the job until you have enough papering to justify the cost of getting the right gear.*

Tools of the trade

The most important item in any wallpapering tool kit is a good sharp pair of papering scissors. Ordinary scissors won't do, and a craft knife will tear all but the heaviest papers. Use the backs of the shears to crease the paper into corners prior to trimming.

A pasting table is also worth buying; you could improvise, but it's not really worth it. While you're at it, buy a cheap plastic seam roller for flattening the seams between strips and a decent smoothing brush – smoothing the paper with your hands or with a cloth could easily damage it. You also need a plastic bucket for mixing the paste or for wash water. Always clean and dry tools at the end of a session before the wallpaper paste dries hard or causes the tools to rust.

Stretch a length of string across the rim of your paste bucket and tie it to the handle anchor points. You can then rest your pasting brush over the bucket, not in it, and use the string to scrape off excess paste.

You must have some means of marking vertical lines on the wall. The traditional way to do this is with a plumbline, but in a pinch you could get away with penciling the lines against a carpenter's level. Always use a pencil; ink can bleed through the paper.

Optional extras

Depending on the wallcovering, you may also need a breakaway knife and a metal straightedge for trimming. A small pair of scissors is useful for dealing with loose ends. And of course, if the room is carpeted, you'll need some means of protecting the floor – either dropcloths or disposable plastic sheets and newspaper. Don't forget that you may need access equipment if you're papering a ceiling or a stairwell, where it's even more important to have a secure platform than for painting. Otherwise you can probably get by with a stepladder, but it needn't be full size – a 3-step stepladder is more convenient for normal height rooms.

■ The full wallpapering toolkit
*doesn't amount to very much, so it's
worth buying. Don't forget that you
may have to rent access equipment if
you're papering a stairwell or ceiling.*

Stepladder

Pasting brush

Bucket

Dropcloths

Sponge

Wallpapering
scissors

Small scissors

Seam roller

Utility
knife

Plumb bob

Straightedge

Pasting
table

Smoothing brush

How to hang wallpaper

YOU'VE BOUGHT THE WALLPAPER *and all the tools; now you just have to get the stuff on the wall! Hanging paper is not difficult if you take your time. Get the first strip right and everything else should follow smoothly.*

Pasting and folding

Cut a strip of paper to length allowing about a 1½-inch overlap top and bottom. Lay it on the pasting table so that one long and one short edge overlap the edges of the table. To apply the paste, brush out from the middle of the strip in a criss-cross pattern towards the overlapping edges. If it is prepasted paper, place the roll in the water tray until the adhesive is activated.

Hanging the strips

On every wall, always hang the first strip less than a strip's width away from a corner, door, window frame, or fireplace so that you have a fair amount of waste at each end. It is essential that you align the first strip that you hang against a vertical line drawn on the wall with a plumbline or level. That way, you know that the seams and pattern will look right; corners themselves are rarely as true as they seem, and errors will be compounded.

HANGING THE STRIPS

(1) Plumb a line

Use a plumb bob to mark a vertical guideline for the first strip. Add 1½ inches to the drop to allow for trimming, not including pattern repeats.

(2) Align the first strip

Use your fingertips to ease the edge of the pasted and folded strip against the line. Brush back to the far edge to remove air bubbles, and trim.

The art of cornering

Don't panic when you come to your first corner. Follow the simple tips below.

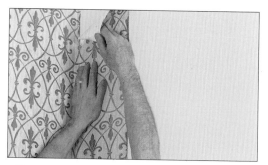

a Internal corners

Cut the end strip to turn the corner by no more than 1 to 2 inches. Hang the overlapping strip to a plumb line, trim vertically, and smooth.

b External corners

Turn about 1 inch around the corner. On both inside and outside corners, you need to slice the top of the strip to allow for smoothing.

Both prepasted and dryback papers should be folded back to back – a process called "booking" – after pasting or wetting. Leave folded for about 5 minutes or as long as the manufacturer recommends. On ceilings and stairwells, where you're using very long strips, you'll need to fold them accordian-style.

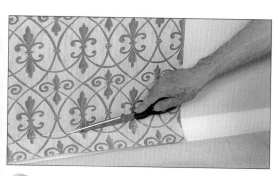

3 Crease and trim

Crease the wallpaper with the back of your shears to mark the trimming line, then pull away and cut along the crease. Smooth back the flap.

4 Subsequent strips

If the first strip hangs vertically, so will all the others on that wall. But don't forget to match the pattern when butting the strips together.

Papering problem areas

A GOOD RULE *for papering problem areas is: don't! Paint them instead. But even the boxiest rooms have their obstructions and window recesses, in which case the tips shown here will help save your sanity.*

Reducing problems

Plan ahead to reduce headaches. For example, move the starting point of your first drop of paper to avoid having to hang nasty narrow strips around doors and windows. Remove everything you can from the walls, and make sure the walls themselves are free of dust. If you've made repairs, coat the surface with wallcovering primer to keep the wallpaper from drying out too fast while you wrestle to trim it round those awkward areas.

If you have to overlap strips vertically – as in a window recess – make sure the exposed edge faces the window so that it doesn't cast a shadow. If you are using vinyl papers, always use vinyl-to-vinyl adhesive where the strips overlap.

Arches and radiators

Arches are best papered with a plain or random-patterned paper, as pattern-matching is impossible between the curved and flat surfaces. Paper the walls either side of the arch first, trimming to leave a 1-inch overlap. Then make "V" cuts every 2 inches and stick down the flaps. Finally, cut the inside strips to width, pattern-match them to the walls at the bottom, and butt-join them at the crown of the arch. Around a wall-mounted radiator, hang full lengths of paper as far as possible to each side of and between the brackets. Then slit the remaining strips to fit over the brackets.

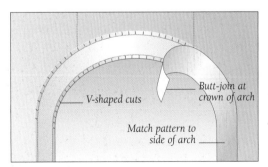

Butt-join at crown of arch

V-shaped cuts

Match pattern to side of arch

■ **To paper neatly** *around an arch, trim the inside strips exactly to the wall thickness.*

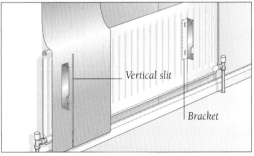

Vertical slit

Bracket

■ **Cut vertical slits** *in the wallpaper so you can fit it around the brackets behind a radiator.*

DEALING WITH WINDOWS

■ **Paper a recess** *in the order shown here. For a shallow recess, make release cuts in the last length of paper, then fold it around and trim to the frame. Fit extra top corner pieces and side pieces in a deep recess and turn the facing paper over the edge.*

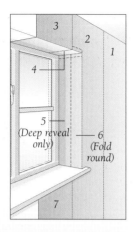

1 Making release cuts

Brush the paper against the the door frame or windowsill to mark the projection. Cut into the angle with the wall so that the paper lies flat.

2 Trimming to the sill

Make further release cuts into each part of the molding, then press the paper into the projection and trim it to fit.

3 Brushing into position

Add more paste if it has dried out, then brush the paper back into place, using the tips of the bristles to push it into the angles.

Switches and fittings

Having turned off the electricity, loosen the faceplate of an electrical fitting just before you paper around it. Then paste up the strip, let it hang loosely over the fitting, and press gently on the paper to mark the four corners of the faceplate. Now make four release cuts from the center of the fitting back to the marks and tear off the waste to leave 2-inch wide flaps. Brush these under the faceplate and screw back down. It's as simple as that!

■ **Dealing with light** *switches is much easier than you might think.*

Wallpaper borders

PAPER BORDERS *are a great accent to your wallpaper, or for a painted room. They come in the same range of types as wallpaper, and most are prepasted for ease of use. You can also create your own by cutting a border strip from your favorite wallpaper. Tape up a cut before committing yourself; borders can easily overpower a room.*

HANGING WALLPAPER BORDERS

1 Prepare and fold

Cut the desired length of border, allowing for overlap at corners and seams. Paste or activate the adhesive on back, then book the strip.

2 Hang to a guideline

Draw a horizontal guideline on the wall, align the edge of the strip against it, and unfurl, smoothing out any air bubbles as you go.

3 Overlap at seams

Allow enough overlap on any subsequent strips to match the pattern. Smooth down, then trim through both strips at once to remove the waste.

4 Roll the seams and edges

Use a seam roller on seams and edges to make sure they are firmly stuck to the wall. Sponge off any excess adhesive before it dries.

Hanging techniques

Make sure the walls are smooth and clean, then pencil a horizontal guideline around the room. Use a carpenter's level to ensure the line is level, unless the border is going close to the ceiling, in which case make the line parallel with the ceiling instead.

When pasting borders, lay lining paper over the table to protect the surface, and paste from the middle of the strip outwards over the edges. Soak prepasted borders in a water tray, just like prepasted wallpapers.

Matching the pattern on a corner can be tricky, so practice first. Fold two spare strips of border so that they form the desired angle, making sure the pattern is symmetrical along the seam.

Along seams, overlap the strips so that the pattern matches and cut through both layers at once. To form corners, adjust the overlap to the desired angle and cut through both layers. To form a strip of border around a curve, cut V-shapes halfway into the inside edge and smooth down.

A simple summary

✓ Surfaces need to be clean, sound, and non-absorbent. For best results, or if the surface is a little uneven, hang lining paper first.

✓ Always order more rolls than you think you need – if you take them back before too long your supplier should refund you for any unused rolls.

✓ Make sure you have all the necessary equipment on hand, including extra ladders and scaffold boards for access.

✓ Always hang the first strip on each wall against a vertical line, having checked how much waste this leaves at either end.

✓ Plan ahead to make papering problem areas less of a problem. Always turn off electricity before loosening switch and outlet faceplates so that you can trim the paper behind them.

✓ Wallpaper borders are an easy and cost-effective way to revamp a room's decoration.

Chapter 8

Ceramic Tiling

FOR PERMANENCE, DURABILITY, AND EASE OF CLEANING, ceramic tiles are still the number one choice for walls and floors. But tiles will only be as good as the surface they go on – so preparation is the key.

In this chapter...

✔ Choosing tiles and estimating

✔ Tiling tools and materials

✔ Preparing surfaces

✔ Splashbacks and borders

✔ Cutting ceramic tiles

✔ Laying ceramic floor tiles

✔ Grouting and sealing

✔ Whole walls

CERAMIC TILES: HARD-WEARING, EASY TO CLEAN, AND THERE FOR KEEPS!

Choosing tiles and estimating

CERAMIC WALL AND FLOOR TILES REPRESENT *a sizeable investment, and once installed they are there to stay. So take your time in selecting tiles and be sure to order enough to complete the job.*

Buying tiles

You can find a wide selection of both *glazed* and *unglazed* ceramic tiles in large home centers or you can shop at specialty tile stores for a more diverse selection. Generally speaking, you'll find basic colors of machine-made tiles at great prices at home improvement chains. Smaller tile outlets will offer hand-made styles in unique colors and designs (some hand painted) at higher prices. If you're on a budget, reserve these specialty tiles for small areas, or for decorative borders and panels.

Ceramic tiles come in all shapes and sizes, the most popular being 4¼ inches square. A variety of other types of tiles are available including bullnose tiles with one edge finished in a curve, cap tiles to use as an edging along a tiled wall, and cove tiles for along the base of a tiled wall. You can also choose smaller mosaic tiles, which come in panels attached to backing sheets. As a rule, small tiles look better in small areas and are much easier to cut and fit around awkward corners. On the other hand, the larger sizes give a cleaner, less cluttered look

It's best to avoid garishly patterned tiles or extremely offbeat colors: you may like them, but they could adversely affect the resale value of your home.

Estimating quantities

The best way to estimate quantities is to measure width times length to find the square footage of your area. Tile stores and home centers sell "field" tiles (the square tiles you use to cover the wall or floor) in boxes marked to cover a given area. Buy more than you need to cover breakage, and then buy specialty tiles – such as cove base, or corner tiles – individually.

It's a good idea to have the tiles delivered because they are bulky and heavy – and if some get broken on the journey, the store will replace them free of charge. Within reason, they should also refund you for unused tiles.

> ### DEFINITION
>
> *Ceramic tiles come **glazed** or **unglazed**. Glazed tiles are nonporous and have a gloss or matte finish. Unglazed tiles have a more natural look but absorb water and grease and so are harder to clean and are unsuitable for wet areas.*

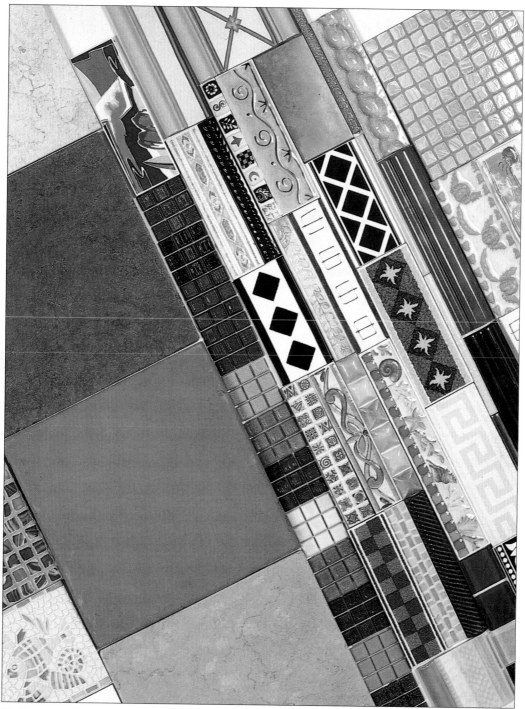

■ **There is a huge selection** *of types of tile available, including machine- and handmade ceramic tiles (both glazed and unglazed), mosaic tile panels, and plain and molded edging tiles.*

Tiling tools and materials

YOU WILL HAVE NO TROUBLE buying or renting all the tools and materials you need to set the tiles. Most specialized tiling tools are inexpensive enough to be used on a one-time basis, but a lever-operated snap cutter is a good investment if you have a large area to cover or if the tiles themselves are especially thick.

SPECIALIZED TILING TOOLS

A "score-and-snap" tile cutter: this is fine for the smaller sizes of wall tiles, but is hard work on tiles measuring more than 4 inches square or ⅜ inches thick. Inexpensive "all-in-one" gadgets do the same job, but are not all that much easier than snapping tiles over a piece of wood.

A lever-operated snap cutter: this will make short work of larger wall tiles and floor tiles, and can be rented from tool rental stores. For cutting and shaping thick, glazed quarry tiles, you may want to rent a wet saw and a stone cutter.

Tile nippers: use these in conjunction with a cutter to remove small pieces of tile for cut-outs. Alternatively, use a tile saw, which is time-consuming but reduces the risk of breakages. Use a hardened ceramic tile bit for drilling holes in tiles, taking care to avoid the edges.

A profile gauge: this useful tool molds itself to the shape of awkward gaps, allowing you to trace the shape of the cut-out on the tile in felt-tip pen. In some places it is easier to make a cardboard template of the gap.

A grout float and a squeegee: you'll need these to apply and smooth the grout between the tile joints. Tile adhesive is spread with a notched trowel in one of two notch sizes; follow the manufacturer's recommendation.

TILING MATERIALS

Wall tile adhesive (mastic): this is generally sold ready mixed in tubs. Some types double as grout, which is handy for small areas. Thin set mortar is stronger and is sold dry for mixing with water.

Grout: this comes ready mixed or in powder form for mixing with water. You can buy colored grouts to match tiles or decor, latex grout for super-water resistance, or epoxy grout for extra chemical or stain resistance.

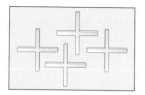

Plastic X-shaped tile spacers: these are sold in various thicknesses; generally speaking, the smaller the tile, the narrower the gap. Plastic edging strips are sold for finishing edges and external corners but can look tacky.

On a surface like a tiled countertop that needs to be both sanitary and waterproof, seal the grout with grout sealer. Wait until the grout has fully cured, then apply the sealer to the grout seams with a foam brush to prevent any from getting on the tiles.

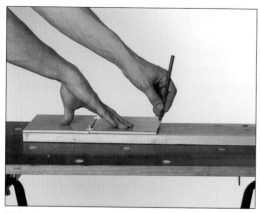

■ **Make your own tile gauge** *using a wood batten marked in whole tile widths. Don't forget the grout gaps between the tiles.*

■ **Colored grout** *can look very effective with dark tiles. The grout comes in pre-mixed packages in a wide range of colors and formulas.*

Preparing surfaces

AS WITH ALL DECORATION JOBS, thorough preparation will prevent problems later and ensure that the tiles stay firmly stuck. Tile adhesive is a pretty forgiving material, so there's no need for surfaces to be absolutely flat. But make sure that the underlying surface can't move or flex, otherwise the grout will start falling out in no time at all.

Playing smart with surfaces

Tiles are a fairly permanent fixture, so install them to last. Any semi-permanent fixtures are better removed than tiled around and if you're thinking of entirely remodeling the kitchen or bath, now's the time to do so: if you postpone it until later, you may be faced with unsightly gaps in the tiling.

Don't make the mistake of thinking that tiles will cover up moisture. Eventually, the dampness seeps through the joints and creates a moldy, musty smell. Be extra careful in applying adhesive – make sure there is no way that water can seep under the edges of the tiles.

Tiling is difficult in areas full of nooks and crannies or plumbing and wiring. Box in service pipes and augment built-in features such as pillars so that they become more regular in shape; it not only makes the job easier, but looks better, too. Build boxes with a wooden frame, screwed to the wall, and surface with water-resistant cement board or waterproof drywall. You can build a recess for a luxurious semi-sunken bath in the same way.

Tile bath panels and other wall access panels separately. Fix the panels to their backing framework with domehead screws – the type with screw-on chromed caps to cover the heads. For necessary access to plumbing, cut out individual panels in the plywood facing and tile separately.

Plan the way you're going to handle the joints with adjacent surfaces. Wherever tiles join a surface that might move – a bath, for example – fill the joint with caulk. If the gap is too wide, close it with partial tiles embedded in caulk. On a tiled floor, the chances are that the surface will be raised at door thresholds. The best way to deal with this is to screw down metal or wood threshold strips. Fill the gaps around baseboards with caulk, smoothing down the surface with a finger. Finish the edges above a half-tiled wall with wooden molding (use caulk along the joint) or a row of bull nose or decorative border tiles.

WHICH METHOD FOR WHICH SURFACE?

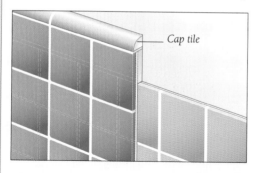

Cap tile

a Existing tiles

Although it's generally recommended that you remove existing flooring down to a clean and level subfloor surface, you can tile over existing tiles, providing they are firmly fixed and the surface is clean and dry. Finish the top edge with cap tiles.

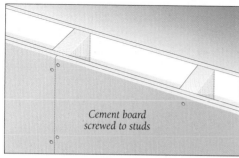

Cement board screwed to studs

b Drywall surfaces

Drywall is fine to tile on, but around baths and shower stalls you may want to take extra precautions. Use dry-set mortar and, if possible, install cement board around the area.

Skim-coating

c Plaster walls

Make sure the plaster is sound and free of dust or flaking paint. Strip any wallpaper and patch all holes and cracks. If the surface is slightly uneven, skim coat it with a light layer of plaster to make it easier to set the tiles.

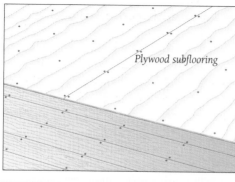

Plywood subflooring

d Floors

Level uneven concrete floors with self-leveling compound. On wood floors, remove boards down to the plywood subfloor. Replace rotted or uneven plywood. Be sure to allow access for pipes and conduits.

Splashbacks and borders

A TILED BORDER behind a basin or sink is the ideal place to practice your tiling skills. With luck, you won't have to cut any tiles. And on jobs of this size, there's no need to fit a base batten to support the bottom row.

Tiling small areas

Modern tile adhesive is so effective that for small jobs you don't even need to nail a batten to the wall to support the first row. Even so, you'll find a vertical batten helpful to keep the tiles straight; check it with a level and leave the nail heads sticking out so that you can remove them without disturbing the tiles. The secret of putting up tiles is to apply the right amount of adhesive, and to make sure that it's properly grooved. The grooves create suction that helps the tiles to stick; they also allow for movement, so that the tiles can be made to lie flat. People used to space tiles with matchsticks, but ready-made X-shaped plastic spacers are cheap to buy and far easier to use. At internal corners between walls, simply trim off one arm of an "X" to form a "T."

If one tile sticks out from the surface, don't try to force it to lie flat – you'll probably crack it. Instead, remove the tile, scrape off the adhesive from both the tile and the wall, lay a fresh bed of adhesive, and try again. After you've laid the first few tiles, you'll quickly get used to applying the adhesive to the right thickness.

Trivia...

In 1840 Englishman Richard Prosser patented a technique for producing clay buttons in a press. Ten years later the same process kicked off the Victorian tile craze: decorative tiles appeared in nearly every type of new building, and even on furniture such as washstands and dressing tables.

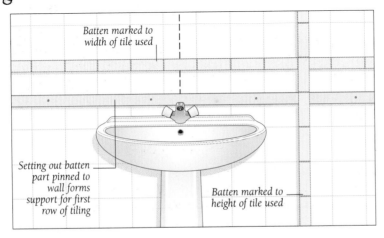

Batten marked to width of tile used

Setting out batten part pinned to wall forms support for first row of tiling

Batten marked to height of tile used

■ **On larger jobs**
plan where to lay the tiles so that they look centered and don't leave you with odd cuts at edges and corners. The easiest way is to use a batten marked in whole tile widths, allowing for grout lines. Check both horizontal and vertical, then mark where the first tile goes.

TILING A SPLASHBACK ABOVE A SINK

1 Setting out the tiles

Use a batten marked out in whole tile widths – allowing for the gaps – to gauge where to lay the first row of tiles so they're centered.

2 Spreading adhesive

Part-nail a batten vertically to one side to act as a guide. Then use a notched spreader to comb adhesive over the area to a depth of ¼ inch.

3 Laying the first tile

Starting at the vertical guide batten, lay the first tile. Push it with a twisting motion into the adhesive bed and check that it lies flat.

4 Fitting a spacer

Push a tile spacer into the adhesive at the top corner, then continue laying tiles in the same way. Start each new row at the guide batten.

5 Laying border tiles

For a more professional look, remove the guide batten and finish the splashback with oblong border tiles or, as here, contrasting mosaic tiles.

6 Caulking the joint

Apply grout with a float and wipe off excess with dry cloth. Rub down joints, then use a caulk gun to seal joint along the sink (above).

Cutting ceramic tiles

THE THICKER THE TILES, *the harder they are to cut and to shape in order to fit them around awkward corners. So choose your tools wisely: at the very least, you'll avoid lots of costly breakage.*

MAKING STRAIGHT CUTS TO TILES

 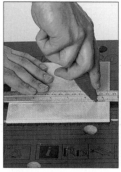

1 Marking the cut

To mark tiles for cutting, first lay the tile to be cut over the last whole tile, then cover the gap with another tile and mark along its edge.

2 Score and snap

Score down the cutting line with a tile cutter against a metal rule, then lay the tile on a piece of wood or wooden dowel, and snap.

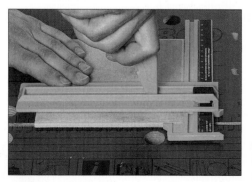 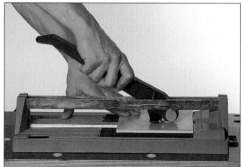

3 All in one

"Score-and-snap" tile cutters provide a guide for the tile scorer. After scoring, simply press down on the tile.

4 Snap cutter

Cut thicker tiles in a lever-operated snap cutter. Position the tile with the cutting line centered below the levered snapper, and push.

Dealing with awkward shapes

Awkward shapes are trickier than straight cuts and may call for a combination of techniques. Don't make the cuts too complicated or you risk the tile cracking; the grout or caulk will disguise a certain amount of unevenness. Mark curves and gaps with a profile gauge (see below) or a cardboard template (snip the edges to make it follow the line of the curve). Then mark the tile in felt-tip pen.

Create small recesses using the "score-and-nibble" technique. Otherwise, use a tile saw. You can use a tile saw – or quicker yet, a wet saw – to cut square or rectangular cut outs in a single tile. Make several cuts from the edge of the tile to the desired depth, and then use your nippers to bite off the small bits one at a time. If you want to avoid sharp cut edges, smooth them with a rubbing stone.

Cutting tiles to fit around obstacles

With the right equipment, shaping tiles to deal with obstacles is not too tricky.

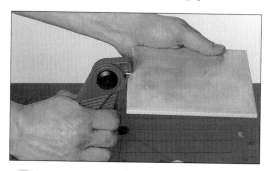

1 Match the shape

To use a profile gauge, first let the sliding feelers mold themselves to the shape of the gap.

2 Mark the tile

Then hold the gauge against the tile and trace the profile in felt-tip pen.

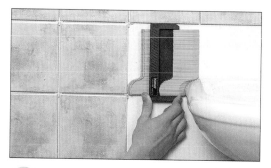

3 Nibble out recesses

If the recesses are small, score the waste with a tile cutter and then use nippers to snip it off.

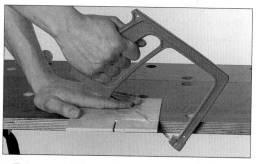

4 Cut shapes with a tile saw

If dealing with L-shapes and deep recesses, where the tile might crack, it is safer to use a tile saw.

Laying ceramic floor tiles

CERAMIC FLOOR TILES *are laid in much the same way as other types of tile, with the added complication that you have to get them level. But again, modern thin-set mortars make this an easier job than it once was.*

Setting out the tiles

Clear the room, prepare the floor, and use a chalkline to mark a cross in the center of the room. Lay rows of whole tiles along the arms of the cross (not forgetting to allow for the grout gaps) to see where the cuts fall around fittings and at the edges. Wherever you're left with unsightly or narrow cuts, try to get rid of them by adjusting the layout of the tiles. If you have to compromise, do so where it will show the least. When you're happy, mark new chalk lines to lay the tiles along.

If the room isn't a regular shape, set out the tiles to run along the line of the most visually dominant wall as seen from the door. Otherwise, there is a risk that the joints will look askew.

Laying, leveling, and finishing

Starting in a corner, apply the floor tile adhesive with a notched trowel over an area of about a square yard. Spread it to a depth of roughly ¼ inch unless otherwise recommended and make sure it is well notched. Then lay out the first few whole tiles, using block spacers to form the grout gaps. Press each tile lightly into place with a slight twist. When the area is filled, check for level with a spirit level and if necessary tap the tiles with a block of wood wrapped in padding.

If a tile is badly out of line, lift it, add more adhesive, and re-lay it. Continue in this way until you've laid all the whole tiles. Leave to dry for a few hours, then fill in with cut tiles. This time spread the adhesive on the backs of the tiles, not the floor, and check for level each time. Leave the floor for 24 hours before grouting and caulking the edges.

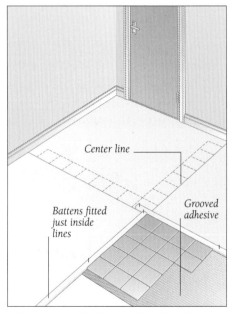

Center line

Battens fitted just inside lines

Grooved adhesive

■ **Set out guidelines** *and nail two battens at right-angles to form a bay. Start tiling the section farthest from the door.*

FLOOR TILING TIPS

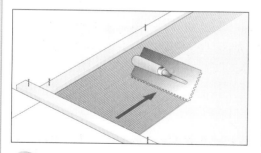

a Spreading adhesive

Cover an area of 1 yard at a time with adhesive, then draw the notched edge of the trowel through it, holding it at 45° to the floor.

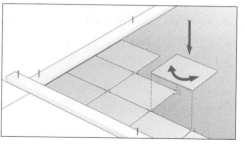

b Laying ceramic tiles

Lay the first tile butting up to both the battens. Don't slide it, but bed it down with a twisting motion. Work outward from the corner.

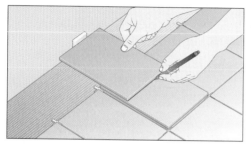

c Cutting tiles at edges

Lay the tile to be cut over the last full tile. Place a spacer between another whole tile and the wall, and mark the cutting line along its edge.

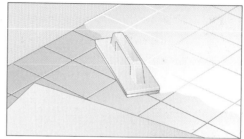

d Grouting the joints

Kneeling on boards, work grout into the joints using a rubber float or a squeegee. Sponge off tiles, and polish with a dry cloth when dry.

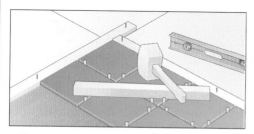

e Laying quarry tiles

Bed quarry tiles into thin-set mortar and level them by tapping with a cloth-wrapped wood block. Use ¼ inch-diameter dowels as spacers.

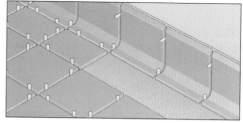

f Setting cove base tiles

Molded cove base tiles form a neat edge for quarry tiles. Be sure to set them in place before cutting the edge tiles.

Grouting and sealing

GROUTING THE GAPS *between tiles is the most satisfying part of the whole job, but don't forget to seal around the edges of the surface.*

Every base covered

Leave tiles to dry for at least 24 hours before grouting. Afterwards, fill expansion gaps – areas around the edges where movement may occur – with caulk. The exposed edges of thicker wall tiles can be finished with plastic edging, although this usually has to be bedded down at the same time as the tiles. Special outside corner tiles are a better option. Plastic cove baseboard molding or cove wall trim tiles will cover up any gaps around the edges of the floor. Mix large batches of grout with a mortar mixer attachment on your drill to save time and effort. Use a grout bag – which looks like a large pastry bag – for grouting joints that can't be reached with a grout float or squeegee.

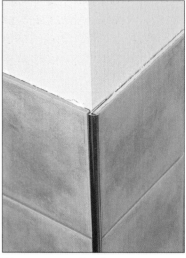

■ **For a smooth edge**, *plastic edging strip is embedded into the tile adhesive before laying the final row of tiles. On horizontal edges, some form of border tile is better.*

GROUTING THE TILES

1 **Applying**

Apply the grout with a float or squeegee, working it across the surface and into the joints.

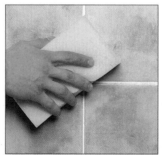

2 **Washing off**

Remove the excess with a damp sponge, taking care not to lift grout out of the joints.

3 **Smoothing**

Smooth the joints to a slightly concave finish using a finishing tool. Leave to dry, then polish.

Whole walls

TILING LARGER AREAS is all about setting out the tiles so that you don't leave unsightly cuts – especially around a window.

Double-check the layout

Whole walls – and even more so whole rooms – need extra-careful laying out to avoid cuts. Windows are often the trickiest places, so plan the tile layout outward from the main window using the order shown here as a guide. The best place for cuts is behind a door.

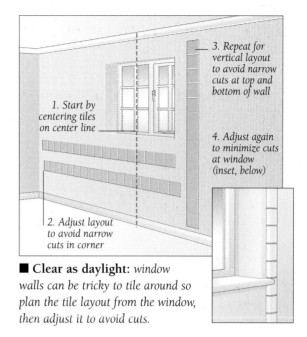

1. Start by centering tiles on center line

2. Adjust layout to avoid narrow cuts in corner

3. Repeat for vertical layout to avoid narrow cuts at top and bottom of wall

4. Adjust again to minimize cuts at window (inset, below)

■ **Clear as daylight:** *window walls can be tricky to tile around so plan the tile layout from the window, then adjust it to avoid cuts.*

If you're installing heavy tiles, work upwards from horizontal and vertical support battens nailed to the wall along the lines of the first rows of whole tiles. After the whole tiles are dry, remove the battens and fill in the gaps with cut tiles. Support any special-purpose tile, such as a soap dish, by taping it temporarily to its neighbors.

A simple summary

✔ Ceramic tiles are a permanent and quite costly feature.

✔ Tiling tools are inexpensive and tile suppliers should stock them.

✔ Make sure the surface is flat, dry, and clean before tiling.

✔ Splashbacks and borders are good for practicing tiling skills.

✔ Avoiding costly breakages is your reward for careful cutting.

✔ Ceramic floor tiles can create an elegant but informal ambience.

✔ Sealing and grouting makes a satisfying conclusion to the job.

✔ When tiling whole walls, windows present a challenge.

Chapter 9

Staining and Varnishing

A S WELL AS BRINGING OUT OUT THE BEAUTY and richness of natural wood, staining and varnishing performs an important protective function – indoors against dirt and wear and tear, outdoors against the elements. But unless the wood is new, your first task will be to strip the existing finish – a time-consuming but ultimately rewarding job.

In this chapter...

✓ Indoor stains and varnishes

✓ Stripping wood

✓ Sanding and finishing floors

✓ Preserving outdoor woodwork

BRING STRIPPED FLOORS TO LIFE WITH PAINTED PATTERNS AND VARNISH

Indoor stains and varnishes

STAINS FOR INDOOR WOODWORK can be divided into those that enhance or slightly modify the natural color and grain of the wood and those that hide it completely. Varnishes, like paints, are either oil-based or water-based. The most popular type is polyurethane, which is easy to use and durable.

Stain without pain

The golden rule is to test the **wood stain** on a piece of scrap – preferably a large one. Softwoods such as pine absorb stain at an uneven rate, which can cause blotchiness. And with hardwoods such as oak, you can end up with a color that's far from what you imagined.

Surfaces for staining must be clean and dry. In general, treat softwoods with a sealer before staining to avoid blotchiness. Apply the stain in thin coats with a paintbrush or soft cloth, following the grain of the wood. Apply, wipe off any excess, and let the stain dry, repeating until you have the appearance you desire. If you are staining drawers, cover them inside and out to prevent warping.

> **DEFINITION**
>
> **Varnishes** *form a protective coating over the wood.* **Wood stain** *is a dye that colors wood, although some stains also have preservative properties.*

STAINING A FLOOR BORDER

1 Marking out

Mark the area to be stained with a chalkline. If the design crosses the grain, score along the line to prevent the stain from bleeding.

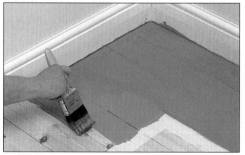

2 Brushing on

Use masking tape to protect the surrounding boards. Apply the stain with a paintbrush, following the grain of the wood.

Varnishing tricks

The secret of applying varnish is patience – in other words, taking the time to build up multiple thin coats rather than a single thick one, and sanding between coats to get a really smooth finish. Always follow the instructions on the can, especially with regard to drying times.

Traditional shellacs and lacquer finishes are for furniture only. Apply several coats with a cloth pad or polisher's mop. Then rub down with fine steel wool and wax-polish or "lift" to a gloss finish by rubbing lightly over the surface with a pad soaked in mineral spirits (a job requiring skill).

Modern polyurethane can be applied with a brush and comes in flat, satin, and gloss finishes. Traditional spar varnish is thicker and much harder. With both, sand between coats for a smooth finish.

Oiling and waxing wood

Furniture oils and wax are more labor intensive, but more natural-looking, alternatives to varnish, but they are not as protective. Wax marks very easily, and so is unsuitable for outdoor use or surfaces that are likely to have things put on them.

Linseed oil or tung oil are ideal for protecting garden furniture, wood paneling, or floors against moisture. They create an attractive warm glow. Hand rub the oils into the wood. The surfaces will require continual maintenance. Penetrating oil is a more durable, less labor intensive alternative, but it has a pungent odor.

APPLYING VARNISH

1 **Prepare the surface**

Remove grease and dust by wiping down the surface with a rag soaked in rubbing alcohol, then apply the first coat of varnish.

2 **Sand down**

When dry, lightly sand down the surface using a sanding block and fine grade sandpaper. Remove dust with a tack cloth.

3 **Apply next coat**

Apply one or more full-strength coats of varnish, finishing with the grain. Sand down again between coats.

Stripping wood

HIDDEN BENEATH LAYER UPON LAYER of old paint, there may be beautiful woodwork just waiting to be rescued – and even if you plan to repaint, there comes a time when old paint just has to go. But if you're varnishing, proceed cautiously: you don't want to damage the wood.

The choice is yours

You can strip paint by hand, or remove the offending item and have it professionally dipped in a bath of caustic soda. Stripping by hand is much more laborious, but generally gives better results; dipping tends to make most woods go "flat."

1 **Chemical stripper:** this is available in brush-on liquid and gel form, or as a paste which you apply with a putty knife. All involve slow, messy work. These products can have different effects on different woods, so test on a small patch first. Modern water-based strippers are a lot less hazardous than the old solvent-based types. Even so, use in a well-ventilated room, wear a respirator, and follow the manufacturer's instructions.

2 **Heat stripping:** this is fast and efficient on flat surfaces, but be careful not to scorch the wood. Using a heat gun is safer, but slower, than a propane torch.

3 **Scraping and sanding:** these are hard work, even with power tools, as paint tends to burn or clog the sander. But it's often the only way to remove the last traces of chemically- or heat-stripped paint without damaging the wood grain.

If possible, on old doors and built-in furniture strip an unobtrusive area to see how easily the paint comes off: old wood was sometimes primed with a plaster-based filler, in which case you'll need to get the item dipped. Bear in mind, too, that some doors and moldings were not meant to be left bare, so you'll have to judge whether the wood is attractive enough to be varnished.

Easy does it

Varnishing accentuates the natural grain of wood, so the last thing you want to do is ruin the grain in heavy-handed attempts to remove the old paint. A variety of scrapers are available for chemical and heat stripping, and the more of them you have on hand the better. Use a stiff-bladed paint scraper for flat surfaces, and a hook scraper for getting into the crevices of decorative moldings. Always scrape with the grain of the wood and never force stubborn patches: stop, and apply another coat of stripper. After stripping, finish off by giving the wood a light sanding with medium- to fine-grade sandpaper to remove any remaining paint.

If you use a propane torch, keep all flammable materials well way from the area and be sure to wear protective clothing. Use a heat-proof metal shield or fireproof fabric to protect vulnerable areas such as glass window panes or plastics, and catch the drips of melted paint in an old metal can.

A heat gun takes longer, but is safer and more controllable. Even so, you still need a heat shield to protect window glass from cracking

■ **Be patient** *with chemical stripper: you may need two or three applications to get through very thick paint.*

Never heat strip old paint that you think might contain lead – it could emit poisonous fumes. Likewise, sanding can release toxic dust. Use a bonding chemical stripper instead, and always wear a respirator.

USING A HEAT STRIPPING GUN

1 **An integral stripping tool**

A gun with an integral stripping attachment makes short work of flat surfaces. Lay down foil to catch the paint drips and flakes.

2 **A separate scraper**

Then use a hook scraper to deal with more intricate moldings and the awkward corners with adjacent surfaces.

Sanding and finishing floors

STRIPPED AND FINISHED wood floors look fantastic and are a lot cheaper than a new carpet if you do the work yourself. Even using rented power tools, however, it is hard work – but the rewards more than justify the effort.

Sanding down

It almost goes without saying that you should assess the condition of the floorboards before stripping. If they are too badly damaged, you're better off replacing them. And if you're in doubt about the color, test a small area first. Think about the noise implications, too. Bare floors can be very noisy for those in the rooms below unless entirely covered in rugs. Carpeting might be a better option in such cases.

To strip the bulk of the floor you need to rent a drum sander. For the edges, rent a smaller orbital edge sander. Make sure you wear full protective gear, including ear protection, and keep the room well ventilated at all times. Bear in mind that the floor may be out of action for a day or more.

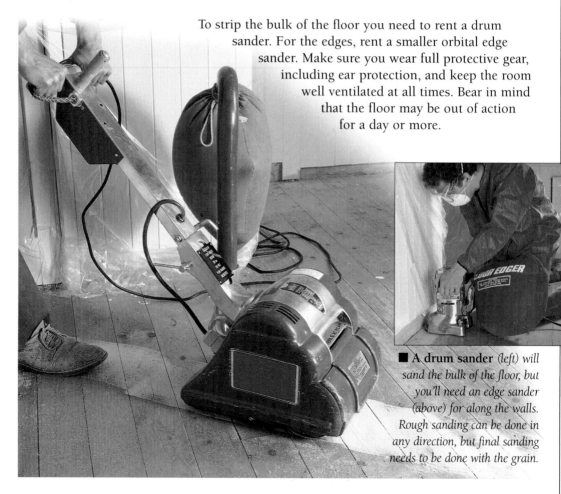

■ **A drum sander** *(left) will sand the bulk of the floor, but you'll need an edge sander (above) for along the walls. Rough sanding can be done in any direction, but final sanding needs to be done with the grain.*

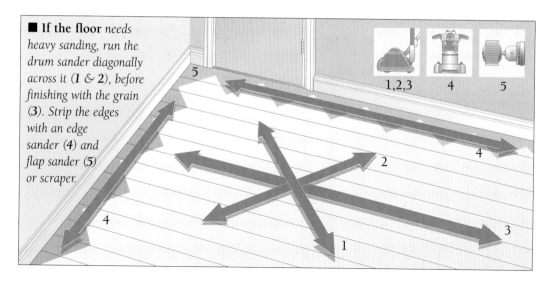

■ If the floor *needs heavy sanding, run the drum sander diagonally across it (1 & 2), before finishing with the grain (3). Strip the edges with an edge sander (4) and flap sander (5) or scraper.*

Before you start, clear the room and tape up the doors to stop dust from spreading. Nail down loose boards, sink raised nail heads, and fill any cracks. Replace damaged boards with new planks of the same type.

Start with a coarse abrasive sheet on the drum sander. If the boards are very rough, or heavily coated, slowly run the sander diagonally across the boards, working back and forth across the room. Otherwise, run with the direction of the grain. Then switch to a finer-grade sanding belt and work along the grain of the boards. Sand along the walls with an edge sander and finish in corners with a small flap sander on an electric drill or a hand scraper.

Never switch on a drum sander while the drum is in contact with the floor or you'll damage the boards. Tilt the sander backwards, switch on, and gradually lower it as you move forward. Likewise, lift the sander off the floor at the end of each pass, and drape the power cord over your shoulder to avoid accidents.

Sealing

Remove all dust and grime from the floor and ventilate the room thoroughly. Seal the floor with a penetrating sealer appropriate for the type of polyurethane you will be using (water- or oil-based), using a dry, clean rag. Buff the sealed wood with a floor polisher fitted with a buffing pad. After the floor is sealed, apply the polyurethane. Use a brush on small floors, or a painting pad on larger floor areas. Sand between coats with a fine-grade abrasive belt or abrasive pad, working in the direction of the grain. Allow each coat to dry according to the manufacturer's instructions, and let the floor cure for 24 hours after the final coat.

Preserving outdoor woodwork

PRESERVING EXISTING LUMBER *is a lot simpler and cheaper than replacing rotten wood. The trouble is, it has to be done on a regular basis because otherwise the effects of previous treatments will soon wear off.*

Pretty tough stuff

Preservative stains can help to brighten the outside of your home, but their main function is protection – against the elements, fungi, and insect attack. All outdoor wood structures should be treated with a waterproofing sealer or wood conditioner once a year, and you should treat any new lumber before you use it – particularly the cut ends of fence posts and rails. Naturally oily woods such as cedar and teak, or truly durable redwood, are tough enough to do without staining or preservatives, but even these should be regularly treated with waterproofing sealer to protect against the elements.

You can buy lumber that has been pressure-treated with preservative at the factory. If you're concerned about this material's effect on the environment and health, buy finish-quality lumber and treat it yourself as soon as you get it home.

Outdoor options

There's a vast array of exterior preservatives on the market, each with slightly varying properties, so read the manufacturers' recommendations before you buy.

1 **Exterior stains:** these are much like interior stains, but with more protection against water and the elements. Water-based types are the most common, but oil-based are available as well. Exterior stains are clear, semi-opaque, or opaque.

2 **Wood toners:** these seal and condition the wood, offering some protection against the elements. Most are not suitable under stains or varnishes.

3 **Waterproofers:** these are wood-conditioning agents that protect against the bleaching caused by UV damage, and many include fungicides in their formulas that protect the wood against mildew, mold, and fungus. Remember that these products should never be used with stains or varnishes.

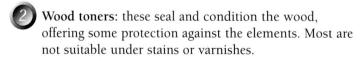

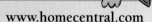

INTERNET

www.homecentral.com

Presented by Sierra Home Network, this site has a wealth of material on decks, lumber, and outdoor projects. It also includes multiple materials estimators.

METHODS OF TREATMENT

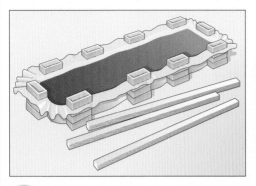

a **Homemade preservative bath**

Make one for lumber components out of a sheet of heavy-duty polyethelene and building bricks.

b **Spray gun**

Hire one to spray large areas of outdoor woodwork, but protect nearby plants.

Although preservatives are harmless to humans and animals when dry, they can be dangerous when wet. Keep family pets out of bounds when treating outdoor woodwork and cover water features such as fish ponds. Avoid all contact with your skin.

A simple summary

✔ Surfaces for staining and varnishing need to be free of grease and dust. Test a stain on a large piece of scrap to see how evenly it absorbs and how the color turns out.

✔ Always check that doors and floorboards are suitable for stripping, if necessary by testing an unobtrusive area first.

✔ Nearly all varnishes give a better finish if sanded down between coats – but be sure to remove all traces of dust.

✔ Outdoor woodwork needs regular treatment with preservative. Otherwise you will leave it vulnerable to attack by mold and insects – as well as at the mercy of the elements.

Chapter 10

Laying Floorcoverings

Balance durability against decorative effect when thinking about new flooring and consider the wear and tear that's likely to be inflicted. Does the floor need to be waterproof? Will it be regularly trampled on by muddy boots? And how important is it to have a soft, comfortable surface underfoot?

In this chapter...

✓ *Laying sheet vinyl*

✓ *Foam-backed carpet*

✓ *Tufted carpet*

✓ *Laying a floating wood floor*

✓ *Parquet flooring*

✓ *Vinyl floor tiles*

SHEET VINYL IS INEXPENSIVE, EASY TO FIT, AND CONVINCINGLY MIMICS MORE EXPENSIVE COVERINGS

Laying sheet vinyl

FOR SHEER VALUE FOR MONEY, *you can't beat sheet vinyl in rooms that get messy or wet – like the kitchen and bathroom. Modern sheet vinyl not only rivals more expensive materials for looks and durability, but it is incredibly easy to lay and forgiving of mistakes. Unfortunately, the same can't be said of linoleum; laying this is best left to a professional.*

Rooms with straight edges

In most rooms you can simply lay the vinyl and trim to fit. Unroll the sheet and let its weight mold it to the floor. Align the pattern with the most visually dominant wall or run of cabinets, and adjust so that the pattern is balanced all around the room. Roughly trim the vinyl with a utility knife to leave a 2-inch overlap all around. Then make release cuts at external and internal corners (see below) so that the vinyl lies flat enough to be trimmed to the walls. Most types of vinyl must be fixed to the floor with adhesive, applied with a notch trowel. Check the manufacturer's recommendation for the flooring you buy.

Before you actually lay the sheet vinyl, leave it unwrapped and loosely rolled in a warm room for at least 2 days. This will make it more flexible and easier to handle.

TIPS FOR LAYING SHEET VINYL

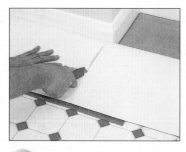  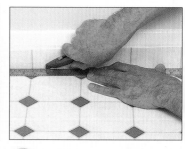

a **At external corners**

Roll back the vinyl over a piece of hardboard. Starting 2 inches from the bend, cut back to the edge.

b **At internal corners**

Pull down and cut along the center of the V-shaped fold, and overlap the resulting flaps.

c **Along baseboards**

Starting at an internal corner, push a straightedge into the angle and trim along it at 45°.

Complicated floor areas

In rooms with lots of obstacles, it's easier to make a paper template and use this to cut the vinyl to fit. Make the template from sheets of heavy brown paper taped together. Cover the entire floor, leaving a 1-inch gap around the edges and around obstacles. Then scribe around the walls and each obstacle using a block and pencil to leave a clear impression on the template.

Remove the template and lay it over the flattened-out vinyl sheet. Using the block to follow the lines you've just scribed on the template, reverse-scribe back onto the vinyl to leave pencil marks showing you where to cut it. This may seem like magic, but believe me, it works! All I would advise is that you cut generously to the waste side – you can always make adjustments by carefully trimming the vinyl once it's in place.

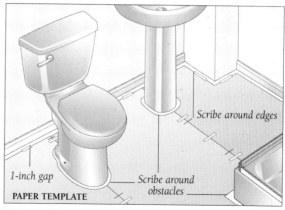

Scribe around edges

1-inch gap

Scribe around obstacles

PAPER TEMPLATE

■ **Tape sheets together** *to a rough fit. Scribe around the obstacles using a block of wood, then scribe back from these lines onto the vinyl.*

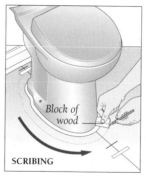

Block of wood

SCRIBING

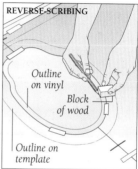

REVERSE-SCRIBING

Outline on vinyl

Block of wood

Outline on template

ⓓ At door molding

Make vertical cuts to the floor at each change in profile of the molding, then trim off the excess.

ⓔ At thresholds

Trim the edge of the sheet to the middle of the threshold, then screw a metal threshold strip to the floor.

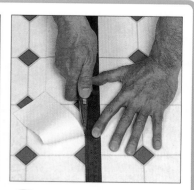

ⓕ Cutting seams

Overlap the sheets and match the pattern. Cut through both layers, then stick the edges to the floor.

Foam-backed carpet

SIMPLE TO LAY *and highly versatile, foam-backed carpet can be used virtually anywhere in the home. You may have to search hard to find it – most carpets sold are tufted – but you'll be rewarded.*

Added backing

Foam-backed carpet, as the name suggests, has its own built-in pad, although I'd still advise you to fit felt paper or *spun polyester underlay* beneath it. This added barrier will stop the foam from sticking to the floor, which in turn will make lifting the

■ **Foam-backed carpet** *is a boon to do-it-yourselfers, because it doesn't need stretching.*

carpet far easier if the need arises. It's also a good idea to draw a scale floor plan of the room to be carpeted, showing all recesses and doorways, before cutting.

Foam-backed carpet is available in several widths. Where possible, try to pick the width that translates to as few seams as possible in the space you're covering – even if this means considerable waste. Where seams are unavoidable, as in a large L-shaped room, keep them away from heavily used areas, and make sure the pile faces the same way. Foam-backed carpet is largely priced according to durability. Inexpensive light duty types are right for bedrooms; heavier types are suitable for living rooms, halls, landings, and stairs.

One of the secrets of successful carpet laying is to fit a new blade to your knife after every 2 yards or so of cutting. It may seem wasteful, but believe me, it's worth it!

Before fitting, unroll the new carpet outside or in a larger room. Following your scale plan, use a trimming knife to trim it roughly to the shape of the room leaving about 8 inches waste all round. Be careful not to let the rolled carpet buckle under its own weight when you move it around or you may damage the foam backing, resulting in unsightly creases in the pile.

Reaching the threshold

Carpet grippers are used on door thresholds to provide a smooth transition from one floor surface to another. Made of metal or wood, these strips also protect the edge of the carpet for both aesthetic and safety reasons.

Use a carpet gripper without spikes for foam-backed carpet and cut to fit the width of the door opening with a junior hacksaw. Fix the strip to the floor with nails or screws.

LAYING FOAM-BACKED CARPET

1 Felt pad

Stick double-sided tape around the edge of the room and staple or tape the pad to the floor.

2 External corners

Make a straight release cut to the edge of the corner over a piece of wood.

3 Internal corners

Make triangular release cuts at internal corners, as far as it takes for the carpet to lie flat.

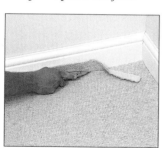

4 Trim to baseboard

Score along the edge with the back of the knife then trim to the baseboard.

5 Joining strips

Lay the second strip over the first and cut through both layers against a straightedge.

6 Taping the seam

Fold back the first strip, lay double-sided tape along the seam, and press both onto it.

Tufted carpet

TUFTED CARPET *should always be laid on a separate carpet pad. Unlike foam-backed carpet, tufted carpet also needs to be stretched during laying so that it will be held taut by the tackless strips that are used to secure it around the edges of the room.*

Get a gripper

Don't be fooled into purchasing a cheap carpet pad: a thick, high-quality foam or natural fiber pad will prolong the life of the carpet and feel better underfoot.

Be careful when cutting your carpet. Mark a cutting line between slits made on the edges, and cut loop-pile carpet from the face, and cut-pile carpeting from the back.

Trivia...

It's estimated that around 10 percent of the weight of an average 2-year-old domestic carpet consists of dust mites and their droppings! So if you were thinking of replacing that old carpet, maybe now's the time. There again, perhaps a total change of floorcovering is in order…

Tufted carpet is stretched and fastened onto spiked "tackless" strips, which you nail around the edges of the room. To do the stretching, you need to rent a special tool called a knee-kicker, plus a stretcher. Use the knee-kicker on two sides of the room and use the stretcher to stretch the carpet against the other two sides. A carpet that is not stretched properly may bind up and wear unevenly. Tackless strips allow you to simply unhook the carpet and try again if this happens.

■ **Use a knee-kicker** *and cold chisel to push the carpet tightly onto the tackless strips.*

Start on the wall containing a doorway. Trim and slide the carpet into the strips along this edge, then spread the rest of the carpet out toward the far wall. Trim the adjacent walls next, using the knee-kicker to push the carpet toward the strips and to secure it on the spikes using the bolster. The knee-kicker does not require great force – just give it a firm tap. Finally, check that the carpet hasn't bound up anywhere in the room and use a stretcher to fit it to the far wall.

LAYING TUFTED CARPET

1 Nail down strips

Nail tackless strips around the room, leaving a gap two-thirds the thickness of the carpet.

2 Fit the pad

Trim the pad with scissors to butt up to the strips, and staple it to the floor.

3 Trim to baseboard

Trim and fit the carpet along the wall, changing the blade every 2 yards or so.

4 Push behind strip

After stretching and trimming, use a cold chisel to tuck the cut edge behind the strip.

5 Binder bar

Nail the binder bar to the floor, then trim along a line running down the middle.

6 Moldings

Make vertical cuts down the molding, then push the edge into the threshold strip.

Joining carpet sections together

Joining sections of any type of carpet is best avoided if you can. But in an odd-shaped room full of recesses and alcoves, tufted carpet can work out very expensive unless you make use of some of the larger remnants. Try to position seams in little-used or unobtrusive places.

You should use special double-sided seaming tape to join seams together. Position the length of tape under the seam and, using a seaming iron, melt the tape's adhesive and follow along with the carpet edges, pinching the seam closed. Although the bond formed by the tape is reasonably strong, you must be careful not to break the joint when stretching the carpet.

Laying a floating wood floor

LAMINATED WOOD STRIP FLOORING *consists of interlocking pre-finished wood floor strips that are snapped or glued together to "float" on an existing floor. Though not as tough – or as expensive – as standard wood strip flooring, it has the advantage of being easy to lay and maintain.*

Before you start...

The floor must be level and dry. Level uneven subfloors with latex patching compound or plywood and lay a plastic moisture barrier over concrete floors. Removing the baseboards will give you a much neater finish around the walls. The wood strips will raise the height of your existing floor slightly, so you may need to trim the bottoms of doors. Some systems include matching threshold strips.

Mind the gap

Begin by covering the existing floor with foam underlayment. Lay the flooring panels along the longest or most dominant wall first, leaving a ¼-inch gap between floor and wall. Use spacers to keep this gap as you glue or snap subsequent rows in position. The final row may have to be cut lengthways, in which case don't forget to allow for the gap. This gap allows the boards to expand with changes in humidity, and is often filled with a cork strip that will be covered up when you replace the baseboards. If it isn't practical to remove the baseboards, cover the expansion gap with shoe molding, nailed to the baseboard. Leave the floor to set for 24 hours before walking on it if glue was used.

There's no need to cut strips to fit around door moldings. Just cut away the base of the molding to the same depth as the floor strip and slide the strip underneath.

■ **Sunset strip:** *pre-finished wood flooring is both decorative and durable.*

LAYING THE FLOOR

1 Leaving room for expansion

Lay the first section against the longest wall using wedges to keep a ¼-inch gap all around.

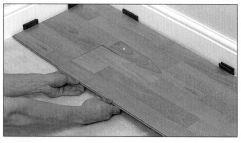

2 Laying subsequent sections

Begin the second row with a spacer and snap or glue the tongue and groove into position.

3 Protecting tongues

Hammer the boards together using a grooved block of wood to avoid damaging tongues.

4 Finishing off

Use a pry bar and hammer on the final row to secure it in place. Be sure to leave the gap.

Fitting at edges

The last bit of the job is the most satsifying – neatly edging your new floor.

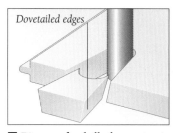

Dovetailed edges

■ **Pipework:** *drill, then cut out a dovetail shape, leaving ⅛ inch clearance around the pipe.*

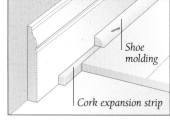

Shoe molding

Cork expansion strip

■ **Baseboard:** *fit a cork strip, and nail shoe molding covering the strip.*

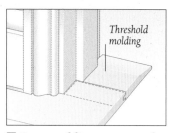

Threshold molding

■ **Door molding:** *cut away the base of molding to allow the woodstrip to fit beneath it.*

Parquet flooring

ELEGANT, DURABLE, AND LUXURIOUS, *parquet flooring comes in a range of stains and woods. It's ideal for hallways and living areas – including kitchens, if well sealed – but is not recommended for bathrooms.*

Preparing and planning

Wood parquet tiles – single tiles combined in patterns – vary in detail, but the fitting method is basically the same for all interlocking loose tiles. Whether working with square or rectangular tiles, you leave a ¼-inch gap for expansion around the edges of the room creating a "frame" of tiles laid end-to-end. Then you fill in the center with tiles in your chosen pattern. Lay down the tiles in a bed of wood tile adhesive. You can also buy peel-and-stick tiles, which you lay just like vinyl tiles.

Prepare the room as you would for wood strip flooring. Remove all the baseboards and threshold strips if at all possible. Your supplier will advise on quantities, based on your chosen laying pattern (see opposite), and on a suitable underlayment if you need one. Ask your supplier about the appropriate adhesive at the same time. Laying the blocks won't require much in the way of special equipment, but with a herringbone pattern, it definitely makes sense to rent a table saw to make the 45° cuts in blocks; sawing by hand is hard work and much less accurate.

LAYING TILES IN A HERRINGBONE PATTERN

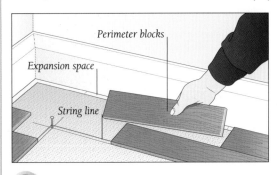

Perimeter blocks

Expansion space

String line

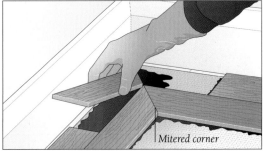

Mitered corner

1 **Set up guidelines**

Mark a ¼-inch expansion gap around the edge of the room, then set up chalk lines two blocks' widths in from there, and dry-lay the perimeter tiles.

2 **Lay the perimeter tiles**

Trowel adhesive around the perimeter, trim the grooves off the whole tiles, and lay. Then cut and trim the corner tiles to fit before placing them.

Laying the tiles

With most patterns, it's customary to lay the tiles around the edge of the room and then fill in the pattern, finishing at a doorway. The exception to this rule is a basket weave pattern, where you arrange the tiles in "panels" and lay those panels that fall around the edge of the room. Cut away the base of any door frames with a saw to accommodate the tiles. Afterward, replace the baseboards to hide the expansion gaps, or else cover it with shoe molding and paint or stain to match the wall color of trim shade.

Unfinished tiles will have to be sanded and finished once laid.

■ **Three popular laying patterns:** *basketweave, stretcher, and herringbone, which requires more cutting but looks great.*

When laying tile flooring, particularly if working on perimeter tiles last, make sure you don't stand directly on the newly laid tiles. Kneel on a piece of plywood to spread your weight evenly.

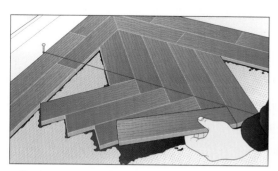

3 **Start the herringbone pattern**

Set up a string guideline for the apex of the outer row of tiles. Dry-lay them first, then miter the other end to fit at the perimeter.

4 **Fill in the gaps**

Lay the tiles, one herringbone row at a time, over the whole area. Fill the gaps at the edges by marking the tiles in place using a combination square.

Vinyl floor tiles

RESILIENT VINYL TILES are inexpensive and easy to fit, even in a small room with obstructions. The advice here also applies to cork and carpet tiles.

Dry lay and fit

Make sure the surface to be tiled is clean and level. Whether you're laying glue-down tiles or the self-adhesive type, begin by dry-laying them to center the pattern and ensure equal-width cuts at the edges. Starting in the quarter of the room farthest from the door, fix the whole tiles in place. Press down from the center outwards to avoid trapped air. Lay all the whole tiles, then fill in the straight-cut gaps. Tackle any awkward corners last.

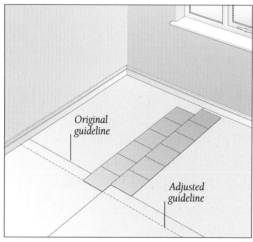

Original guideline

Adjusted guideline

■ **As with ceramic tiles,** *mark a cross in the room and then dry-lay the tiles to see how the cuts fall. Adjust the lines if necessary.*

TILING EDGES

1 Mark border tiles

Lay the tile to be cut over last full tile. Use a second tile to mark the border cut.

2 Cut the tile

Place the tile on a piece of board and cut using a linoleum knife and straightedge.

3 Fit and smooth

Slip the cut tile into place and smooth out to remove any air bubbles.

Corners and curves

To fit a tile around an external corner, use a second tile to mark the cut for one side of the corner, then repeat for the other side. Cut along the lines to form an L-shape. At an internal corner, mark from both walls and cut to form a square.

To tile around plumbing fittings, either scribe the shape onto the cut tile, as when laying sheet vinyl, or cut a cardboard template of the gap and use this to mark the tile: cut slits in the card and press against the outline.

1 **Mark first side...**

Place the corner tile over the last full tile on one side of the corner. Mark with a second tile.

2 **...then the second**

Repeat for the other side of the corner, again working from the last full tile.

A simple summary

✓ Sheet vinyl is cheap, relatively simple to lay, and easy to keep clean. It's ideal for kitchens and utility rooms.

✓ Foam-backed carpet is wonderfully versatile, at home virtually anywhere in the house. Although easier to lay than tufted carpet, it is not so durable.

✓ Tufted carpet requires more effort to lay than foam-backed but it is longer lasting.

✓ Floating wood flooring is relatively easy to lay, hard-wearing, and can be laid on top of existing hard surfaces.

✓ Parquet flooring is ideal for living rooms and halls. It is easy to maintain, but may warp if subjected to excess moisture.

✓ Resilient vinyl tiles are inexpensive and highly versatile. They are easy to lay, and are considerably less wasteful than other coverings.

PART THREE

Chapter 11
Doors and Windows

Chapter 12
Floors and Staircases

Chapter 13
Shelves and Storage

Chapter 14
Walls and Ceilings

Chapter 15
Heating and Ventilation

Doors and Windows

D OORS AND WINDOWS ARE THE MOST IMPORTANT moving parts of a home and, like all mechanical devices, they need regular maintenance to keep them in good working order.

In this chapter...

✓ Sticking and warping

✓ Casement window repairs

✓ Repair double-hung windows

✓ Repairing frames and sills

✓ Hanging a new door

✓ Door hardware and locks

✓ Window hardware and locks

✓ Weatherproofing

Sticking and warping

WHEN A DOOR OR WINDOW STICKS, *it's the first sign of a potentially more serious problem. So, before you reach for your plane or sander, see if you can trace the cause.*

Stick with it

Consider planing or sanding as a last resort – after all, once you've done it, there's no going back. Seasonal sticking suggests that the wood is inadequately protected, in which case wait until a spell of dry weather, repaint or refinish, and then see if the problem goes away. If it doesn't, or if you can rule out swelling due to moisture, check the hinges. Loose hinge screws and poorly gained hinges are two common reasons for sticking and are easily dealt with. Often, chiseling out or shimming the hinge mortise is the easiest way to deal with paint build up, too. More of a problem is sticking due to rotten wood or to loose joints. Fix these as soon as possible (they can only get worse), then plane to fit and rehang the door or window.

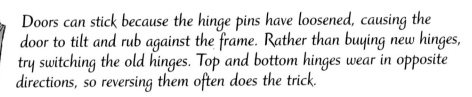

Doors can stick because the hinge pins have loosened, causing the door to tilt and rub against the frame. Rather than buying new hinges, try switching the old hinges. Top and bottom hinges wear in opposite directions, so reversing them often does the trick.

CURES FOR STICKING DOORS

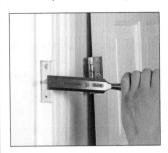  

a **Loose screws**

Fill old screw holes with glued dowels or golf tees and chisel flush, then drill new holes.

b **Sticking shut**

Chisel out a hinge mortise to cure sticking on latch side, but don't remove too much wood.

c **Springing open**

If the door springs open without latching, shim with a piece of cardboard.

Planing down

Don't attempt to plane down a door or window in the frame; remove it and support it securely on a workbench or sawhorses. Paint build-up is best removed with a surform or a power sander; if you need to remove more than 1/16 inch or so, use a block plane.

When planing the bottom of a door, work from the outer edges inward to stop the visible faces from chipping. And be sure to repaint or reseal afterwards, or the problem will recur.

Avoid planing the side edges of a door or window casement if at all possible, otherwise you might find yourself having to reposition the hinges, latch, or other hardware. Adjusting existing hinge positions is a better move.

■ **Power tools** *make short work of planing the base of a door; work from both edges toward the middle to avoid chipping.*

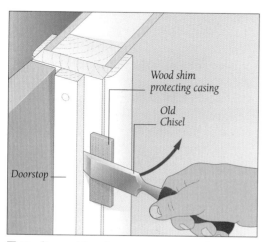

Wood shim protecting casing

Old Chisel

Doorstop

■ **Dealing with minor warping** *in a door is best done by removing the door stops and repositioning them.*

Cures for warping

Serious warping in a door or window casement is nearly always due to inadequate protection from the elements. If the problem has gone too far, you may have no choice but to remove the affected item, lay it flat in a dry environment, and weight it down with bricks. Given time and dry weather, the door should return to its proper shape within a few days, after which you can repaint or reseal it before rehanging. But check first that the joints haven't opened up or loosened in the meantime. Unless the exposed surfaces of the door have a continuous unbroken seal, the warping may recur.

Casement window repairs

DEFECTS IN HINGED *casements often show up as sticking, or as localized drafts that can add up to a small fortune in heating bills. So unless you want to see your hard-earned cash fly out of the window, don't delay in making the necessary repairs.*

Tracing the problem

A sticking window that is constantly forced shut is likely to develop more serious faults over time, as is one that rattles in its frame or lets in drafts. So the first thing to do is to trace the cause of the problem.

Rust-proof metal L-plate

Homemade clamp

Glued dowel

Sliding wedges

■ **Secure loose joints** *in a casement window with recessed metal corner braces, or with glued dowels driven into the mortise-and-tenon joints.*

● **Loose hinges:** are often the result of being slammed shut. Tighten the screws, or refit with a larger screw size.

● **Gaps in the putty:** clean out the old putty and replace before moisture gets into the wood.

● **Broken glass:** a serious safety and security risk and should be dealt with immediately. Remove the broken pane and replace with new glass (see opposite).

● **Paint build up:** very common with casement windows. Sand down to bare wood, prime, and repaint.

● **Warping and loose joints:** another result of constant banging, they can also occur after prolonged exposure to the elements. The only solution is to remove the casement and weigh it down on a flat surface. Clamp the frame so that the joints are forced back together, then reinforce them with metal L-plates or glued dowels (see left).

When repairing a window, particularly at ground level, start early in the day. A window that can't be closed is an open invitation to a burglar, so leave yourself plenty of time to finish the job. If not, board the window up overnight.

REPLACING A PANE OF GLASS

1 **Remove old glass and putty**

Wearing gloves, remove the broken glass and chip out the putty with an old chisel held flat.

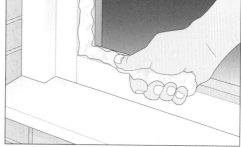

2 **Prepare the frame**

Clean the channel and coat with linseed oil, then roll out glazing putty and lay it in.

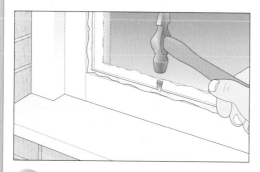

3 **Fit the new pane**

Press the new glass into the putty at the edges. Tap in a glazier point every 9 inches.

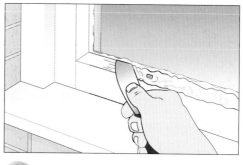

4 **Seal with putty**

Push rolled putty into the channel and smooth with a putty knife. Paint after a week.

Sliding windows and patio doors

Sliding windows and patio doors run in channels that are secured to a frame, which in turn is fixed into the window box. If you experience sticking with this type of window or door, check that these channels are clean and free of obstructions. If not, spray them with a light lubricating oil. If the sticking still persists, check that the joints are tight and that the frame is square within the box; often, retightening the fixing screws can make all the difference. As a last resort, with wooden frames, you should be able to lift them out of their runners and sand down. If you sand back to bare wood, make sure you repaint it before re-installing it or moisture will get into the wood, causing it to swell or warp.

Repair double-hung windows

WHEN A DOUBLE-HUNG WINDOW *sticks or stops working, it's a sign that the window needs a general overhaul. Once you know how double-hung windows work, the job's easier than it looks – but you will need a helper to lift out the sashes, and you should prepare yourself for some redecorating.*

> **DEFINITION**
>
> A **double-hung window** is a vertically sliding window that is counterbalanced by weights or springs hidden in its frame.

Removing the sashes

Begin by prying the sash stop away from the frame; run a knife blade down the edge of the stop to help release it from layers of old paint. Now pull the inner sash away from the frame. Tie a length of string to each sash cord, then cut the cord between string and sash and lower the counterweight to the bottom of the jamb box. Remove the outer sash in the same way, having first released it by prying out the parting strip between the two sashes. Note which weights are for which sash.

Not all double-hung windows have cords; newer ones use spiral spring balance mechanisms. Check which you have before removing the sashes. Spiral-system sashes rarely need maintenance, but the springs can break. Buy a special tensioning tool to re-balance the springs.

■ **Pry the sash stops** *off with a pry bar, starting in the middle of each. When refitting, put the first nail 5 inches from the corner.*

Replacing sash cords

If a sash cord breaks, causing the sash to go "loose" on one side, replace both cords together. The pockets giving access to the jamb box may be screwed, nailed, or just slotted in place, but the chances are they will be covered in layers of old paint that will have to be cut or scraped out first. Pull the counterweights out through the pocket and sever the old cord. Then tie the old cord end-to-end to the new one with a piece of string, and use the old cord to draw the new cord up the jamb box and through the pulley. Attach one end of the new cord to the weight, then nail the other end to the top of the sash.

A DOUBLE-HUNG WINDOW

A traditional double-hung window is a mechanical marvel: make sure you treat it with respect! You should know how the window is constructed before attempting an overhaul. Replacement pulleys, sash cords, and weights are obtainable from hardware stores; so are replacement springs for the newer sprung-balance type.

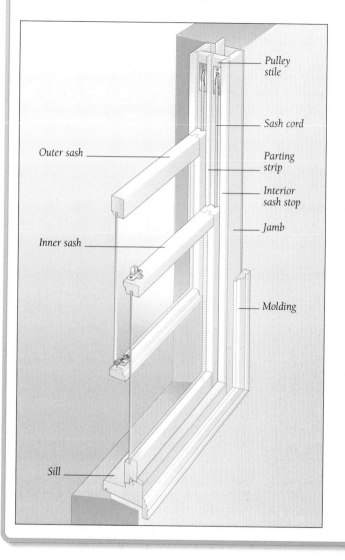

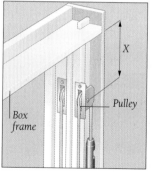

■ **Measure from** *the pulley to top center of the box frame when replacing cords.*

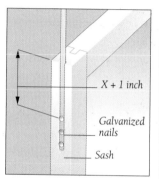

■ **Add 1 inch** *to the above distance when nailing new cord to sashes.*

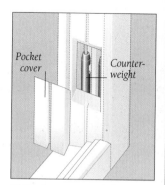

■ **Pocket covers** *behind the sash stops hide counter-weights within the jamb box.*

Repairing frames and sills

EXTERIOR WOODWORK IS FOREVER *at the mercy of rain and that,*
ultimately, means one thing: rot. Guard against moisture penetration by
checking door frames and windowsills regularly, and deal with any patches of
rotten wood promptly, before the damage spreads.

Checking for rot

Inspect all exterior woodwork at least once a year for signs of wet rot. Spot flaking or
bubbling paintwork – this is often a sign of moisture retention, but don't rely solely on
visual indicators. Test wood with an awl: if the wood is soft and the awl can penetrate
easily, you've got a repair job on your hands. If detected early, you may be able to cure
damp patches by using new borate fungicides, then reconstitute the damaged wood with
an epoxy filler. But be warned: this will keep the specific area rot-free, but the
underlying condition that caused it must be treated to stop future recurrence.

If you encounter rotten wood that is dry, powdery, and covered
in a white fungus, call in a specialist immediately. You may have a
serious case of dry rot – a fungal condition that can spread unless
treated with powerful fungicides.

Dealing with rot

If you find evidence of rot in your woodwork, be sure to treat it as soon as possible.

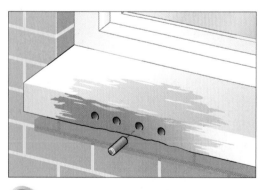

a **Insert fungicidal rods**

Extreme cases of rot can be treated with fungicidal
rods, along with borate preservatives. Drill holes in
the affected area and insert plugs.

b **Repair, prime, and paint**

Repair softwood sills with an epoxy wood filler,
sand down when dry, prime with an epoxy sealer
or paintable preservative, and paint.

Patching frames

Door frames are most likely to suffer lower down, so you should be able to patch rather than replace. Chisel out the affected area and then make a stepped cut into the undamaged wood (see below). Shape a new piece of wood to fit and coat it in wood preservative. Screw the wood patch in place, countersinking the screw heads and covering them with wood filler. Sand the repair to shape, coat with preservative, and repaint. Seal the space between the frame and wall with paintable exterior caulk.

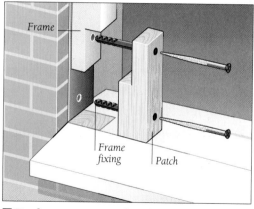

■ **Replace rotten wood** *at the base of a door frame with a patch, secured to the walls with frame fasteners, and sealed with non-setting glue.*

Patching sills

If moisture penetration is severe in a window sill, cut out the damage, and make a replacement block to fit. Place this while you mark the position of a drip groove underneath the sill. Chisel out the groove, coat the new patch with preservative, then glue and screw it to the sill. Cover the screw heads with wood filler, sand the patch to shape, and prime and repaint the sill.

If you can't get a clean cut when chiseling out a patch of rotten wood, it's probably because the wood is damp. Try cutting farther back into good wood.

Rotten door threshold moldings are seldom worth patching: it's better to saw through the saddle, remove the center, and work the ends free from underneath the jambs. Be sure that no rot has spread to the bottom of the jambs and stops.

Buy a metal saddle molding from a home center and cut it to fit snug against the jambs. Make sure that the door clears the new saddle and plane the door if necessary. Make certain that the molding is screwed down tightly enough so that the gaskets create a seal.

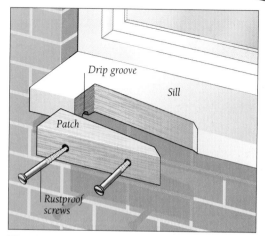

■ **When inserting a patch,** *cut diagonally back into the good wood to give the repair strength.*

Hanging a new door

ALTHOUGH MOST DOORS *are sold pre-hung – complete with frame and buck – you can easily replace just a door if that's the only problem. Most doors are a standard 6 feet 8 inches by 3 feet, but other sizes are available and you can custom order, or trim to fit.*

Measuring and preparation

Measure the height and width of the opening and then subtract a small amount for clearance before transferring the measurements to the new door; take ⅛ inch off the top and sides, and ¼ to ⅜ inches from the bottom. When trimming to length, take equal amounts from the top and bottom of flush doors, but only trim the bottom edge of a paneled door. Trim small amounts with a block plane, working from the corners toward the middle to avoid chipping the edges. If you need to remove more than ¼ inch, use a circular saw and finish with a plane.

Test-fit the door in the opening before you proceed by standing it on wooden wedges. Doors are heavy, so you may need help.

When you are happy with the fit, remove the door to install the hinges and other hardware. If you're starting from scratch, gain the upper hinge 7 inches from the top of the door and the lower hinge 10 inches from the bottom. On a fire door, gain a third hinge 4–5 inches below the top one.

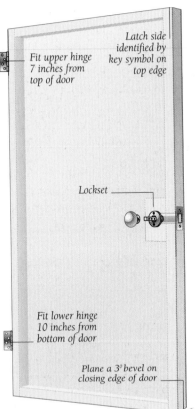

Fit upper hinge 7 inches from top of door

Latch side identified by key symbol on top edge

Lockset

Fit lower hinge 10 inches from bottom of door

Plane a 3° bevel on closing edge of door

■ **A flush door** *must be hung facing the right way so that the latch will be bedded in solid wood.*

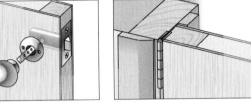

■ **The latchbolt** *(left) should be set approximately 38 inches from the bottom of the door; a butt hinge (right) needs to be centered between the door and frame.*

GAINING DOOR HINGES

1 Marking

Lay the hinge on the door edge and mark around the leaf with a pencil or knife.

2 Mark depth

Mark the depth of the hinge mortise on the face of the door using a marking gauge.

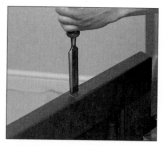

3 Score lines

Carefully drive the chisel in along the marked lines to the same depth as the mortise.

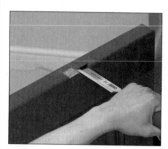

4 Chisel out

Chisel the mortise, working from the line on the face, with the beveled edge up.

5 Test and clean

Test-fit the hinge; then clean up the mortise until you get a perfect fit.

6 Fit hinge

Mark and drill pilot holes for the hinge; then screw the leaf in position.

Fitting to the frame

After fitting on the hinges, wedge the door in the doorway at the correct level and carefully mark the hinge positions on the frame. Reinforce or extend the old hinge mortises as appropriate. Gain new mortises as you did for the door. Try the door with one screw in each hinge and test. If it sticks, try fractionally increasing the depth of the hinge mortises and test again. When you are satisfied with the fit and that it opens and closes freely, screw in the remaining hinge screws, replace the stops (if necessary), and add locks and handles as required. If it is an exterior door, make sure that you prime and paint or seal the door immediately, before moisture can enter the wood, causing it to warp.

Door hardware and locks

YOU'VE HUNG YOUR NEW DOOR, it opens and closes perfectly, and it's been given a coat of paint. Now all that remains is to secure it against prying fingers or the outside world.

Door hardware

A door lockset, comprising handles, latchbolt and spindle, is the minimum requirement for an internal door, and is very easy to install (see right). Rooms where you may need some privacy, such as a bathroom, can be fitted with simple surface-mounted bolts, and you may want to attach door closers to keep the warmth in. Doors leading to garages should always be fitted with locks. Door locksets for external doors are also sold in sets, which may include a knocker, handle, and strikerplate. You may also want to consider a letterbox, security chain, and peephole viewer.

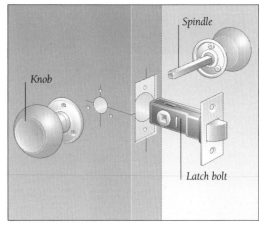

■ **Door locksets** *and latches come in all shapes and sizes. Where security is an issue, you should consider installing a deadbolt.*

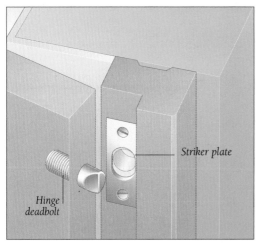

■ **Hinge deadbolts** *offer added protection against hinges and locks being forced, or the frame itself being jimmied.*

Locks and security

A door is only as strong as what's around it. Fitting hinge bolts (see left) will prevent the hinges from being forced – simply drill circular recesses in the door and frame. Buy screw-on metal bars to reinforce the frame itself. The minimum requirement for exterior doors is a deadbolt lock, but you'd be well advised to fit a mortise lock as well. This is fitted in the edge of the door, which must be at least 1-inch thick. Narrow-stile versions are available, however, for use-on glazed doors. Create the mortise by drilling overlapping holes to the depth of the recess, then clean up the sides with a chisel – the lock should be a snug fit.

FITTING A DEADBOLT LOCK

1 Position lock

Mark the position of the lock and holes on the door, using a template if provided.

2 Drill cylinder hole

Drill the cylinder hole from one side; then, when the bit breaks through, from the other.

3 Fit the bolt

Position the horizontal bolt on the door and fix in position using woodscrews.

4 Trim connecting bar

Fit the cylinder in the hole and mark the bar for length. Trim with a junior hacksaw.

5 Position strike plate

Fit the lock and mark where it strikes the frame. Position the strike plate accordingly.

6 Chisel mortise

Chisel out the mortise for the strike plate in the door frame, test-fit, then screw in place.

Fit a rim lock one-third of the way down the door and a mortise lock one-third of the way up for maximum strength.

Test the lock with the bolt extended so that you can pull it out again. Having fitted the lock, cut a recess in the jamb for the keeper (the metal plate or box that receives the latch). Don't weaken the frame wood when you do this.

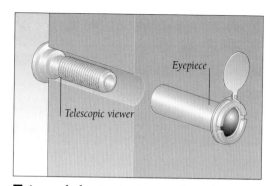

■ **A peephole viewer** *gives a wide-angle view to the outside. Slide the threaded section from outside, then screw on the eyepiece.*

Eyepiece

Telescopic viewer

Window hardware and locks

MANY DOMESTIC BREAK-INS are done through a window. If you don't want to be included in the statistics, install window locks.

Installing window hardware

Window hardware, in the form of latches and handles, will keep your windows open and closed but not secure. Always install locks, too. Some window locks – such as track stops, security pins, and screw stops – can be used with existing hardware, but if in doubt I advise you to buy new. Choose lockable handles and screw-type stops. Keyed turnbuckles and keyed bolts are good for sash windows. For added security, make sure surface-mounted locks can't be dismantled. Use tamper-proof screws, or choose locks with casings that cover their attachments.

■ **Key safety issue:** *never leave keys in locks. Remove after use and keep close at hand, but out of sight.*

Choosing and installing window locks

The design of a window largely determines which locks to fit, but you should also consider ease and frequency of use before buying. Security bolts are unobtrusive, and ideal for wooden casement windows. The bolt is recessed into the edge of the casement and operated by a splined key through the face of the casement. Double-hung windows are secured in many ways, the most popular being rod locks, which are fitted through both sashes, and ventilating locks, which are mounted on the inner sash to permit partial opening.

As with doors, window locks are only as good as their mounting surfaces, so make sure the woodwork is in good condition before installing.

It may seem obvious, but don't leave the keys to window locks in or around the locks where they could be reached from the outside by breaking a pane of glass. Always keep the keys out of sight, but make sure they can be easily found in case you need to open a window in an emergency.

LOCKING CASEMENT WINDOWS...

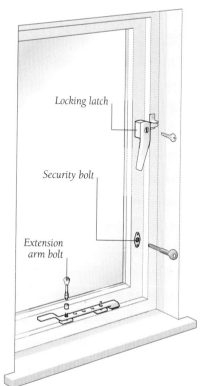

Locking latch

Security bolt

Extension arm bolt

The type of casement lock required will depend on what make of window you have and where it is situated. For frequently opened windows, use an automatic lock (see right). You will need a key to open the window, but it will lock on its own when closed.

AUTOMATIC LOCK

...AND DOUBLE-HUNG WINDOWS

For maximum security it's best to install sash locks in pairs. Older double-hung windows are usually wooden, so security bolts and ventilation locks are good options. Surface-mounted sash bolts (see right) are also popular. They don't require a key to lock, but can't be opened without one.

SASH-BOLT

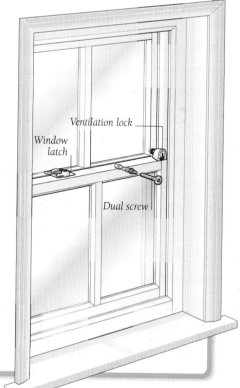

Ventilation lock

Window latch

Dual screw

Weatherproofing

IF YOU WANT TO KEEP THE HEAT IN *you've got to keep the cold out. Sealing doors and windows to prevent drafts could cut your heating bills by 10 percent, so what are you waiting for?*

Search and seal

Use the flickering flame of a candle to locate the source of drafts and fix any cracks or gaps around doors and windows. Seal any gaps around frames with flexible waterproof caulk and repaint where necessary. Clean door frames and window sashes and install weatherstripping. Doors should also be fitted with threshold sweeps. Be sure to check other inconspicuous areas such as letter slots, dog and cat doors, and keyholes.

Windows must remain easy to open after weatherproofing. Providing adequate ventilation around the home is very important, as it reduces the risk of damp and condensation.

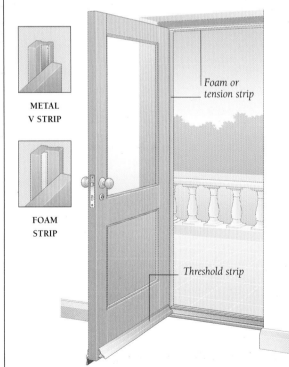

METAL
V STRIP

FOAM
STRIP

Foam or
tension strip

Threshold strip

Weatherproofing doors

There are two basic types of weatherstripping for door frames: metal or vinyl tension V strips and foam or rubber weatherstripping. If the door closes against a doorstop use self-adhesive foam weatherstripping; if it moves across the frame, attach a sweep or threshold gasket. The choice depends on how your door opens and the size of the gap to be sealed. For modest gaps, you can use foam compression weatherstripping on the bottom of the door.

■ **A wide variety** *of door weatherstripping is available, including sweep gasket, foam or rubber compressible strips, and two-part interlocking seals.*

SWEEP GASKET

METAL SPRING

TWO-PART

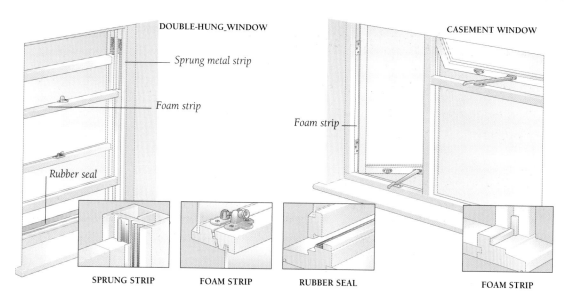

DOUBLE-HUNG WINDOW

Sprung metal strip

Foam strip

Rubber seal

CASEMENT WINDOW

Foam strip

SPRUNG STRIP   FOAM STRIP   RUBBER SEAL   FOAM STRIP

Weatherproofing strips for windows

Foam or vinyl strips are self-adhesive. Sprung metal strips are
nailed to the runner grooves of double-hung windows, then
"sprung" with a special tensioning tool. Tubular vinyl or rubber
gaskets are nailed to the parting strip of double-hung windows.

■ **You can
weatherproof** *your
windows in several
different ways. The
diagram above
illustrates what you can
use and where to use it.*

A simple summary

✔ Don't rush into sanding down a
sticking door or window: there
may be an easier means of repair.

✔ Carry out repairs sooner rather
than later: they'll only get worse.

✔ Repairing double-hung windows
isn't as difficult as it looks.

✔ Keep an eye out for rot. Dry rot
requires specialist attention.

✔ Most doors are sold pre-hung in
a frame, but you can replace
only the door.

✔ Exterior doors should have a
deadbolt lock and mortise lock.

✔ Install locks on all your upstairs
and downstairs windows.

✔ Weatherproofing can save 10
percent or more on heating bills.

Chapter 12

Floors and Staircases

CREAKS IN WOODEN FLOORS AND STAIRS don't only make things go bump in the night; they also cause premature wear in whatever is laid over the top and, in extreme cases, lead to accidents. Get to grips with any repairs before you lay a new floorcovering, or go the whole way and give the floor a brand-new level surface.

In this chapter...
- ✓ Fixing staircase problems
- ✓ Repairing stair banisters
- ✓ Wood floor repairs
- ✓ Installing a wood subfloor
- ✓ Laying a self-leveling subfloor

A CREAKING STAIRCASE MAY BE DAUNTING...BUT IT CAN BE FIXED

Fixing staircase problems

CREAKING STAIRCASES *tend to be annoying rather than portents of disaster, and are usually easily fixed. Cracked treads and split or worn nosings are a different matter, and should be fixed immediately.*

Tracing the problem

Wear and tear and changes in humidity cause all wooden structures to "give" and creak a bit over time, and staircases are no exception. If possible, attack the problem from beneath the stairs. Tap loose wedges back into place, and replace any missing ones with pieces of wood fashioned to the same shape. Weak joints can be reinforced with steel angle brackets or pulled tight with screws. Watch out for missing blocks, too. Replace any that you find missing.

Replace any rotten wood as a matter of course. You should be able to loosen damaged treads from underneath, which will make for a more solid repair.

I've heard it said that talcum powder squirted between the treads and risers is a good way to cure creaks, although I have to confess it's never worked for me!

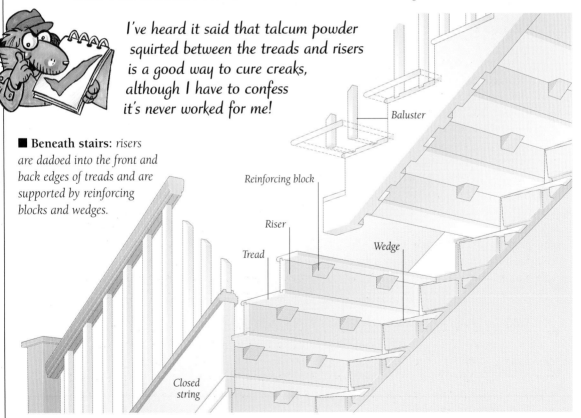

■ **Beneath stairs:** *risers are dadoed into the front and back edges of treads and are supported by reinforcing blocks and wedges.*

Baluster

Reinforcing block

Riser

Tread

Wedge

Closed string

REPAIRING STAIRS FROM UNDERNEATH

Creaks are usually the result of loose or missing supports. Repairing or replacing them may do the job, but extra screws may be necessary. Here's how to deal with them:

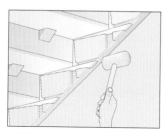

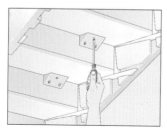

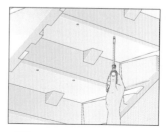

a Wedges

Tap loose wedges back into place. New ones can be made from slivers of wood.

b Blocks

Glue and screw back reinforcing blocks, or make new ones.

c Screws

If the back of the tread has warped, screw up through the tread into the riser.

Repairs from above

The undersides of many staircases are often inaccessible, leaving you with no choice but to make repairs from above. Close open joints between the backs of treads and the risers above with metal angle brackets recessed into the wood. Secure the front of a tread to the riser beneath by flooding the joint with woodworking adhesive, reinforced with countersunk woodscrews.

On some stairs, the nosings (the overhanging parts) of the treads are separate from the treads themselves, in which case they can be pried off and replaced if worn or split. Otherwise, cut the damaged tread back to a line of good wood and then make a replacement nosing from a separate piece. Glue the patch to the cut edge of the tread, reinforced with dowels at 3-inch intervals. Let dry for 24 hours, then plane and sand to match the profile of the other treads. On stairs with open stringers, it may be possible to pry and replace the entire tread, having first released the balusters that are housed into it and cut through any fixings.

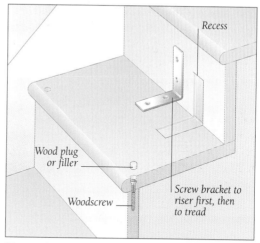

Recess

Wood plug or filler

Woodscrew

Screw bracket to riser first, then to tread

■ **Reinforce joints between** *risers and treads with covered screws and recessed brackets.*

Repairing stair banisters

IT SHOULD COME AS NO SURPRISE to learn that the most often used safety feature in homes with stairs is the banister. Handrails, balusters (spindles), and even the supporting newel posts can all become loose over the years, necessitating urgent repairs.

Checking for problems and making repairs

The most common banister problem is a loose baluster. Although some movement in balusters is to be expected, you should attend to breakages and balusters that fall out without delay. In staircases with closed stringers (the sloping timber supporting the treads), the balusters are housed into grooves in the stringer and the underside of the handrail, where they are separated by wooden spacers. On open stringers, the feet of the balusters are housed in the treads behind "planted" moldings.

Broken balusters can sometimes be repaired without being taken out. Pry the split sections apart and apply wood glue, then press together and clamp tightly. Likewise, you may be able to secure a loose baluster by driving screws at an angle into its housing.

More worrying are loose handrails and newel posts. A handrail can be secured at the newel post end by reinforcing the existing joint with a 3-inch wood screw, pilot-holed and driven in at an angle. Afterwards, cover the screw with a plug of matching wood glued in place. Where the end of a handrail is built into a wall, you can secure it with a metal angle bracket; or, for a proper repair, remove the plaster around the rail, wedge it tight where it is cut into the masonry, then repair the wall.

■ **On closed-stringer staircases,** *balusters sit in the handrail and are held in place by spacers (top inset). The stringer is grooved and also uses spacers (middle inset). On open-stringer staircases, balusters are notched into the tread and held in place with moldings (bottom inset).*

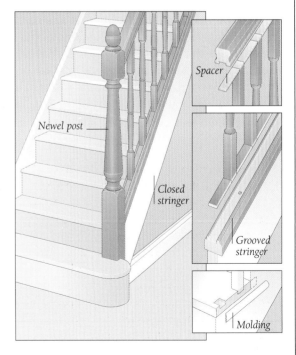

Newel post

Spacer

Closed stringer

Grooved stringer

Molding

REPLACING CLOSED-STRINGER BALUSTERS

 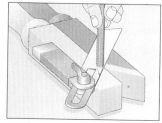 

1 Take out spacer

Pry out bottom spacer in front of the baluster and the top spacer behind it.

2 Cut angles

Use a sliding bevel to transfer joint angle to new spindle, and replace in banister.

3 Replace and finish

Nail spacers back in place, top and bottom, with a finishing nail in the center of each.

REPLACING OPEN-STRINGER BALUSTERS

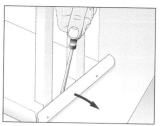 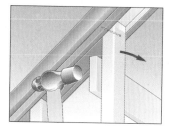 

1 Remove molding

First pry off the molding that holds the baluster in the tread, with a screwdriver or pry bar.

2 Hammer free

The baluster will be nailed to the handrail, so tap free against a woodscrap.

3 Nail back

Cut new baluster and replace. Nail molding back in place and nail the handrail in.

Loose newel posts are the most serious problem, as they are structural members that support the banister. If you can gain access from underneath, bolting the newel post to the adjacent floor joist is the most satisfactory repair. Otherwise, screw the post to the stringer with long No.10 countersunk wood screws. If the cap of a newel post becomes loose or gets knocked off, drill the base to accept a length of dowel; then glue back in place.

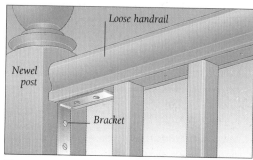

Loose handrail

Newel post

Bracket

■ **Loose handrails** *can be fixed by securing to a newel post or wall with a recessed metal bracket.*

Wood floor repairs

RAISED OR DAMAGED FLOORBOARDS *are a safety hazard, as well as annoying, so don't delay in fixing them. Use the same techniques to gain access to pipes and cables under the floor.*

Creaking and damaged boards

Floorboards are prone to swelling and splitting over time. This can cause the nails to work loose and the boards to creak, and can lead to excessive carpet wear. If you're lucky, loose boards can be secured with additional nails or screws, but badly damaged sections may have to be removed and replaced. To do this, you'll have to cut across a board in place, which is best done with a circular saw. Set the saw bed to the exact board thickness to avoid touching pipes notched into the joists. The cut should fall exactly halfway over a joist, which you can gauge by checking where other joints between boards are; double-check by inserting a piece of card into the gaps. If the board is tongue and groove, you'll have to saw down one edge as well. Afterward, it should be possible to pry up the cut end, insert a batten underneath, and lever the damaged section free.

Before making repairs to isolated floorboards, check the flooring as a whole. If the entire floor appears to have bowed or warped, it may be due to a joist problem. This must be looked at by a professional.

LIFTING SQUARE-EDGED BOARDS

1 Cut at a joist

Use a circular saw, set to the thickness of the boards, to isolate the damaged section.

2 Lift the end

Trim uncut edges with a chisel, then pry the end free with a claw hammer and pry bar.

3 Spring the board

Slip a batten under the board and stand on the raised end to free the other end.

REPLACING TONGUE-AND-GROOVE BOARDS

1 **Remove the tongue**

Sever the tongue from the board by cutting on one edge with a circular saw.

2 **Pry out**

Pry up the edge of the board with a chisel, using scrap wood as a fulcrum.

3 **Cut to size**

Cut off the lower (thinner) side of the groove on new board. Fit it tongue first and nail down.

Patching boards and filling gaps

Gaps between boards can be filled with slivers of wood, cut lengthways to a wedge-shape with a circular saw. Glue the slivers, tap into the gaps with a mallet, then sand flush with the surrounding boards. As a final precaution, use a nail set to drive nail heads below the surface of the boards.

If you can't find an exact replacement for the existing boards, buy boards that are wider and thicker. Trim them to length and width, then chisel notches in the ends to accommodate the joists so that the patch sits flush with the other boards.

Other types of wood floor

Use a similar technique to cut out damaged sections from a plywood floor, being careful to note where the joints between the boards fall. Floors of this type rarely cause trouble unless they get wet and swell, in which case the chances are that all the boards will be affected. Where possible, remove the baseboards first, then lift entire sections and replace them; cutting out small sections is not advised because it can weaken the floor and may lead to creaking.

■ **Nail into joists** *at an angle (left) with cut floor nails parallel to the grain. If for some reason you can't nail directly into a joist, attach a batten to the side of it (right) and screw into this.*

Installing a wood subfloor

INSTALLING A SUBFLOOR *over an existing floor using hardboard or plywood is a lot easier than replacing the floor itself, and will feel better underfoot as well as prolonging the life of the new floorcovering. If you're laying sheet floorcoverings or parquet flooring, it's an essential first step.*

Preparing the existing floor

Although subfloors are usually installed over bare joists, you may want to install on top of an existing floor. This essentially means that the subfloor becomes the "underlayment" – a cushioning layer between a subfloor and final floorcovering.

Hardboard is ideal for most floorcoverings, but if you're planning on laying ceramic tiles, nail down ¼-inch exterior-grade plywood instead. For sheet floorcoverings, carpets, and soft floor tiles, lay 1-M-1 hardboard to the baseboard, leaving a ⅛-inch gap. For hard floorcoverings it is advisable to first remove baseboards and cut the bottom of door moldings, then replace baseboards over the completed flooring.

Laying underlayment over existing floor makes ventilation more critical. Check that the crawl space or basement allows air to circulate freely around the floorboards.

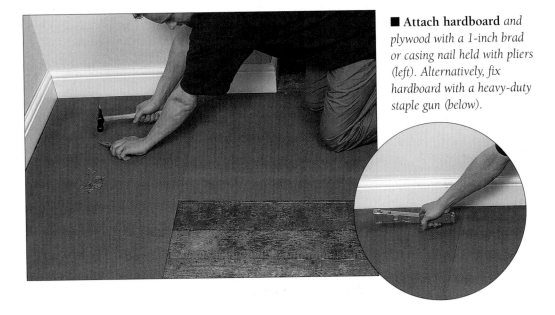

■ **Attach hardboard** *and plywood with a 1-inch brad or casing nail held with pliers (left). Alternatively, fix hardboard with a heavy-duty staple gun (below).*

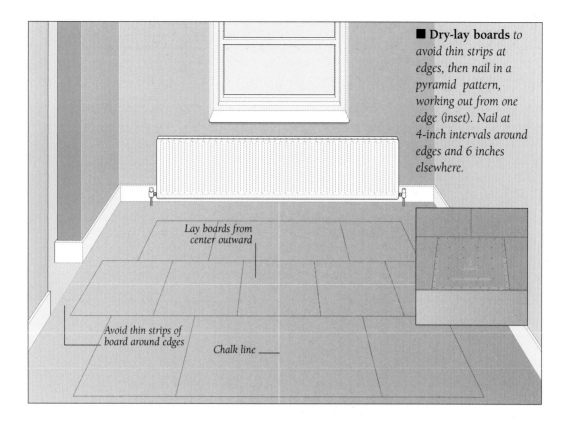

■ **Dry-lay boards** *to avoid thin strips at edges, then nail in a pyramid pattern, working out from one edge (inset). Nail at 4-inch intervals around edges and 6 inches elsewhere.*

Lay boards from center outward

Avoid thin strips of board around edges

Chalk line

Fitting the sheets

After your hardboard is delivered, unwrap it and allow it to stand in the room prior to laying for 48 hours. Hardboard comes in 4 x 4 foot flooring panels, which are easier to handle than full 8 x 4 foot plywood sheets. Mark the center lines across the floor and dry-lay sheets outward from there, staggering the joints between rows. If you're left with narrow strips of less than a floorboard's width around the edges of the room, adjust the layout accordingly. Hardboard should be laid rough side up if you are planning to lay tiles, to provide a key for the adhesive, otherwise lay it smooth side up.

It's important to check the level of underlayment as you go along. The best way to do this is with an 8-foot straightedge — a length of pipe or the uncut edge of a plywood sheet works well.

Once you are happy with the layout, attach the sheets, working from one edge outwards in all directions to prevent the board from bowing up. Then cut pieces to fit the gaps around the edges. Check the level of the floor at regular intervals, and if necessary shim underneath the edges of the sheets with thin wallboard.

Laying a self-leveling subfloor

GIVE A ROUGH CONCRETE FLOOR *a smooth, level surface before tiling using self-leveling compound – a remarkable latex-based powder that finds its own level when mixed with water and dries to a tough finish.*

Using self-leveling compound

The existing floor should be free of dust and dirt, and must be completely dry. Fixtures or fitted units should be unscrewed and propped clear so that the compound can be spread beneath them. If not, make sure you protect them with tape. Before you start, use a level to check the floor for high and low spots. Mark these, so that you can pick a "route" for pouring the compound that starts at the lowest point and ends at the door. Fit wood dams across doorways to contain the liquid. After mixing, pour the compound over the floor and feather with a trowel. Work quickly so that the first batch doesn't harden before you've finished pouring. Depending on the floor, it may take two applications to get it absolutely level.

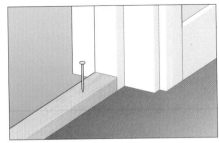

■ **Fit wood dams** *across doorways to contain the compound. You can remove them when it has fully hardened.*

Leveling a floor

Using self-leveling compound makes leveling a solid floor a surprisingly simple job.

1 **Surface preparation**

You apply self-leveling compound over tiles, but whatever the surface, apply a special latex primer. On porous surfaces, thin the primer with water.

2 **Sealing cracks**

Fill any cracks and gaps in the floor surface with mortar. Allow to dry thoroughly before using self-leveling compound.

3 Pour out compound

Pour the self-leveling compound onto the floor, starting in the lowest spot. Don't attempt to cover too large an area at once.

4 Feather

Feather edges with a flat trowel and move on to next section before dry. When done, check level and fill any low patches with a thin mix of compound.

Mixing a large batch of self-leveling compound is often wiser than trying to quickly mix small batches before what you've poured dries. Use a drill with a mixer attachment and be prepared to use the compound as soon as it is mixed. The key to laying an excellent subfloor with self-leveling compound is speed.

A simple summary

✓ Creaking floorboards and stairs don't always signal damage, but check to be on the safe side.

✓ Secure stair banisters are absolutely essential for home safety.

✓ Damaged floorboards and stairs are dangerous: fix them before an accident occurs.

✓ Provide a smooth base on wood floors for floorcoverings by laying hardboard; for heavier floorcoverings such as ceramic tiles, use plywood to support the extra weight.

✓ Self-leveling compound makes the job of leveling solid floors straightforward. Simply pour it over the floor surface.

Chapter 13

Shelves and Storage

ENOUGH STORAGE SPACE IS SOMETHING few homes have – and even when they do, it's not long before it runs out. Making the most of empty wall space is often the answer, using shelves for the things you want to display and built-in cabinets or closets for items that you'd rather hide.

In this chapter...

✓ Adjustable shelving

✓ Built-in shelving

✓ Changing cabinet doors

✓ Installing kitchen cabinets

✓ Building in cabinets

✓ Building in a closet

ALCOVE UNITS AND RECESSED SHELVING CAN CREATE A LUXURIOUS AMBIENCE

Adjustable shelving

ADJUSTABLE SHELVES are
quick and easy to install, and have the
advantage that the shelf heights can be
changed to suit your storage needs.

The standard way

Adjustable shelves and their brackets
come in all shapes and sizes, from simple
metal standard-and-bracket systems to
wood types with matching shelves. All
work on the same ingenious principle,
which transfers the load on the shelves
along the length of the standards and

■ **Adjustable shelving** *is the perfect way to keep*
pace with changing storage needs.

makes them very strong relative to the size of the components used. An adjustable
system can be enclosed within an alcove, or installed along an open wall with attached
shelf ends to stop things from falling off. Virtually any kind of board can be used for the
shelves, with plywood, glass, veneered pressed wood, or melamine-coated
particleboard being the most popular.

One problem you might encounter when installing adjustable shelves
is a wall badly out of plumb, which you can spot by running a
straightedge across the surface. Rather than risk a poor fit, level the
"low" areas with wood shims under the standards.

Designing an adjustable system

The danger with adjustable shelves is that they will sag if overloaded. Avoid this by
fitting standards at a minimum of 16-inch intervals or, on a stud wall, by screwing a
track to each stud, which are normally spaced at 16-inch intervals (12 inches in older
homes). If you anticipate extra-heavy loads, use 1-inch board for the shelves; for books
and other display items, ¾-inch board should be fine. Packs of shelves are often sold
pre-cut and edged in popular shelf widths, which saves a lot of work.

If the shelves are to go on an open wall, position the standards at least 2 inches in from
the ends; if they are enclosed by an alcove, position tracks 4 inches in from the ends. As
a rule, choose brackets that extend the full width of the shelves – unless you are using a
shelf clip system, which won't support as much weight. Always check the standard
manufacturers ratings for maximum weight bearing load.

Installing the standards

When installing the standards, you need to consider the surface to which you are mounting. On masonry walls, use screws and plastic wall anchors and space the standards every 16 inches. On a stud wall, use a stud finder to locate studs and use 3-inch wood screws to attach the standards. If you hang shelves over hollow wall spaces, use metal wall anchors and don't use shelves over 12 inches wide, to avoid too much stress on the supports.

After installation, the tracks can be left as they are, or painted the same color as the wall to hide them. You can even rout out 1 x 2 inch hardwood strips to nest the standards in. In practice, once the shelves are full you won't notice them anyway.

INSTALLING ADJUSTABLE SHELVING

1 Position

Position the first standard and mark the top hole. Remove the standard, drill a hole, and anchor if necessary.

2 Install and let hang

Screw the standard to the wall loosely, then let it swing under its own weight until it hangs vertically.

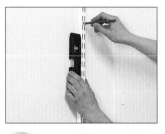

3 Mark screw holes

Use a level to check that the standard is plumb, then mark the positions of the remaining screw holes on wall.

4 Install the standard

Move the standard to one side and drill the holes. Screw the standard securely to the wall, using anchors if necessary.

5 Position next

Fit brackets at identical points on both tracks. Use a shelf on edge and a level to mark the position of the next standard.

6 Secure shelf

Install all standards and hang the brackets and shelves, then drill pilot holes in the shelves and screw from below.

Built-in shelving

IF YOU HAVE A SPARE ALCOVE OR RECESS, consider building in shelves using two or three of the walls for support. Depending on what supports you choose, and on how you finish the shelves, you can give the shelving a substantial finished look, or a "floating" look for displaying ornaments.

Design a system to suit

Built-in shelves aren't as easily adjustable as track systems, so think carefully about what you want to display on them and space the shelves accordingly. In addition to the usual shelf board materials, you could also consider solid wood planks, or 3/16 inch tempered float glass for displaying light ornaments or collectibles.

SHELVING OPTIONS

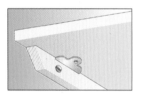

Shelf clips: use these or recessed dowels to secure wood shelves invisibly to battens. The clips are recessed in and screwed to the side battens, then screwed into the shelf from below. Angle the front of the battens to make them less apparent.

Aluminum angle strip: if you have flat walls, you can give the shelves a "floating" look by making the end supports from pre-drilled aluminum angle strip. Don't forget to allow for the thickness of both angle strips when measuring and cutting shelves to length.

Wood cleat: for extra strength, screw an additional cleat to the underside of the shelf, and screw to side cleats.

Molding: strips of wood molding, nailed and glued to the front edges of the shelves, will give the system a built-in look, as well as hiding the ends of the cleats.

Never assume that the sides of a recess will be square. If you are installing wood shelves, make an allowance for waste at either end and measure and cut each shelf individually to fit. You should do the same if you're using glass, allowing ⅛ inch clearance at each end, and then give the measurement to your glass supplier. If the sides of the alcove are badly out of true, consider lining them with wooden boards before you fit the shelves. Screw the boards to the wall and shim to plumb. Hide the gaps afterward with wood molding.

INSTALLING ALCOVE SHELVING

1 Fit the rear cleat

Decide on the height of your first shelf and cut a piece of 1 x 2 inch board to fit along the back wall. Drill screw holes in the cleat over stud positions, then mark the hole positions on the wall using a level on the cleat. Fasten the cleat.

2 Fit the side cleats

Butt the side cleats up to the back cleat and cut slightly shorter than the depth of the shelves. Miter the exposed ends to a 45° angle. As before, drill screw holes, mark the wall, and screw in place.

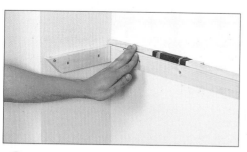

3 Measure the shelf length

Measure the width of the alcove front and back using pinch rods – two overlapping wood sticks bound together. Slide the rods out to touch the side walls, clamp them together, then transfer their combined length to the shelf.

4 Check the angle

If the sides of the alcove are badly out of square, use a sliding bevel to establish the angle between the supports and transfer this to the shelf ends. Be sure to mark and cut each end of the shelf to waste.

Changing cabinet doors

TRANSFORM YOUR KITCHEN *for minimal outlay by changing the doors on the existing units. There's a vast range available, and because kitchen units come in modular sizes, there should be no problem finding doors to fit.*

Re-using the hinges

Unless they're worn or broken, it makes sense to re-use the existing hinges. Most modern kitchen units have overlay or "Euro" hinges, which bring the door flush with the edges of the face frame. Some patterns of overlay hinge simply screw to the door and body; European, or invisible, hinges, have a large circular boss that is mortised into the door, or bodies mortised into the door and body edges.

REFITTING INVISIBLE HINGES

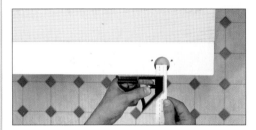

1 **Transfer the hinge positions**

Use a combination square to transfer the mortise positions from the old door to the new.

2 **Drill the mortises**

Mark the mortise center on the new door, then drill to the required depth using a guide.

3 **Mark screw holes**

Mark the hinge screw holes, drill pilot holes, and screw the hinges squarely to the new door.

4 **Attach to cabinet**

Screw the hinges back on the cabinet. Adjust the position of the door with the adjuster screw.

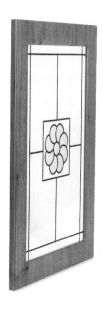

■ **The choice** in *replacement cabinet doors includes (from left to right), glazed, wood-veneered, laminated, and solid wood.*

Refitting invisible hinges will mean drilling new mortises, unless the doors have been pre-drilled. You'll need a special drill bit called a hole saw.

Traditionally constructed cabinets may use butt hinges instead. These allow the doors to sit within a face frame, in which case transfer the measurements of the old door to the new one before you mark the hinge positions and cut mortises for them. You may have to plane the edges of the new door to get it to fit.

Making new doors

If your cabinets are non-standard sizes and you can't readily find premade doors to fit, never fear. Large home centers, lumber yards, and door manufacturers all offer custom sizes. You can order doors made to fit out of veneered particleboard, MDF, or melamine. A more expensive option is soft or hardwood doors. Order them unfinished and you can paint or stain them the color of your choice.

ADJUSTING HINGES

a **Horizontal adjustment**

Adjust this screw to adjust the angle of the door so that it sits square when shut.

b **Vertical adjustment**

Slacken the fixing screws to move the door up or down relative to the cabinet.

Installing kitchen cabinets

BECAUSE KITCHEN CABINETS are modular and come in standardized sizes, it's relatively easy to swap new for old. The important thing is to work in the right order: after you've removed the old units, inspect the plumbing and wiring and make any necessary alterations. Also, repair any damage to the walls behind the units or you'll forever be plagued with dust or pests.

Installing the cabinets

Position the base cabinets first (see below), but don't attach them. Mark vertical lines on the wall to show the locations of studs and positions of the wall cabinets above. Draw a horizontal line not less than 18 inches above the work surface to mark where the wall cabinets will sit. Remove the base units and attach temporary support battens along this line. Starting at a corner or end unit, lift the first wall cabinet into position and mark the drill holes; if the cabinet isn't level, shim under the support batten with wood shims. Attach all the wall cabinets in the same way and, if necessary, join them together with connectors. Then attach the base units to the wall, double-checking that they're level. Finally, install the drawers and hang the doors.

Before removing old units, turn off the electricity and water and disconnect all wiring and plumbing. On wall cabinets, remove the doors to reduce the weight. Get help to support the doors while releasing fasteners.

FITTING A FRAMELESS BASE CABINET

1 Assembling the body

Fit the hardware to each panel and join them together. Then fit the back panel and feet, if any.

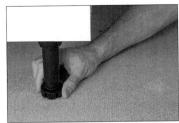

2 Leveling with feet

Position the corner unit and adjust feet, or shim under base until the top aligns with your guidelines.

3 Attaching

Mark the drill holes and screw the ledger board directly into wall studs. Check level again.

Installing a countertop

Installing lengths of straight countertop is relatively easy, but a cutout for a cooktop or sink is more complicated. Support the back edge on a wall-mounted batten. To make the cutout, first drill a starter hole for your jigsaw blade at each corner. Screw a guide batten to the waste along one side, cut this side out, then repeat for the opposite side. Now repeat the process for the other two sides. If necessary, join lengths of countertop using concealed connectors drilled and cut into the underside to pull the lengths together.

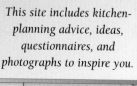

INTERNET

www.homestore.com/
Home_Improvement/
Remodeling/kitchens/

This site includes kitchen-planning advice, ideas, questionnaires, and photographs to inspire you.

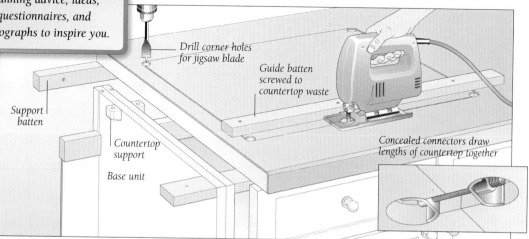

Drill corner holes for jigsaw blade

Guide batten screwed to countertop waste

Support batten

Countertop support

Base unit

Concealed connectors draw lengths of countertop together

■ **To make a cutout** *in a countertop, start by drilling a starter hole in the corners. By fixing a guide batten parallel to the edge to be cut, you ensure that your jigsaw cuts dead straight.*

4 **Fitting around pipes**

If pipes obstruct the unit, mark the side panel to fit, leaving ¼ inch clearance all round.

5 **Notching a side panel**

Cut in from the edge and cut out the notch with a jigsaw. Cut to the exact shape in an exposed panel.

6 **Adding a plinth**

Shape the plinth to fit around the baseboard. Screw clips onto the centerline to align with the feet.

Building in cabinets

LIKE SHELVES, A CABINET *can be built into a recess to make the most of an otherwise "dead" area. Add shelves above and finish with decorative wooden moldings for a traditional "dresser" look.*

Designing the cabinet

If the recess is deep enough and is reasonably square, you can opt for the simplest form of built-in cabinet: alcove shelving with added doors. Install the shelves first, then add a supporting framework for the doors and top. But if the walls of the recess are uneven, badly out of square, or simply not deep enough to provide usable storage space, add side panels to create a square, self-contained frame for the shelving. Cover the gaps between the side panels and the wall with strips of molding, nailed and glued in place.

Cut doors from the same material as the top and shelves, and hang in the frame using ordinary brass butt hinges. Install magnetic catches on the center stile. Finally, cut the top to overhang the doors and fix it to the top of the door frame using wood corner braces.

Don't forget that installing a built-in cabinet may cover a much-needed electrical socket, or else make it difficult to use. If necessary, relocate the socket or reposition it higher up in the cupboard.

MAKING A SIMPLE CABINET FRAME

1 **Attach cleats**

Attach base cleats onto the base molding to support the base of the new cupboard.

2 **Build frame**

Build the cabinet frame from 2 x 2 inch boards. Assemble the frame with simple butt joints.

3 **Install cabinet base**

Cut the base to fit over the cleats and finish the front edge. Install other shelves above it.

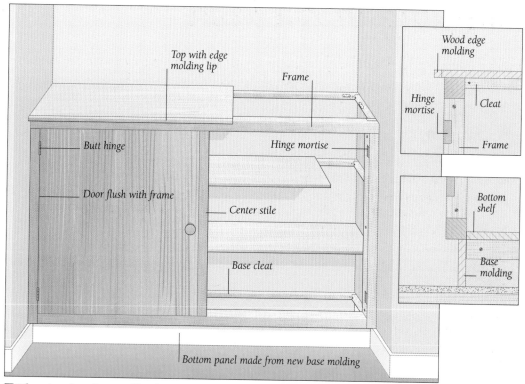

Top with edge molding lip

Frame

Wood edge molding

Hinge mortise

Cleat

Frame

Butt hinge

Hinge mortise

Door flush with frame

Center stile

Base cleat

Bottom shelf

Base molding

Bottom panel made from new base molding

■ **The simplest form of built-in cabinet** *consists of a butt-joint frame over alcove shelves supported by cleats. Finish the edge of the top with a strip of pinned-and-glued wooden edge molding (top inset), and use matching base molding to finish the base (lower inset).*

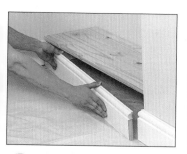

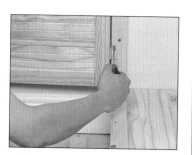

4 **Install new molding**

Cut a new piece of base molding to length and screw and glue to the ends of the cleats.

5 **Install frame**

Position frame on top of base molding and screw to wall, checking for square and plumb.

6 **Cabinet doors**

Cut doors to fit the frame, then mark and cut hinge mortises in the stile.

Building in a closet

CREATE MORE BEDROOM STORAGE *with a ready-made sliding door kit. All you need is a wall with about 2 feet of usable space in front of it.*

Installation considerations

Sliding door kits come in standard sizes and a range of finishes, including mirrored. Some include track shims to ensure the doors fit securely and may even include decorative valances to cover gaps between the doors and ceiling. The most important consideration is that the top track is screwed to a header or secure head jamb. Install premade closet components, according to what you need to store.

INSTALLING SLIDING DOORS

1 **Cut tracks to fit**

Once you have carefully measured from wall to wall, cut the tracks to length.

2 **Install top track**

Shim as necessary and screw in the top track. Be sure it can hold the weight of the doors.

3 **Secure bottom track**

Use a plumb bob to center the bottom track and screw it to the floor through the carpet.

4 **Attach valence**

A decorative valence may be needed to hide the top track. This simply clips in place.

5 **Insert doors**

Lift the sliding door and insert the roller mechanism into the channel in the track.

6 **Secure door**

Secure the door in the bottom track and test that the door closes smoothly.

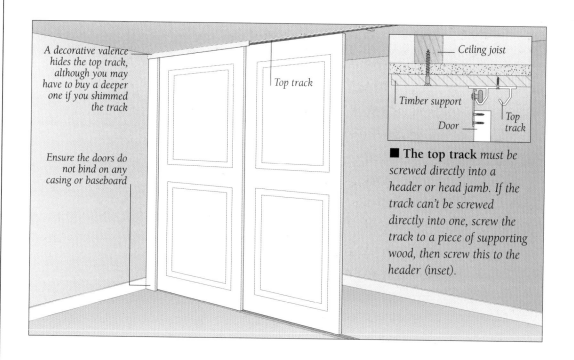

A decorative valence hides the top track, although you may have to buy a deeper one if you shimmed the track

Ensure the doors do not bind on any casing or baseboard

Top track

Ceiling joist

Timber support

Door

Top track

■ **The top track** *must be screwed directly into a header or head jamb. If the track can't be screwed directly into one, screw the track to a piece of supporting wood, then screw this to the header (inset).*

A simple summary

✓ Adjustable shelf systems are easy to assemble and the spaces between the shelves are easily moved to keep pace with the family's changing storage needs.

✓ Fit shelves and built-in cupboards in alcoves and recesses, where they will intrude least on existing living space.

✓ Changing cabinet doors is an effective and affordable way to brighten a tired kitchen.

✓ When installing kitchen cabinets, use the base units as a guide for positioning the wall units, but fit the wall units first.

✓ Transform a room and make the most out of a recess or alcove by building in a cabinet.

✓ Extra bedroom storage is easily created with a ready-made sliding door kit. Always secure the tracks for the sliding doors to a header.

Chapter 14

Walls and Ceilings

S TRUCTURAL WORK ON WALLS AND CEILINGS is best left to a builder – if only because of the mess involved and the potential hidden pitfalls. But don't despair: building a new partition wall is well within the scope of the do-it-yourselfer, as is adding decorative molding.

In this chapter...

✓ Paneling walls

✓ Changing walls

✓ Building a partition wall

✓ Decorative plasterwork

✓ Repairing molding

✓ Installing cove and cornices

✓ Tracing moisture problems

195

PLASTER CORNICE AND WOOD DOOR CASING: THE FINISHING TOUCHES TO A PERIOD-STYLE ROOM

Paneling walls

IF YOUR WALLS ARE IN POOR CONDITION *or covered with pipes and wires, but are free from moisture problems, consider paneling them with tongue-and-groove boards, square plank paneling, or sheet paneling. And you can use the same techniques to box in pipes with paneling over a wood frame.*

Preparing for plank paneling

Tongue-and-groove plank paneling is normally nailed vertically against supporting rows of horizontal cleats or furring strips, but there's no reason you can't put plank paneling up horizontally, or even nail boards diagonally. The key to an invisible installation is to nail each strip through its tongue before slotting the next strip in place (called blind nailing). You can buy special moldings to finish inside and outside corners and to finish the top of wainscotting. Ideally, you should remove all baseboards, door casings, and other moldings before you start and then replace them once the paneling is in place. In practice, this isn't always possible, and you may find yourself having to fit additional moldings around doorways to hide the gaps.

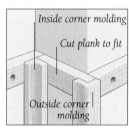

Cove molding

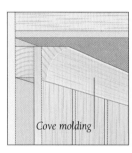

Inside corner molding

Cut plank to fit

Outside corner molding

■ **Leave an air gap** *for ventilation on full-height paneling (top). Finish outside and inside corners with special moldings (above).*

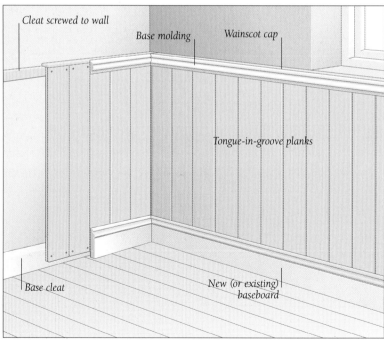

Cleat screwed to wall

Base molding

Wainscot cap

Tongue-in-groove planks

New (or existing) baseboard

Base cleat

■ **Install vertical paneling** *to horizontal battens. If you are leaving the existing baseboard in place, it can act as one of the battens.*

INSTALLING TONGUE-AND-GROOVE PLANKS

1 Installing cleats

Screw the cleats to the wall. Use a spirit level to check they're level and flat.

2 Mark edge planks

Measure for any edge planks. If necessary, mark the planks and trim to fit the wall.

3 Blind nailing

Face-nail the groove edge of the first plank, and blind nail through the tongue at an angle.

4 Subsequent planks

Use a piece of scrap to knock subsequent planks together, then blind nail them.

5 Dealing with corners

Attach inside corner molding, then measure the gap and cut a plank lengthways to fit.

6 Outside corners

Do the same at outside corners, then nail the decorative edge molding in place.

Sheet paneling

Sheet paneling is fiberboard or other thin base covered with a wood veneer or paper that simulates a wood grain. It is glued rather than supported on cleats. Although inexpensive, it as robust as wood plank paneling. Sheet paneling is easy to work with and install; simply set a chalk plumb line, apply panel adhesive to the back of the sheet in bands around the edges, and at 2-foot intervals in between, and hang. Cut the sheets to fit with a jigsaw. Leave a space about the width of a dime at the joints between sheets, to allow for expansion. Just as you should with plank wood paneling, store sheet paneling in the room in which it will be hung for a few days, so that it can season before installation. Stack them with spacers so that air circulates around the sheets.

Changing walls

AS YOUR NEEDS CHANGE, *you may want to add or remove a wall, or create a new door opening. If the wall is loadbearing (see below), then it's time to get professional help. But non-structural walls are easily created or rearranged using drywall over a framework of wood studs.*

Removing a partition wall

Non-structural partition walls are usually wood framed, but they may just as easily be brick or concrete block. Similarly, in a timber-framed house, a stud wall may be loadbearing. The illustration on the right should help you check – but if you are in any doubt at all, get expert advice.

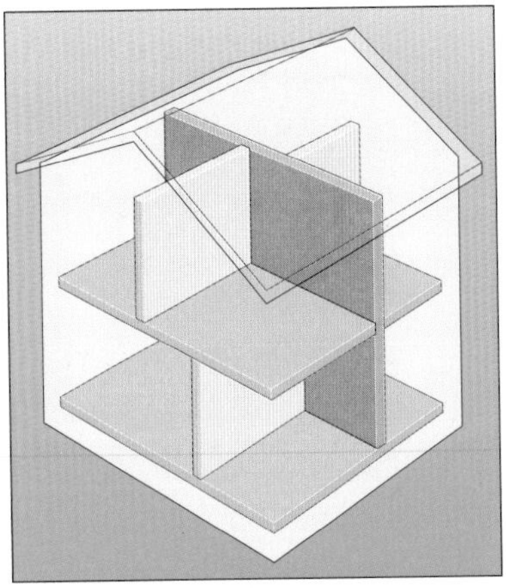

Removing any type of wall creates clouds of dust. Clear the room as much as possible, seal off, and wear a cartridge respirator.

First, remove any baseboards and moldings. Then, with the electricity disconnected, remove any light switches, outlets, and wiring. Reconnect the outlets and tie or tape them safely out of the way until you're ready to relocate them. On a masonry wall, loosen the brick or blocks with a sledgehammer and chisel and try to remove it with the plaster intact to keep down the dust. On a wood frame wall, pry

■ **A wall that rises continuously** *through a house is probably loadbearing and shouldn't be removed.*

away the drywall with a claw hammer or wrecking bar, then dismantle the framework – horizontal headers first, followed by the vertical studs, and then the top and sole plates. Repair any holes in the other walls and ceiling with new drywall.

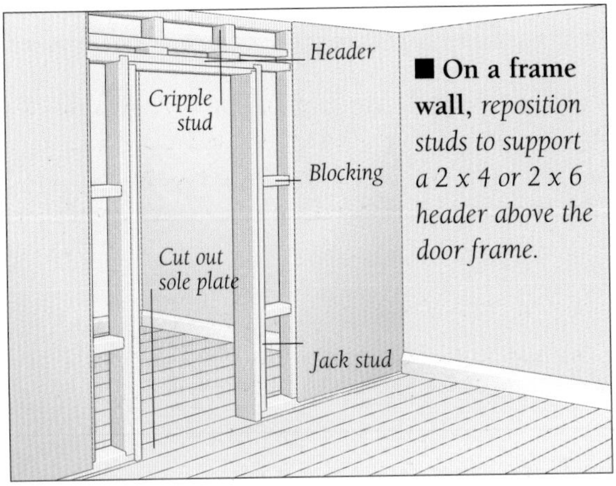

Header

Cripple stud

Blocking

Cut out sole plate

Jack stud

■ **On a frame wall,** *reposition studs to support a 2 x 4 or 2 x 6 header above the door frame.*

Opening up a doorway

You can save yourself a lot of work here by buying a pre-hung interior door with the appropriate swing. On a stud wall, cut back the drywall to

CREATING A DOORWAY IN A FRAME WALL

1 **Brace door lining**

Nail a brace diagonally across the door frame to keep it exactly square.

2 **Mark position**

Cut away the drywall and mark the height of the frame on the exposed studs.

3 **Construct top frame**

Cut through the wall studs and a header under two cripple studs above.

4 **Rebuild side frames**

Strengthen the frame on either side of the door with blockers nailed through the studs.

5 **Install frame**

Install the frame against the jack studs, shim in place, and nail through shims into studs.

6 **Finish wall**

Resurface around the frame with drywall. Finish with case molding and paint.

create the door opening with a trimming knife, mark the position of the doorway, then cut the studs to allow for the door jamb. Cut cripple studs to support a 2 x 6 inch header above the door frame and rebuild the frame with supporting jack studs. Finally, wedge the door in the opening, check that it is square, then attach to the frame and finish the wall.

On a masonry wall, mark the position of the prehung door. Then use a sledgehammer and chisel to chop a slot in the brick or blockwork immediately above the doorway to accommodate a 2 x 6 inch header extending 8 inches to each side. Bed the header on mortar and leave to dry. Then cut away the rest of the opening and screw the door frame in position about every 16 inches, being sure it is plumb and square.

Building a partition wall

A NON-LOAD-BEARING STUD PARTITION wall is the quickest way to create two rooms out of one. Build the framework from 2 x 4 studs screwed to the floor and ceiling joists, then simply clad with plasterboard.

Positioning the wall

The position of the wall is governed by the sole plates (see right), which on a timber floor must be screwed through the floorboards and into the joists. If the wall is to run parallel with the joists, locate the nearest joist and site the sole plates directly over the top. Follow the same principle for the top plate. If the ceiling joists run parallel and "miss" the plate, install solid bridging between the joists from above to provide a secure attachment.

Building the wall frame

Aside from the sole and header plates, the rest of the frame can be nailed together using 3-inch nails. As when creating a new doorway, save yourself time by using a prefabricated buck for the door opening, with short studs to either side supporting a trimmer above. Elsewhere, space the studs at 16-inch intervals, toe-nailing them to the sole and wall plates. Then brace the spaces in between the studs with blocking, staggered so that you can nail through the studs into the ends.

CONSTRUCTING THE FRAMEWORK

1 **Attach top plate**

Get help to support the top plate while you screw it to the joists – or along one joist.

2 **Attach sole plate**

Hang a plumbline from the top plate to make sure that the sole plate goes directly beneath it.

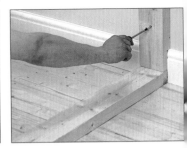

3 **Secure end studs**

If necessary, cut out sections of baseboard, then screw the studs to the adjacent wall.

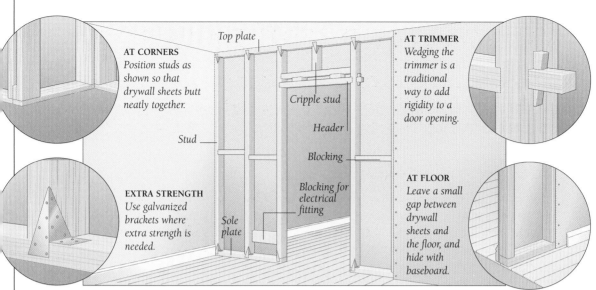

AT CORNERS
Position studs as shown so that drywall sheets butt neatly together.

Top plate

Cripple stud

Header

Blocking

Blocking for electrical fitting

Stud

EXTRA STRENGTH
Use galvanized brackets where extra strength is needed.

Sole plate

AT TRIMMER
Wedging the trimmer is a traditional way to add rigidity to a door opening.

AT FLOOR
Leave a small gap between drywall sheets and the floor, and hide with baseboard.

■ **Key design features** *of a stud wall; use stud brackets and wedge trimmer for extra strength.*

Cladding the frame

Nail drywall to one side of the frame, arranging for the joints to coincide with the frame members where possible. If desired, make the wall sound less "hollow" and improve the soundproofing by packing in between the frame with insulation batts. Then clad the other side of the wall, and tape and compound the drywall to prepare for painting in the usual way (see p. 62).

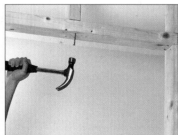

4 **Fit studs**

Toe-nail the ends of the studs to the top and sole plates, taking care to keep them plumb.

5 **Frame the opening**

At an opening, install a header supported by cripple studs, and add blocking as needed.

6 **Install blocking**

Install blocking between the studs, staggered so that you can nail into the ends.

Decorative plasterwork

PLASTER MOLDINGS *add the finishing touch to a period-style room, and can be repaired, too.*

Attaching ceiling medallions

Use a ceiling medallion with a pendant lamp or chandelier, or as a stand-alone feature. Plaster medallions are simply attached using gypsum adhesive, and most are predrilled with screw holes so that you can secure the medallion to ceiling joists. Before attaching the medallion, you must make sure the ceiling is completely clean and free of dust, and stable enough to hold the weight of the plaster. Fill over the heads of the fixing screws and smooth off.

■ **A ceiling medallion** *provides a focal point in a period-style room, especially when complemented by a chandelier or elegant pendant light.*

ATTACHING WALL MOLDINGS

Buy polyurethane or plaster moldings and work the same way in attaching them. Attach polyurethane moldings with latex adhesive caulk, and plaster with a plaster mix or gypsum adhesive. For both, use a sandable, non-shrinking filler.

1 **Apply adhesive**

Spread adhesive over the back of the molding with a small putty knife.

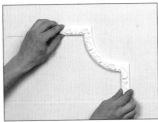

2 **Start at a corner**

Position the first corner molding against your pencil guidelines.

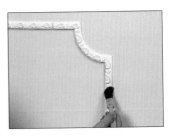

3 **Finish the joints**

Press filler into the joints with your finger, then smooth with a damp brush.

Repairing plaster moldings

If you must replace all plaster molding in a room, you'd be wise to choose polyurethane molding, which is extruded to look just like plaster, but much easier to work with. If your house is old, and a section of molding is damaged, you have two alternatives: remove the existing molding and replace it all; or else make up a mylar template to match the profile of the existing molding and use this to shape a plaster patch.

A repair is only feasible if the damaged section is less than about 12 inches long. Stiffen the mylar with hardboard and screw on a handle. Transfer the profile of the molding to the template using a profile gauge and cut it to shape with a coping saw or jigsaw. Then screw on a wood frame, handle, and guide piece (see below), so that the template can be held in the correct position on the wall.

Fill the damaged section with patching plaster, using pieces of steel mesh for support where necessary; the batten underneath the molding will hold the plaster in place. Then, while the plaster is still wet, draw the template across it to shape it to the correct profile. Smooth the surface with a wet sponge.

Do any final shaping and finishing when the plaster has dried. If you feel you want to secure the patch more firmly to the wall, use a drill equipped with a masonry bit, and screw and plug the repair to the wall. Drive the screws below the plaster, fill over the heads, and finish the surface with fine grade sandpaper.

REPAIRING A PLASTER CORNICE

1 **Make a template**

Use a profile gauge to copy the cornice profile onto a mylar sheet, and build a wood frame.

2 **Apply plaster**

Nail a batten to the wall below the cornice, then fill damaged area with patching plaster.

3 **Shape the profile**

Run the template along the batten so that it molds the repair to the cornice shape.

Repairing molding

BASEBOARD MOLDINGS, DOOR CASE MOLDINGS, and other wooden decorative features are available in countless sizes and profiles from home centers and lumberyards. Replacements are simply nailed to the wall with finishing nails, but repairing original moldings may require more ingenuity.

Repair or replace?

If large sections of molding are missing, remove the rest and opt for wholesale replacement. Use a pry bar to remove old molding, with a wood scrap to protect the wall. For a repair, your best bet is to match the profile of the original molding using individual lengths of narrow strip molding, then filling the gaps between them.

To avoid damaging the surrounding surfaces when removing moldings, cut through the joint between the molding and the wall with a putty knife before prying it away.

Installing new moldings

- **Casing moldings** form a decorative facing around doors and hide the joint between the door jambs and the jack studs. Nail them in place, corners first.

MITERING DOOR CASING

1 **Miter the side**

Mark inside of miter on the side trim piece, ⅛ inch from the inside corner of the door.

2 **Miter top trim**

Miter and attach sides, then use them to mark the outside miters on the top trim.

3 **Finishing**

Miter the top trim, put it in place, then nail through the miter as shown.

REPAIRING BASEBOARDS

a Removing baseboard

Use a crowbar or chisel and hammer to pry the baseboard away from the wall.

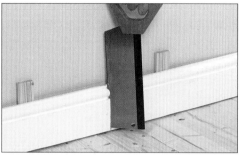

b Removing a section

Wedge the baseboard clear away from the wall and cut into it at 45° at both ends.

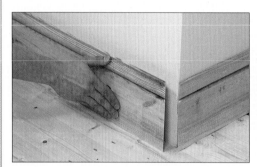

c Mitering outside corners

At outside corners, mark the inside of the miter at the corner of the wall.

d Scribing inside corners

Use a scrap piece of baseboard to mark the profile on the back of the new length.

- **Chair and picture rails** add interest to plain walls and will visually lower a high-ceilinged room by dividing it into horizontal bands. Nail them into place.

- **Baseboards** protect the base of a wall and can be used to disguise the expansion gaps around the edges of floorcoverings. If there is a pipe or other obstruction in the way, create a box by screwing cleats to the wall above and below, then nail the base molding to these.

Other parts of the house, for example staircases and paneled walls, tend to be finished with one or another of the above, often in conjunction with narrower strips.

Installing cove and cornices

CORNICE IS THE GENERAL TERM *for a variety of decorative moldings used to cover the joints between walls and ceiling. Cove or crown moldings usually have a simpler appearance and are consequently appropriate for a wider range of home styles.*

A choice of styles

You should be aware that the terms cove or crown molding and cornice are often used interchangeably. Avoid possible confusion by asking to see suppliers' catalogs and pointing to the items you want. Cornices come in a vast range of styles. Made of gypsum plaster or – more commonly these days – polyurethane foam, most of these are incredibly ornate. Available styles include replicas of ancient Greek, Roman, Georgian, and Victorian designs. Plaster cornices are attached with special gypsum adhesive, while foam replicas are secured with latex adhesive caulk or are nailed to supporting cleats attached along the joint between the ceiling and wall. This type of mounting system is extremely effective in situations where the ceiling line is very uneven, since it allows you to set the battens (and hence the moldings) level and then fill the gaps above.

Some molding manufacturers supply special sections for inside and outside corners with their cove or cornice kits, which eliminate the need to miter the molding.

 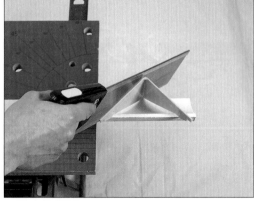

■ **Some makes of coving** *come with a template that hooks over the molding to act as a cutting guide in two planes. Use the different sides of the template for internal miters (above left) and external miters (above right). Clamp the coving securely and cut the miters with a tenon saw.*

INSTALLING PLAIN COVE MOLDING

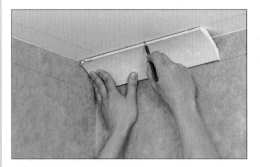

1 Mark guidelines

If the room is wallpapered, use a scrap of molding to mark the wall and ceiling showing where the cove molding will go.

2 Preparing the surface

Cut along the lines with a utility knife, then strip away the paper to the ceiling. Afterward, score lines in the wall plaster.

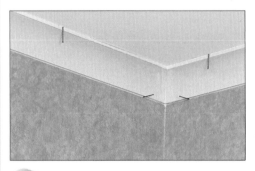

3 Attach molding

If you want to steady molding for final nailing, use finishing nails around the edges to hold the molding in place.

4 Filling the joints

Fill any gaps in between, above, and below the cove with sandable, paintable, silicone adhesive. Smooth with a fingertip.

Attaching cornices

Both the wall and ceiling should be dry, dust-free, and stripped of old wallpaper for installing cornices, regardless of whether you are using plaster or polyurethane. If the ceiling line is very uneven, you may want to do a dry run first to see where the low points are – or even draw a horizontal line around the room and fix the coving to this to ensure that lengths line up. As a rule, start in a corner and work from either side of this to end in the most unobtrusive part of the room. Afterward, fill any gaps with patching plaster or, in the case of polyurethane, the caulk described above.

Tracing moisture problems

MOISTURE RUINS DECORATIONS and can lead to rot in structural members. The trick is to locate the actual source of the trouble and fix it properly – even if that means calling in a professional.

Beware the penetrator

Penetrating moisture, or *wicking*, affects all houses, but is most common in older houses with cracked stucco walls that allow water to seep in slowly and steadily. Houses with wood, vinyl, or metal siding are less likely to be affected, but they are not immune. There are many sources of water damage; the most common include:

- Damaged pointing and broken bricks on a masonry wall.
- Defective *flashings* on roofs and around chimneys.

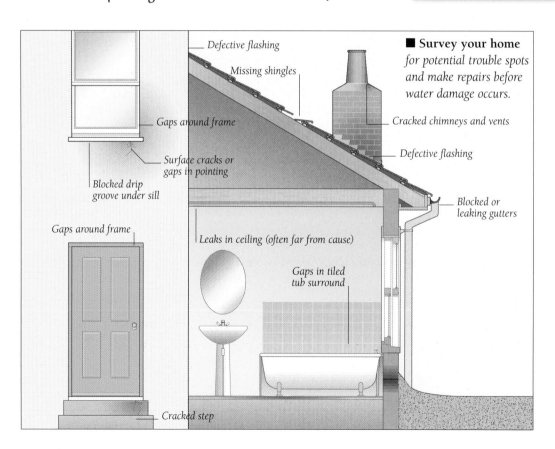

Defective flashing

Missing shingles

Gaps around frame

Surface cracks or gaps in pointing

Blocked drip groove under sill

Gaps around frame

Leaks in ceiling (often far from cause)

Cracked step

■ **Survey your home** *for potential trouble spots and make repairs before water damage occurs.*

Cracked chimneys and vents

Defective flashing

Blocked or leaking gutters

Gaps in tiled tub surround

- Gaps between door or window frames and the surrounding wall.
- Defective gutters and downspouts.
- Defective or blocked drip grooves on the underside of window sills, causing water runoff onto the wall below.

Note that if water gets into a ceiling cavity, it will find the lowest spot to leak through – which may be some distance from the point of entry.

Waterproofing from top to bottom

The two main areas of potential water seepage are roofs and basements. Regularly check roof and chimney flashing and repair any damaged or missing flashing immediately. Basements can leak through floors or walls and many different remedies can be used, depending on the actual source of the water. First and foremost, be sure that the your foundation has an exterior drain field – a perforated drain pipe nested in fabric filter, running the length of the foundation at slight decline toward a runoff area. If you have an older home, you may not have a drain field, and installing one is a simple way to solve many water problems. You should also patch basement cracks with hydraulic cement or mortar, and coat with waterproofing compound.

A simple summary

✓ Tongue-and-groove planks or sheet paneling are great for hiding walls in poor condition – but not where moisture is a problem.

✓ Thinking of knocking a hole through a wall? Check whether the wall is load-bearing first; if it is, leave the job to a builder.

✓ A framed stud partition wall is the easiest way to split one room into two. Make the job even easier by installing a prehung interior door.

✓ Much decorative plasterwork can simply be glued in place.

✓ Match old wooden decorative moldings by combining several different types of strip molding.

✓ If your existing ceiling cornice is badly damaged, you're better off replacing it.

✓ Don't just treat the symptoms of water seepage, pin down the root cause – even if this means calling in a contractor.

Chapter 15

Heating and ventilation

THERE IS NOTHING QUITE AS COMFORTING as a warm, cozy home. But rooms can soon become stuffy without proper ventilation. Keeping the cold out while allowing fresh air in is the name of the game when it comes to any heating system – and if you can allow yourself the luxury of an open fire, then all the better.

In this chapter...

✓ Insulating your home

✓ Ventilation and condensation

✓ Fireplaces and stoves

✓ Renovating a fireplace

✓ Replacing a fireplace border

RECLAIMING AN OLD FIREPLACE CAN TAKE TIME, BUT IT IS CERTAINLY REWARDING

Insulating your home

INSULATION SAVES ENERGY, which should save you money, not to mention the planet. There are plenty of insulation products on the market, all with installation instructions, but it pays to know the facts before you buy.

Setting your priorities

Recent buildings should be insulated to a high standard, but you can make major improvements to older ones, even if they're insulated already. Insulation materials are rated by their R-value – an indication of their resistance to heat loss. So a material with a high R-value will be as effective as a greater thickness of a lower R-value material where space is restricted, such as between the joists of a loft floor. In theory, it's more efficient to insulate the outside of a building; inside the house, insulation reduces the temperature on the cold side, which can lead to condensation problems unless the area is properly ventilated. Start with the roof and walls; exterior walls may require professionally installed, "blown-in" insulation.

The heat loss is greatest from those areas that are hottest relative to their surroundings. That makes hot water pipes and water heaters obvious candidates for insulation. If you're elderly or on a low income, local utilities may offer insulation programs.

PAYBACK TIMES

It can take some time to recoup your investment in insulation. These rough estimates will vary depending on climate and other factors.

Hot water cylinder/pipes	1 year
Loft floor	1–2 years
Radiator foil	1–2 years
Weatherstripping	2–3 years
Flat roof	2–4 years
Floor	3–5 years
Wall cavity	5 years
Window	5+ years
Solid wall	10+ years

Methods of insulation

Use polystyrene foam pipe wrap for pipes and a ready-made jacket with a high R-value for the water heater if recommended by the manufacturer. Fiberglass batting roll is still the most popular choice for insulating between floors and in cavity walls, but it must be handled with great care – always wear a mask and gloves. For insulating between roof rafters and in between ground-floor joists, you'll use fiberglass batts with a foil facing. You'll more than likely need to install styrofoam air channels before insulating attics to ensure adequate air circulation. Exterior blown-in insulation involves a complex procedure that should definitely be left to the professionals.

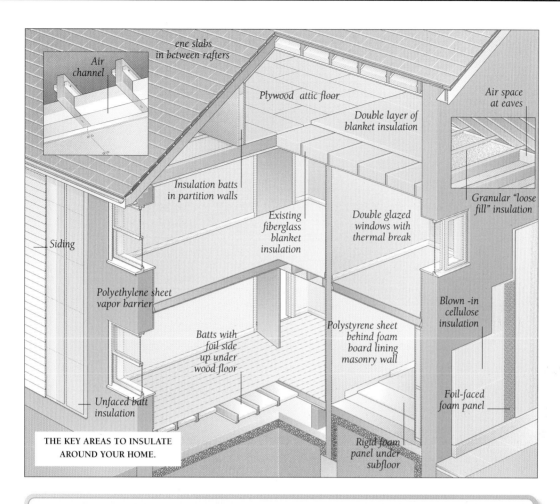

ene slabs
in between rafters

Air
channel

Plywood attic floor

Double layer of
blanket insulation

Air space
at eaves

Insulation batts
in partition walls

Granular "loose
fill" insulation

Existing
fiberglass
blanket
insulation

Double glazed
windows with
thermal break

Siding

Polyethylene sheet
vapor barrier

Batts with
foil side
up under
wood floor

Polystyrene sheet
behind foam
board lining
masonry wall

Blown-in
cellulose
insulation

Unfaced batt
insulation

Foil-faced
foam panel

**THE KEY AREAS TO INSULATE
AROUND YOUR HOME.**

Rigid foam
panel under
subfloor

INSULATING PIPES

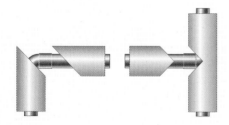

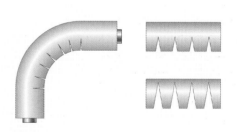

1 **Insulating joined pipes**

*Miter the ends of foam pipe insulation to cover
a 90°bend. Cut matching V-shapes for a T-joint.
Tape or cement all joints and then tape edges.*

2 **Insulating bent pipes**

*Make V-shaped cuts in the slit side of foam pipe
insulation to fit around bends. Gauge the
spacing of the cuts to suit the bend radius.*

Ventilation and condensation

WARM, WELL-INSULATED ROOMS are all well and good, but without adequate ventilation you could find yourself with condensation problems. If not tackled quickly, these can lead to moisture damage and mildew growth.

Damp-busting

Warm air absorbs moisture until it becomes saturated or comes into contact with a colder surface. At this point, some moisture is released causing condensation. A flow of air will prevent saturation while leaving a useful moisture content that holds heat, so open windows regularly. Keeping warm air away from cold surfaces depends on adequate heating and insulation. The most vulnerable areas are those in which there is a dramatic temperature difference between the outside and inside.

Ventilation is critically important in houses with conventional gas or wood fireplaces, both of which need a constant flow of fresh air in order to burn. Make sure that doors and windows allow for cross breezes, and that the fireplace flue is working properly.

■ **The illustrations show the places** *most at risk from condensation. An insulated roof space is particularly vulnerable due to the temperature difference, so make sure it is well ventilated.*

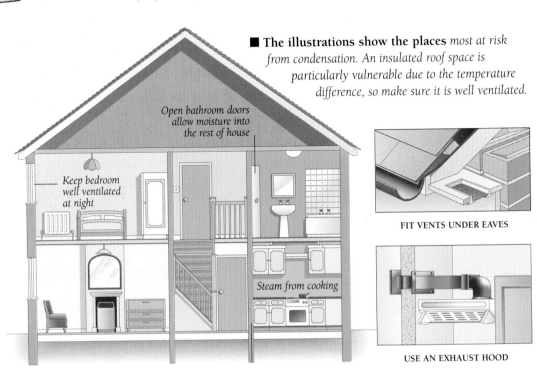

Open bathroom doors allow moisture into the rest of house

Keep bedroom well ventilated at night

Steam from cooking

FIT VENTS UNDER EAVES

USE AN EXHAUST HOOD

Preventing condensation

A combination of warm surfaces and frequent air changes should provide the answer.

■ **Special polystyrene** *ceiling tiles help prevent condensation in rooms where it is a problem.*

■ **Insulating wall liner** *adds a layer of protection, and can be covered with paint or wallpaper.*

■ **Exhaust fans** *are essential to remove moisture from windowless bathrooms. Buy a fan which has a cfm (cubic feet per minute) rating that is suitable for the size of the bathroom.*

■ **A dehumidifier** *extracts water from the air. It collects in a reservoir or can be fed out via a pipe through the wall.*

■ **Add fungicide** *to bathroom paint in bathrooms that are not well ventilated. This will help prevent mold and mildew.*

■ **Plastic sheet** *stapled between unfaced batt insulation and ceilings acts as a vapor barrier.*

Fireplaces and stoves

EVEN IF YOU DON'T PLAN TO INSTALL A FIREPLACE, *it still makes sense to have a basic understanding of how they work.*

The importance of flues

All fireplaces and boilers have two basic requirements: air to keep them lit and a means of expelling smoke and fumes. A chimney is the traditional way to satisfy both needs. A shuttered damper provides an exit for smoke, while at the same time creating an updraft that draws fresh air to the fire. You should regularly have the chimney cleaned, and the flue inspected. A blocked flue can cause fumes and flames to spill back into the room. Many new fireplaces also use outside air intake vents under the fireplace, a good way to prevent the fire from drawing warm air out of the room. Make sure there is adequate ventilation, by installing door or window vents if necessary.

■ **Open fireplaces** *are not especially efficient or easy to clean, but there is no more welcoming sight on a cold winter's night.*

Although gas fireplaces will work perfectly well with a conventional flue, most modern types are designed to work in conjunction with an inlet/outlet vent that expels fumes through a duct in an outside wall, while drawing in fresh air. Obviously, this gives you more freedom with positioning.

Don't even think about hooking up a gas fireplace yourself. Even though gas is scented to aid detection of a leak, improper connection of a gas stove or fireplace can result in an explosion or fast-spreading fire. Leave this job to a licensed plumber.

Assessing the options

As you examine the alternatives in the heating department there are a number of considerations that that should not be ignored.

● **A modern wood-burning stove** is an effective way to heat a small room. It warms both through convection and radiation, and loses less heat through the chimney than a conventional open fire.

Flue liners may need to be upgraded, depending on the age and condition of the liner. Many local building codes require newer ceramic liners and other fire safety measures with a wood or gas fireplace. If you are renovating a fireplace, check with the local zoning board or your contractor.

● **Traditional fireplaces** look great but aren't very efficient: the updraft can draw warm air out of the room.

■ **A gas or independent fireplace** *can be outfitted with an inlet/outlet vent on any outside wall.*

■ **A wood-burning stove** *can't be used with a steel chimney flue lining; you'll need to replace it with ceramic.*

■ **An open fireplace** *simply requires the flue damper to be free of blockages and leaks.*

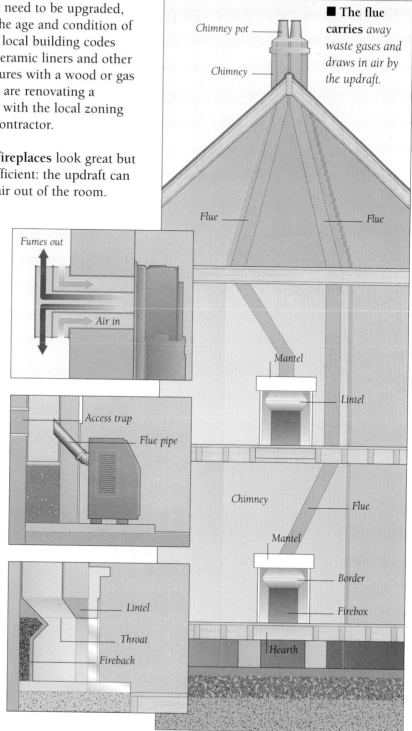

■ **The flue carries** *away waste gases and draws in air by the updraft.*

Chimney pot

Chimney

Flue — — Flue

Mantel

Lintel

Chimney

Flue

Mantel

Border

Firebox

Hearth

Fumes out

Air in

Access trap

Flue pipe

Lintel

Throat

Fireback

Renovating a fireplace

INSTALLING *a new fireplace is a job for a builder, but opening up or renovating an old fireplace is a different matter. Before starting the project, however, get the chimney swept and check local building codes for liner and chimney requirements.*

Refurbishing a fireplace

Refurbishing an old fireplace is relatively simple, but very messy: clear the room as much as possible, and tape up doors to stop dust and soot from spreading around the house. Although this job should largely consist of cleaning and minor repairs, you need to assess the entire structure for any potential damage. This includes the damper, and checking the chimney for cracks and missing or damaged bricks.

■ **The fireplace border** *provides the decorative face to the firebox, and can be embellished with marble, or other material to match the interior of the home.*

Remove surrounding material back to the original opening, then assess the extent of the work ahead. The firebox should be cleaned with hot water and detergent, and small cracks should be patched with refractory mortar. You should also have the chimney cleaned thoroughly; creosote and ash buildup present a fire danger. A CSIA (Chimney Safety Institute of America) certified chimney sweep will not only clean your chimney, but will also be able to perform a general structural inspection and provide you with a list of defects – if any – that must be remedied to bring the fireplace up to code. Many chimney sweeps also offer renovation services.

Some old fireplaces have asbestos in their construction. If you suspect asbestos, have an abatement company test for it. Asbestos must be professionally removed according to local and federal guidelines.

For all their beauty, fireplaces can be extremely inefficient heat sources because most of the warm air goes right up the chimney – often taking warm air inside the home with it. Newly built fireplaces are much more energy efficient, but you can make your fireplace a much better heat source by using heat circulating grates or, for a much bigger investment, installing a fireplace insert that shunts hot air into the living space.

Fireplace caution

The fireplace damper is extremely important. Blockages can force smoke and fumes – not to mention carbon monoxide – into the living space. Ensure that the damper is in good working order. You should also know what kind of liner is installed, because that will affect what can be burned in the fireplace. Gas fireplaces have steel-lined flues, which will corrode if used for burning wood. Changing or installing a liner is a task best left to a professional, not only because it is difficult and dirty work, but because the type of liners used and their installation are both governed by complex sets of local, state, and federal regulations. If you live in a home more than 50 years old, you should have a professional inspect your liner.

INSTALLING A NEW FIREBOX

Replace rather than patch a badly damaged firebox. Most types come in two pieces, which are simply bedded into the fireplace with fire cement. You might also need a few bricks to fill in any gaps.

1 **Prepare surface**
Remove damaged parts of the old firebox. Sweep clean and patch any holes with mortar.

2 **Install first section**
Test-fit the base piece and fill the space around it with bricks if necessary, then bed in place.

3 **Add second**
Lay the top half of the new firebox on a bed of refractory mortar. Mortar any gaps.

Replacing a fireplace border

A NEW FIREPLACE BORDER adds the finishing touch to a renovated fireplace. Alternatively, you may want to change the existing border to fit in with a new decorative scheme.

Out with the old

Old fireplace borders can be very heavy, so enlist help before attempting to remove one. The border may be screwed to the wall through hardware secured in the plaster. Remove the plaster around the border, then pry the border away from the wall with a crowbar. Wood and plaster borders may be attached with additional concealed cleats, but can be removed in the same way.

Brick and stone borders can simply be demolished; cut through any metal wall ties securing the border to the masonry behind. If the removal process causes a lot of damage to the lintel or firebox itself, you may need to make repairs before proceeding. Also check that the hearth and firebox are in good condition and up to code, and make any necessary repairs.

Rent an angle grinder to cut around the edge of a recessed fire border. This will make the border easier to remove from the wall and should cause minimal damage to the surrounding plasterwork.

Installing a new border

A border kit provides the easiest route to restoring the outside of your fireplace.

1 Lay the new hearth

Some border kits come with a hearth slab. Bed this on mortar on a concrete underlayment.

2 Install the border

Use adhesive and position the border to sit squarely above the fireplace; screw it to the wall.

3 Add a mantel

Assemble the mantel on the floor and lift into position. Screw it to the wall.

In with the new

Modern borders and mantels tend to be sold in kit form. You just glue and screw the parts together, then fix to the wall screwing directly into masonry or studs. Brick and stone borders are also sold as kits, often with the parts numbered to aid construction, and are easily customized to fit a particular space.

After installing, fill any gaps between the border, the fireplace, and the surrounding masonry with refractory mortar, which is heat-resistant to prevent cracking. Then complete the look with new paint, new wallcovering, or new fixtures.

■ **Fireplaces with tiled borders** *often come with brass trim to cover the gap between the border and the fireplace.*

A simple summary

✔ Insulating your house properly will save you money in the long run. Insulating your attic floor will pay you back in 1–2 years. Wrapping your hot water cylinder and pipes should pay you back within a year.

✔ When attempting to keep the cold out and the heat in, don't forget that your home also needs to be adequately ventilated. Open fireplaces or boilers with a conventional damper need a steady flow of fresh air.

✔ Make sure that you have your chimney professionally swept and inspected before installing or renovating an old fireplace.

✔ Many older fireplaces used asbestos in their construction. Have an abatement company come and test for it.

✔ Replacing a fireplace border can transform a room and will add the finishing touch to a fireplace you have just renovated.

PART
FOUR

Chapter 16
Fences and Gates

Chapter 17
Paths and Patios

Chapter 18
Walls and Roofs

Chapter 19
Gutters and Drainage

Chapter 16

Fences and Gates

Fences, gates, and decking all have to take the worst that the weather – and the family – can throw at them. No wonder they develop problems! In this chapter, I'll show you how to put up a fence that will last, and how to make repairs to existing wood structures.

In this chapter...

✓ Building a fence

✓ Repairing fences and gates

✓ Repairing decks

Building a fence

PUTTING UP A FENCE *is the quickest and least expensive way to mark a boundary. Fences come in all shapes and sizes, but all of them are built in generally the same way.*

The basic choices

If security and privacy are your main concerns, the choice is between a woven panel or some form of close-boarded fence. But for simply marking a boundary, remember that open fencing will be more stable in high winds and won't need as much maintenance.

Preparing the site

Begin by clearing all obstacles, including rubble, old fence posts, tree roots, and paving. Level the ground; then run a string line to mark the line of the fence, and place stakes where the posts will go. Generally space 4 x 4 posts 6–8 feet apart, and 6 x 6 posts 8–10 feet apart; space posts for prefabricated fence panels according to the width of the panels.

If the site slopes, the height of the fence will have to be staggered to match. This is relatively easy to arrange for open fencing, but for a panel or close-boarded fence, you may prefer to level the site in terraces so that the boards are the same height within a bay. If the fence

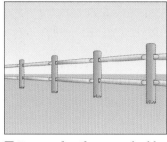

■ **Post and rail:** *easy to build and maintain. Rails can be nailed to or slotted into posts.*

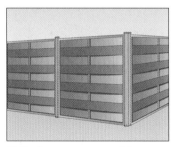

■ **Basket weave:** *good for privacy in sheltered areas. Panels are often available prefabricated.*

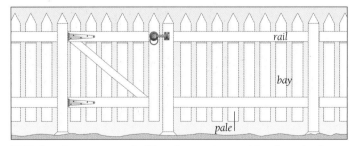

■ **Picket fence:** *easy to build and attractive, a picket fence is often the first choice for the front of a property. Pickets can be pointed or curved and are generally spaced 1 to 2 inches apart.*

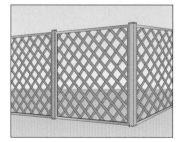

■ **Lattice fence:** *can be built from scratch or from panels. More stable in high winds.*

has to run across a slope, terrace the ground a minimum of 1 foot beyond the higher side.

Setting the posts

Set the posts in the ground, reinforced with layers of packed soil and gravel, or in concrete with a gravel base, or in metal post spikes (see below). A rented gas auger will make digging the post holes easier. Brace the posts with wood braces nailed to stakes in the ground and leave for 24 hours until the concrete has completely set. Fencing terminology dictates that the main posts are the corner and gateposts; between are line posts. The space between two posts is a a bay. Horizontal supports are rails.

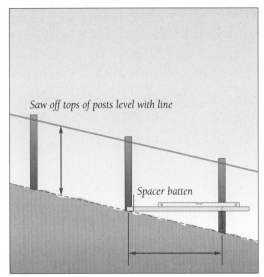

Saw off tops of posts level with line

Spacer batten

■ **On a sloping site,** *use a level and straightedge to ensure the posts stand parallel to one another, and use a string line to mark their heights.*

SETTING POSTS IN POST SPIKES

Setting fence posts in packed soil or concrete is economical, but it is also hard work unless the ground is exceptionally soft, in which case you have no choice. Otherwise use post spikes as shown here. Similar bolt-down sockets are available for continuing the fence across a stretch of concrete.

1 Driving in

Set the spike plumb with a level, then insert an endcut and hammer into the ground.

2 Locating the post

Coat the end of the post with waterproofing, position in the socket, and recheck it's plumb.

3 Install post

In this system, the post is slid into the socket, which also holds the bottom board mount.

Putting up the fence

It's usually easier to build a fence one bay at a time, starting with the first two posts, then the rails or panel brackets, and then the panel itself. But if you're setting the posts in concrete, set them all at the same time using a string line and spacer batten as a guide and double-check that the post spacings match the length of the panels or rails. Attach a post adjoining a wall to the wall itself.

Most types of fence panels are nailed or screwed onto the posts, although some are hung with special brackets. If you have to cut a prefabricated fence panel to size, pry off the frame and saw the paneling, then replace the frame. When the fence is complete, nail caps to the posts to finish them.

On a homemade fence, nail rails to the posts, or for extra durability, secure the rails in mortises in the posts. Mark the positions of the rail ends, drill out the mortises, and clean up the mortise with a chisel. Secure the joints with galvanized nails.

When using pressure treated or pretreated lumber, avoid making cuts where at all possible, as this increases its susceptibility to moisture. Where you do have to saw components to length or chisel mortises in fence posts, coat the cut areas with waterproofing before assembly.

Trivia...

In 1874 Joseph Glidden patented barbed wire, and almost overnight the character of the American Great Plains was transformed. As the open range became fenced in, the cattle drive became a thing of the past – an event later lamented in Cole Porter's song "Don't Fence Me In."

BUILDING A PREFABRICATED PANEL FENCE

1 Set the first post

Drive in a post spike for the first post using a post endcut. Check that it goes in plumb.

2 Secure post

On this system, the post is secured by tightening the clamp bolts on the socket itself.

3 Set second post

Space the second post to the exact length of a panel and check that it too, is plumb.

MAKING AND HANGING A GATE

Many prefabricated fence systems include pre-made gates, but for a homemade picket or close-boarded fence, it's easy to make your own using odd sized pieces of rail and pickets. Build a square frame to the size of the opening, using nailed mortise and tenon joints to hold the frame together. Attach the pickets, then prop the gate in the opening and adjust the frame until it fits. Remove the gate, being careful not to disturb the set of the frame, and cut a piece of rail to fit as a diagonal brace across it. Screw or nail the brace in position, then hang the gate.

1 **Test-fit gate**

Prop the gate in the opening to adjust the fit. Mark the hinge positions at the same time.

2 **Add a brace**

Mark the cuts for the brace directly against the gate, saw to shape, and nail in place.

3 **Recheck the fit**

Double-check the fit of the gate in the opening before attaching the hinges.

4 **Mark bracket positions**

Prop the panel between the posts and mark the bracket positions with a pencil.

5 **Attach panel brackets**

On this system, the brackets come with self-tapping screws that allow you to screw them straight in.

6 **Install panel**

Prop the panel back in place, double-check that it is level, then screw it to the brackets.

Repairing fences and gates

FENCES AND GATES ARE MORE EXPOSED *to the elements than most outdoor structures. Damaged rails or boards, loose or rotten posts, and gates that sag are all-too-familiar headaches for fence owners.*

Stopping the rot

The buried part of wood fence posts, the joints between posts and rails, and the gravel boards along the base of close-boarded fences are all especially vulnerable to rot and insect attack. Below are some typical problems and the best course of action:

● **Rotten fence posts**: these should be replaced if at all possible, but if this will disrupt the structure of the fence, you can fit a sister post instead (see opposite).

● **Rotten boards and panels**: not worth patching; your time is better spent going to a lumber yard to get a replacement.

● **Rotten rails**: these are more of a problem. You can avoid making a wholesale replacement by fitting galvanized brackets (see right). These can be used to strengthen a section of rail or can help support the joints at the post. There are special brackets available for repairing the triangular rails sometimes found on board fences. Gravel boards are designed to rot before the rest of the fence, so be sure to replace them before the rot starts to spread.

Wooden post caps are there for a reason — to stop the tops of fence posts from rotting. So be sure to replace a cap that's rotten or has been knocked off; it's a lot easier than replacing the post.

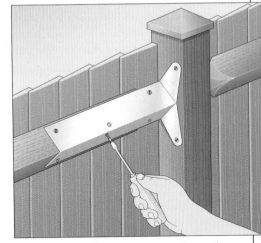

■ **Mending a damaged triangular rail:** *special galvanized brackets are available for mending damaged sections of triangular rail. Secure with galvanized screws.*

Leaning posts and loose rails

If a post is leaning, but otherwise sound, dig around the base to expose the footing. Use a level to ensure the post is plumb, then secure it with three 1 x 2 inch bracing boards

Repairing a Rotten Post

1 **Dig hole for brace**

With a post hole digger or a shovel, dig the hole for the sister post.

2 **Position sister post**

Drop the sister post into position and mark bolt holes through to the post.

3 **Bolt to post**

Bolt the sister to the rotten post. Cut and sandwich a piece of felt paper to wick moisture.

nailed to the post and to stakes driven in the ground. Wedge any gaps between the post and the footing with wood shims coated with preservative, and reinforce the footing with additional concrete to stabilize it in position.

To secure a loose rail, you can use metal or wood block braces at the ends or, to secure the length of the rail, bolt a sister rail underneath the original. Coat both the sister and original with preservative to ensure than no moisture problems occur between the two.

Repairing gates

Fixing a sagging gate is often simply a matter of replacing or refitting the hinges, but if the gate itself is sagging, you should be able to brace it (see right). Check that the gate is square by measuring the diagonals (which should be equal). Brace or reconstruct any loose joints at the same time. If a gatepost is loose, cut a sister post for each side, with a 45° bevel on one end. Position the sister post tight against the loose gatepost and hammer the top of the sister post to drive it into the ground. Repeat for the other side, and secure the sister posts to the main post with bolts.

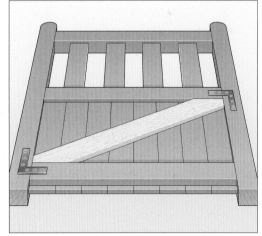

■ **Bracing a sagging gate:** *square the gate and attach a diagonal brace running upward from the hinge side. Reinforce the joints with metal L-brackets for extra strength.*

Repairing decks

DECKS, LIKE OTHER OUTDOOR STRUCTURES, will last for years *if properly maintained. But if the deck has been neglected, you may find yourself having to cut patches for rotten boards or structural members.*

Deck maintenance schedule

1 Clean the deck once a month. Clear out the gaps between boards and joints with a putty knife to prevent wet dirt from becoming lodged there, then hose down.

2 If the lumber is not pressure treated, smooth rough areas with 80-grit sandpaper; use a power sander for large areas. Seal the sanded areas with wood preservative, then refinish the whole area.

3 Replace a damaged board by cutting out the damaged section of a long board over joists – to span at least three joists – or by replacing the entire length of a short board. Treat the new wood before installing.

4 Refasten loose boards by removing the old attachments, clamping the board to the joist, and screwing in new rustproof wood screws.

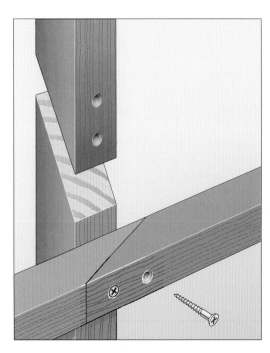

5 Treat rotten wood using wood preservative and epoxy wood hardener (see p. 158). Patch non-structural members using scarf joints (see left), and replace rotten structural members. If replacing a joist or beam, temporarily support the structure with jack posts, spreading the load with a thick top plate.

6 Brace flexing posts with Y- or X-shaped angle braces bolted to the posts and to each other to form a rigid framework.

■ **Repair non-structural members** *using a scarf joint, angling the joint so that the exposed face slopes downward to prevent rainwater from running into it. Secure the joint with waterproof adhesive and rust-proof screws or bolts.*

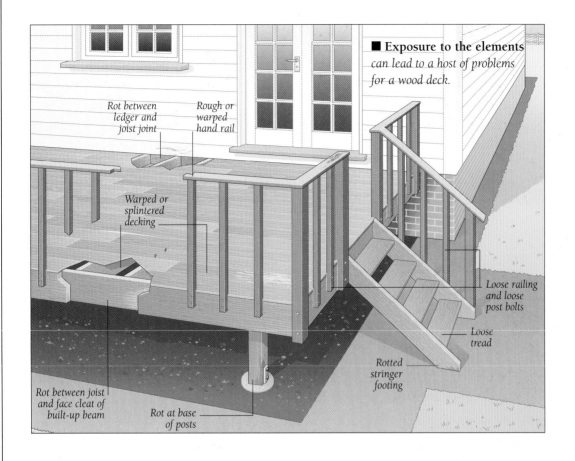

■ **Exposure to the elements** *can lead to a host of problems for a wood deck.*

Rot between ledger and joist joint

Rough or warped hand rail

Warped or splintered decking

Loose railing and loose post bolts

Loose tread

Rotted stringer footing

Rot between joist and face cleat of built-up beam

Rot at base of posts

A simple summary

✔ Fences are the quickest and cheapest way to establish a boundary. Basically, your choice is between a fence built from scratch or one built with prefabricated panels.

✔ Use a post hole digger or metal post spikes to take the hard work out of setting fence posts.

✔ You can buy metal reinforcing brackets and craft sister posts and rails for making repairs to an existing fence without disturbing the structure.

✔ Clean and inspect a deck once a month and treat any suspect wood with preservative at the first sign of trouble.

231

Chapter 17

Paths and Patios

WHEN IT COMES TO CREATING THE RIGHT IMPRESSION, few outdoor improvements have as much impact as a paved path or driveway. And at the back of the house, you can use the same techniques to extend your living space by bringing the "inside out" with a paved patio or sundeck. In all cases, careful planning is the key to avoiding waste and future drainage problems.

In this chapter...

✓ Repairs to paved areas

✓ Planning a patio

✓ Laying pavers

✓ Laying concrete

✓ Building a deck

A PAVED AREA: PERFECT FOR A SMALL GARDEN

Repairs to paved areas

CONCRETE PATIOS AND PAVING SLABS *suffer a lot of wear and tear. If you don't want to go to the trouble of resurfacing them entirely, it will pay you to catch repairs early.*

Replacing a broken slab

Replace a broken slab as quickly as possible to avoid accidents. Pry out the old one with a crow bar, using a block of wood for leverage. If the old slab was bedded in mortar, dig out out the old mortar bedding, level the site, and bed the new slab on new mortar. If the old slab is bedded in sand, add *new* sand to level it out before bedding the replacement.

If you can't find a replacement slab or paver, "borrow" one from a less obtrusive area, taking care not to damage it as you lift it. Fit a new paver in its place, or patch with concrete.

REPAIRING SURFACE DAMAGE

Use premixed mortar to patch large cracks or holes in concrete, adding a little epoxy bonding adhesive to help the mortar stick. Narrow cracks or small holes can usually be filled with vinyl concrete patch mix or, in the case of smaller hairline cracks, with latex crack filler.

1 **Prepare the crack**

Use a steel mallet and cold chisel to open a narrow crack for filling. If you can undercut the edges of the crack, so much the better.

2 **Level the repair**

Open holes to help the repair adhere. Dampen the area and fill with mortar mixed with adhesive. Level with a screed.

REPAIRING ASPHALT

Holes in asphalt are usually the result of wear and tear, and exposure to the elements. Small holes can be easily filled with driveway patch compound. For deep holes, fill to within about 4 inches of the surface with gravel before filling. Mound slightly above the surface if cars will drive over the patch.

1 **Stabilize the hole**

Clean out debris and excavate the hole back to a stable surface. Dampen the hole and fill with gravel base if deep.

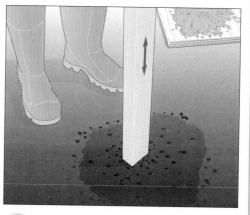

2 **Fill with asphalt mix**

Combine asphalt mix and heavy duty stone, and shovel this mixture into the hole. Tamp down firmly with the end of a wood post.

Getting rid of stains

Oil and other engine fluid stains are the most common problems on asphalt and concrete surfaces. Cover the spill with sand or sawdust and remove as much of the residue as you can. Then apply a degreasing cleanser with a stiff brush and flush with water.

Get rid of slippery green algae growth quickly for safety's sake. Pour a solution of fungicidal concrete cleanser and water over the affected area and scrub with a stiff broom, or use a bleach solution followed by washing the surface with a TSP mixture.

■ **To fix a cracked walkway edge,** *prop a piece of wood as a form for the patch, and clear out any loose debris. Saturate the area with water, then form the patch with an epoxy concrete patching compound.*

Planning a patio

CAREFUL PLANNING is the key to creating a paved outdoor area you can enjoy. Think hard about what the surface will be used for, how you're going to deal with obstacles, and what kind of weather it will have to face.

Choosing a hard surface

Appearance, cost, and durability are all important factors when choosing a hard surface. Concrete is inexpensive, versatile, and strong enough to take the weight of vehicles, but loses out in the looks department. Asphalt and gravel are a cheap alternative for driveways, but need regular maintenance. Next up the scale are bricks, shaped slabs, and concrete or reconstituted stone paving slabs, all of which can be bedded on sand if the ground is stable – if not, cover the site with ½-inch or more of gravel, and bed the slabs or pavers on strips of mortar. At the luxury end of the market are natural stone slabs, to which the same considerations apply. Most suppliers also offer a range of matched edging pieces.

THREE TECHNIQUES FOR OUTLINING

When laying a new paved patio or outdoor surface, it is important to have accurate and clear guidelines to follow.

a Stakes and string

Mark out the area to be paved with wooden stakes and colored strings. Use a line level and straightedge between stakes to check for high spots.

b Sand or lime lines

If the strings get in your way when you try to dig and remove turf, sprinkle sand or lime along them to act as a guide, then remove the strings.

c Marking a curve

To mark a curve, drive a large nail through a length of 1 x 2 inch board to match the curve's radius, then score the line of the curve in the ground.

■ **The area to be paved** *will probably need to be dug up to level the foundation. Use wood stakes, leveled with a carpenter's level and straightedge, to gauge the depth of the excavation and to provide for a slight slope.*

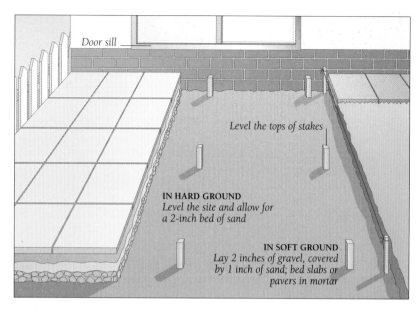

Door sill

Level the tops of stakes

IN HARD GROUND
Level the site and allow for a 2-inch bed of sand

IN SOFT GROUND
Lay 2 inches of gravel, covered by 1 inch of sand; bed slabs or pavers in mortar

Planning considerations

Unless the site is small and square, draw a scale plan on graph paper to help you estimate quantities and plan the steps necessary to lay the paved surface.

① If the paved area is to abut a house wall, make sure it is at least 2 inches below the door sill to keep water from collecting and damaging the woodwork. Paving should slope away from the house to promote water run-off – about 1 inch for every 4 feet.

② Build up areas around access boxes, such as those used for driveway lighting, so that you can pave around them.

③ Terrace a steeply sloping site with "steps" of concrete. You can excavate and cast the steps one at a time, allowing 2–3 days for drying before moving on to the next one. Or create stepped forms for all the concrete terraces and pour all the concrete at once. If you choose this method, rent a power mixer to mix big loads of concrete.

④ Minimize cutting of paving material such as flagstones, both by your choice of paving material and by the way you deal with obstacles. Allow sufficient space for you to pave around obstacles with whole slabs or pavers.

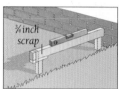

¾ inch scrap

■ **Plan a slope** *by attaching a wood shim to your straightedge.*

■ **Level a sloping** *site by terracing it with steps of concrete.*

■ **Minimize cutting** *when planning spaces around obstructions.*

Laying pavers

LAYING PAVERS OR PAVING SLABS on a bed of sand isn't difficult, but you can make the job a lot easier by renting a vibrating compactor to compact the sand bed and a block cutter to trim pavers for the edges.

It takes two

Providing the site is level – and you don't lose your way with the pattern – it's hard to go wrong paving over a sand bed. Even so, the job is a whole lot easier if you have a helper. Your chief consideration is how to deal with the edges. One option, especially if the pavers are small, is to bed concrete edging blocks on mortar. Otherwise edge the paved area with boards nailed to wood stakes and use these as a guide to levelling the sand bed. Pour the sand, rake it out, and use a screed to level it. Then compact it with the rented vibrating plate compactor and you are ready to lay the pavers. Level the pavers a square yard at a time, adding sand if one sits too low, or tapping with a block of wood if the paver stands above the level of those around it.

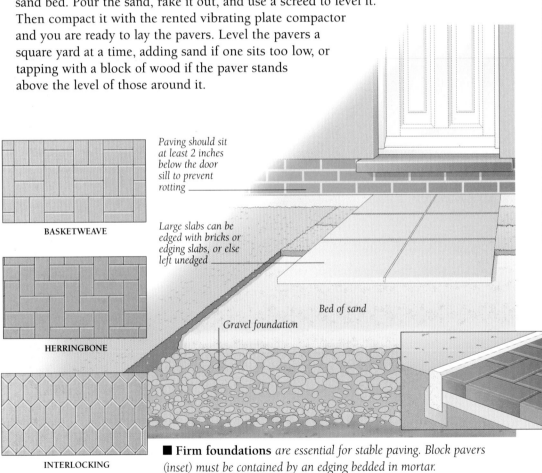

BASKETWEAVE

HERRINGBONE

INTERLOCKING

Paving should sit at least 2 inches below the door sill to prevent rotting

Large slabs can be edged with bricks or edging slabs, or else left unedged

Bed of sand

Gravel foundation

■ **Firm foundations** *are essential for stable paving. Block pavers (inset) must be contained by an edging bedded in mortar.*

PAVING A DRIVEWAY

1 Level the sand bed

Line the edges of the site with boards and use these as a guide to leveling the bed of soft sand.

2 Laying pavers

Lay the pavers according to your chosen pattern. Kneel on a board to spread your weight.

3 Alternate the pattern

Alternate patterns in "panels" if you wish. Use a 2 x 4 as a guide, working from the edges.

4 Deal with obstacles

Obstacles such as access covers need to have their frames reset level with the new surface.

5 Cut pavers to fit

Split pavers to size by scoring them and breaking with a brickset chisel, or rent a cutter.

6 Compact and fill

After laying the pavers, brush sand into the joints and compact with a compactor or tamp.

Laying concrete

LAYING A CONCRETE SLAB or walkway is a quick, effective way to provide a hard surface for just about any area around the house. Sidewalks are generally 3–4 inches thick, while a patio or driveway should be 5–6 inches thick.

Preparing the site

Mark the site boundaries with stakes and string. Excavate the site to the proposed depth, allowing an extra 4–6 inches for a layer of gravel, and then level it out. Lay down the gravel, tamp or compact it, and cover with polyethylene sheet to aid curing and prevent moisture from reaching the slab. Cover this with reinforcing mesh, or rebar for larger spans, and place and secure stop boards to divide sections where necessary. Hold the boards in place by nailing them to wooden pegs.

Use a concrete mix of 1 part Portland cement to 2½ parts mason's sand to 3 parts coarse gravel. This way, 1 cu yd of concrete = six bags of cement + 15 cu ft. of sand + 18 cu ft of aggregate.

CONCRETE PATHS

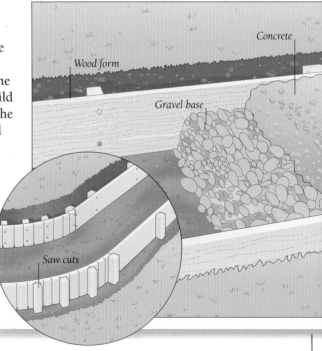

Wood form

Concrete

Gravel base

Saw cuts

On a straight path, dig up and level the site and mark it out with wood stakes. Use a level to ensure that the tops of the stakes are all the same height, then build the wood forms nailing the boards to the stakes. The width of the boards should match the combined depth of the concrete and gravel (normally 4–6 inches). After you've poured the concrete, the boards can be used as level ledges for a screed.

If the path curves (inset), place stakes 3 inches apart along the curve. Use a strip of ¼-inch plywood or hardboard to form the curve. You can make saw cuts in the strip to help it mold to the curve.

Pouring the concrete

If you're laying concrete over a large area, position strips of ½-inch thick expansion joint filler sheet, or plywood every 3 yards. These form expansion gaps that will stop the concrete from cracking or buckling. If the slab abuts a masonry wall, position an expansion joint where they meet. In addition, slice control grooves every 3 feet.

Mix the concrete with a little water at a time, mixing until it leaves the shovel clean and grooves don't flow together. If you are working a large area, it's almost certainly worth hiring a power mixer. Tip the mix into the forms. Spread and level the wet concrete with a shovel or rake, making sure that all corners and gaps are properly filled. Then use a lumber screed to compact the concrete, and saw it off level with the top edges of the form boards. Cover the slab with weighted-down plastic sheets and leave to cure for 3–7 days before removing the forms. In very hot conditions, you should try and dampen the slab daily to prevent cracking. Afterwards backfill around the slab with topsoil and turf as necessary.

Finishing the surface

Finish the surface as the concrete dries. In dry conditions you may not have long before it becomes unworkable.

a **Fine-textured finish**

Mist the surface with water from a hose and smooth with a wooden float; finish with a trowel.

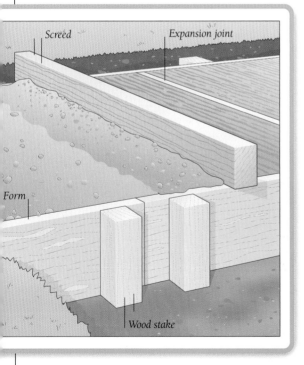

Screed

Expansion joint

Form

Wood stake

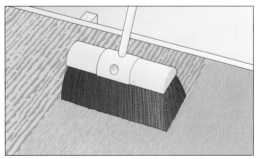

b **Rough finish**

To provide a rougher, less slick surface, lightly sweep over the leveled concrete with a stiff broom.

Building a deck

WOOD DECKS *provide a natural transition from an indoor living space to an outdoor recreation area.*

Building a deck

First decide whether to rest the deck on ground-level joists, or on a foundation of joists supported by 6 x 6 inch posts. Any raised decking should be outfitted with a handrail that meets local building codes, and you will need to provide steps. When choosing lumber, pick redwood or cedar, or pressure treated softwoods. Plot the position of the deck and its support posts, using one at the end of each beam, and one at the middle in runs longer than 12 feet. The beams should slope ¼ inch per foot, down away from the house. Posts are secured by concrete footings; they are either sunk into the concrete or attached to the top with metal brackets. Construct the framework by nailing pairs of joists on either side of the posts, or create built-up beams and place across the shortest spans between posts on braces on top of the posts; nail the joists on edge over these beams, then nail or screw the decking boards down. Lastly, build the stairs and handrails.

It's important to do everything possible to prevent the decking boards from cupping and bowing; lay them bark side up, so that the end-grain annular rings are pointing down.

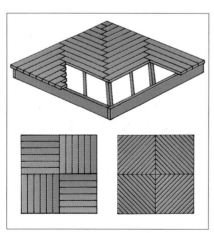

■ **Simple solution:** *prefabricated decking squares are available in a variety of patterns from large DIY stores.*

An easier way

You can also buy prefabricated timber decking panels with wooden slats in ready-made wood frames. Like individual boards, these can be laid over joists resting directly on the ground, or on a framework supported by posts.

The panels tend to look better laid with the slats pointing in alternate directions. Secure the panels to the joists using decking nails.

INTERNET

www.doityourself.com

This site offers advice and product information on a variety of home improvement issues, including outdoor topics such as building and maintaining decks.

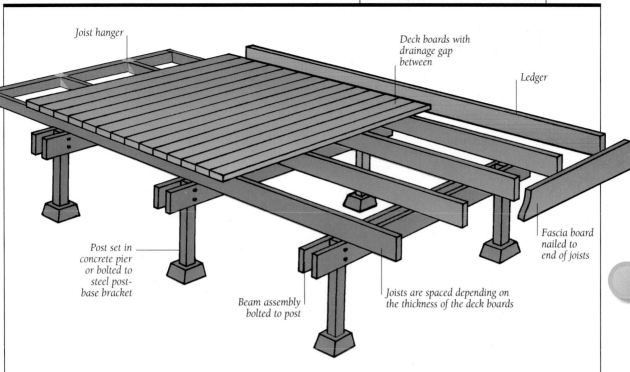

Joist hanger

Deck boards with drainage gap between

Ledger

Post set in concrete pier or bolted to steel post-base bracket

Beam assembly bolted to post

Joists are spaced depending on the thickness of the deck boards

Fascia board nailed to end of joists

■ **Elevated decking** *must be supported on 6 x 6 posts mounted on or in concrete footings. Decks should be attached to houses by means of a 2 x 10 ledger with masonry bolts. A range of specialized decking hardware makes construction easier, but follow local zoning codes as to joist and post spacing.*

A simple summary

✔ Repair a damaged concrete or paved surface as soon as possible, to prevent accidents.

✔ Careful planning of a paved area avoids problems during laying and saves on materials.

✔ Pavers and slabs can normally be laid on a bed of soft sand and finished with edging blocks.

✔ Concrete is a quick and very economical way to create a hard, durable surface. Always lay concrete over an aggregate such as gravel, to prevent problems.

✔ A wood deck is a great alternative to a patio, especially if the ground slopes or is uneven. Regularly maintained, it should last for years.

Chapter 18

Walls and Roofs

REGULAR INSPECTIONS OF THE OUTSIDE of your home will show up any minor problems before they turn into major disasters, and as long as you have a head for high places, there's plenty you can do yourself. But take my advice and stop short of a main roof: working safely at a height calls for special equipment and is best left to a professional.

In this chapter...
✓ Gaining access outside
✓ Repairing masonry
✓ Siding
✓ Repairs to flat roofs

REPAIRS TO LOW ROOFS ARE WITHIN EASY REACH

Gaining access outside

A LADDER IS FINE for making quick inspections, but if you need to do any kind of substantial repairs to the outside of the house, consider renting scaffolding.

Safety

Scaffolding, complete with clip-on ladders, is easy to rent, often with free delivery. Most have tubular sections that slot together easily, with bolt-on crossbraces between them to form a solid structure. Working platforms and kick boards are generally short lengths of 2¼-inch board with brackets for securing to the frame. A tower over 6 feet high needs outriggers to keep it stable or

■ **A ladder stabilizer** *is a worthwhile investment if you use an extension ladder frequently, or if you have doubts about the soundness of the structure.*

should be attached to the house at each level. Remember: erecting a tower is a two-person job. Secure the tower to any structurally integral part of the building, not impermanent fixtures such as downspouts.

ⓐ **Putting up an extension ladder**

Pull out the extension to the right height, hook it over the rungs, then tilt the ladder towards you as you carry it to the wall.

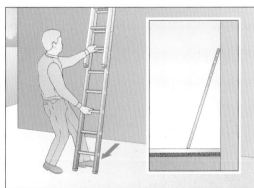

ⓑ **Positioning the ladder for safety**

Pull the ladder out from the wall a minimum of one quarter its total length. Make sure the ladder sits on a firm footing and cannot slip.

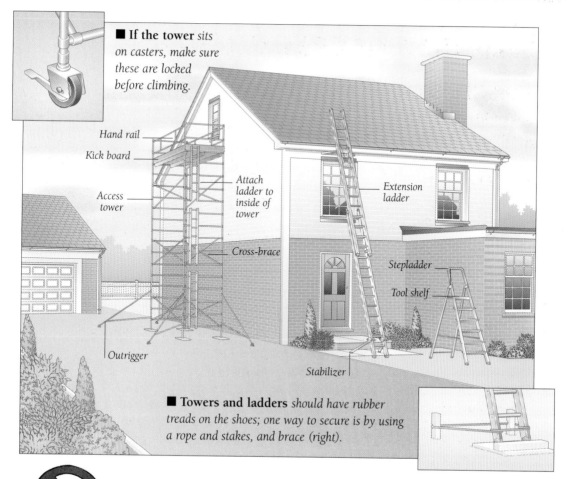

■ **If the tower** *sits on casters, make sure these are locked before climbing.*

Hand rail

Kick board

Access tower

Attach ladder to inside of tower

Extension ladder

Cross-brace

Stepladder

Tool shelf

Outrigger

Stabilizer

■ **Towers and ladders** *should have rubber treads on the shoes; one way to secure is by using a rope and stakes, and brace (right).*

My advice about working on a pitched roof is: don't if it can be avoided. Even if you have a head for high places, the risks involved aren't worth taking. If you have to access your roof, don't step on it; use a board to distribute your weight. And make sure the ladder sticks up four rungs above the edge, so that you can see it at all times.

Working on flat roofs

Most flat roofs aren't designed to be walked on, so protect the existing surface with a walkway of planks or boards. Even if you can gain access from a window, you'll probably need a ladder as well for passing up materials and passing down debris. In this case, make sure the ladder extends at least four rungs above the line of the roof so that it doesn't accidentally get kicked away – and you can see where to climb onto it.

If you need to use a flat roof as a base for a ladder to reach higher up, secure the base of the ladder with a staked 2 x 4 cleat, to stop the feet from slipping.

Repairing masonry

MASONRY WALLS are by no means immune to the effects of the elements, especially pointing – the mortar joints in brickwork – and large, flat areas of stucco. The trick is to make repairs before compromised surfaces allow moisture to penetrate.

Repair, then repoint

Old age and excessive exposure can cause **pointing** to deteriorate. If the whole house needs repointing, you're better off leaving the job to a mason. Often the problem is confined to one small area, in which case try to find the underlying cause. Crumbling bricks, loose flashings, leaking gutters, and blocked drip grooves below window sills are some of the most likely culprits. Chimneys are also vulnerable, due to their exposed position, and should be inspected yearly.

Clear out the old mortar joints with a chisel. Dampen them, then fill in the joint with fresh mortar using a trowel. Flush pointing is rubbed smooth with canvas as the mortar dries. Concave pointing is shaped with an old metal bucket handle or similar tool while the mortar is still wet. Create weather pointing with a trowel held against a batten.

POINTING FINISHES

FLUSH

CONCAVE

WEATHER

Repointing a wall

Repointing protects your home from the elements and smartens up your house.

1 Clean out old mortar

Use a mallet and brickset to clear out the crumbling mortar. Brush clean and dampen.

2 Apply new mortar

Use your trowel to roll the repair mortar into a sausage shape, then force it into the joints.

3 Finish the joints

Create a weather joint with the trowel held at an angle, then trim the mortar against a batten.

PATCHING DAMAGED STUCCO

1 Cut back the damage

Use a steel mallet and cold chisel to chip out the damaged stucco to a strong edge. Repair or replace existing metal lath.

2 First layer

Moisten the area. Lay in the base coat of stucco, about ¼ inch below surface level and leave to dry for 2 days.

3 Second layer prep

Score the base coat to provide a bonding surface for the second layer. Apply the second coat, filling to the surface.

4 Finish surface

Level the surface with a screed and smooth with a float. Leave to dry for 2 days and apply third coat. Once dry, paint to match wall.

Damaged stucco

Cracks in stucco can allow moisture to penetrate, causing the stucco to pull away from the wall. If you leave it untreated, the stucco deteriorates and crumbles away from the underlying surface.

Repair small cracks with stucco compound. For larger patches, use base coats of a stiff mix one part masonry cement with three parts sand, and enough water to hold the mix together. The final coat should be about two parts cement with three parts sand, and water to a creamy consistency.

Siding

EXTERIOR *siding, whether in the form of shakes, shingles, clapboard, or vinyl siding, is your home's front line of defense against the elements. A little tender loving care on a regular basis will ensure that it stays that way.*

Types of siding

- **Clapboard**: siding formed by attaching one course of beveled boards overlapping the course below it. Handsome and durable, clapboard siding must be regularly repainted and inspected for weather damage.

- **Wood shakes and shingles**: these vary in durability according to what they're made of. The best type are made from Western red cedar, which needs virtually no maintenance and weathers with an attractive finish. Asphalt shingles are also available as siding.

- **Board sidings**: these can be attached horizontally or vertically in various profiles, including tongue-and-groove, board on board, shiplap, board on batten, and others.

- **Vinyl or aluminum siding**: this is virtually maintenance-free, requiring only the occasional washing. This makes them a favorite with homeowners who don't want to have to repaint clapboard siding every few years. Properly installed and maintained, these type of sidings can last decades.

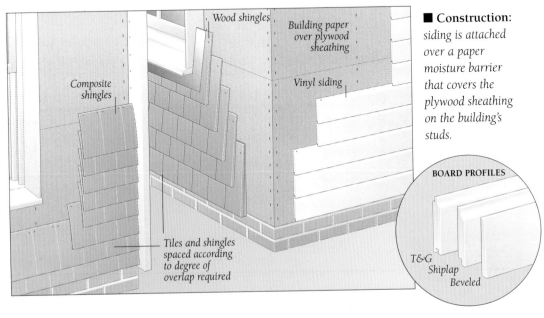

Wood shingles

Building paper over plywood sheathing

Vinyl siding

Composite shingles

Tiles and shingles spaced according to degree of overlap required

■ **Construction:** *siding is attached over a paper moisture barrier that covers the plywood sheathing on the building's studs.*

BOARD PROFILES

T&G
Shiplap
Beveled

REPLACING DAMAGED SHINGLES

As on roofs, shingles are fixed to overlap each other so that the joints are completely weatherproof. When replacing a shingle, hold it in position and mark the cutting line so that the bottom edge will align with its neighbors.

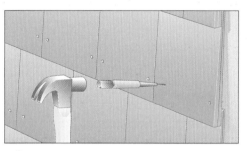

1 **Remove shingle**

Split the damaged shingle with a chisel and pull the nails out with a pry bar or nail puller.

2 **Nail on the replacement**

Slide the new shingle under the ones above and nail it in position in line with adjacent shingles.

REPAIRING DAMAGED CLAPBOARD

Replace a damaged section of clapboard with a piece of wood beveled to the same profile. Nail the new section to the underlying surface, following the position of the rows of existing nails.

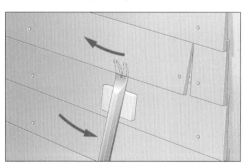

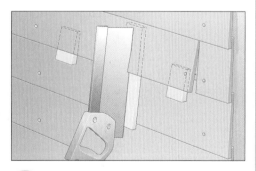

1 **Pry up the board**

Using a pry bar over a wood scrap to protect the board below, carefully pry away the damaged board to loosen the nails.

2 **Cut and fill**

Wedge the board away from the surface and cut away the damage. Cut and fit a matching piece, and nail into place.

Repairs to flat roofs

THE THREE BASIC TYPES OF FLAT ROOF *include asphalt-and-tar laid hot on the surface; roll roofing where one course is laid out overlapping the next, and membrane roofing that can be rubber, mineral surfaced, or some other water resistant surface. Roll roofing is the only type that a home do-it-yourselfer should attempt to install. The others are far too difficult.*

Dealing with blisters and cracks

Once rolled roofing starts to blister, it's only a matter of time before it cracks and allows water to seep down through the boards underneath. Inside the house, the leak may appear some distance from the blister, as water can follow the joist for a long way before settling. Flat roofs are also extremely susceptible around flashing and fascia areas, which should be inspected regularly. Standing water can also be a tremendous problem in sagging roofs; it will rapidly increase the deterioration and extent of damage to the roof. Even flat roofs should be tilted enough for runoff. Address the problem of standing water immediately.

Repair blisters by slitting and applying a patch bedded in roofing cement. Tubes of roofing cement are sold for use in a caulking gun. Make sure you treat all suspect areas at one time, then, when the patches are dry, apply a final coat of the compound.

PATCHING A BLISTER

1 **Slit blister**

Slit along the blister, peel back the edges, and coat with roofing cement.

2 **Nail back flaps**

Nail down the flaps with roofing nails, then apply more roofing cement.

3 **Cover with patch**

Bed a patch over the wet cement, nail the edges, then cover with roofing cement.

Repairing flashings

Flashings, which create waterproof joints between roofs, house walls, and chimneys, are a common source of leaks. Faulty metal chimney flashings should be replaced, including the counterflashing that is embedded in the pointing of the chimney. Unless you're comfortable with working on the roof, have a mason replace these. Valley flashings can be repaired with new rolled aluminum flashing, cemented into place with flashing cement. Older asphalt flashing that is leaking should either be replaced entirely or covered with steel mesh sandwiched between layers of flashing or roofing cement.

a **Repoint the mortar joints**

The mortar joints are the most vulnerable areas around metal flashing. As long as the metal itself isn't damaged, repoint as you would for brickwork.

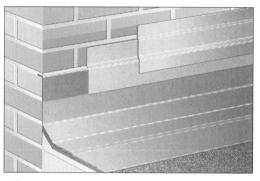

b **Using aluminum flashing**

Replace mortar flashing with rolled aluminum flashing cemented into place with flashing cement. Apply it in overlapping strips and roll flat.

A simple summary

✓ Use a ladder for inspections and minor repairs only. For major repairs, rent scaffolding to give you safe access.

✓ Before repointing mortar joints or patching areas of cracked stucco, look for any structural faults that may have caused them to deteriorate prematurely.

✓ The big risk with siding is that moisture will penetrate behind the boards. Repair any damage as soon as you spot it.

✓ Repairs made to flat roofs should only ever be regarded as a stop-gap. When the roof starts to blister, it's a sign that it needs replacing.

Chapter 19

Gutters and Drainage

FAULTY GUTTERS AND DOWNSPOUTS are some of the most common causes of water damage in homes, usually because they have suffered years of neglect. Inspecting your drainage systems once a year may sound like a chore, but believe me, it's a small price to pay compared with the cost of fixing a ruined wall or replacing rotted wood members. In this chapter, we'll also look at how to clear blocked drains, and what to do if your garden isn't draining properly.

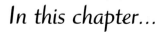

In this chapter...
- ✓ *Fixing gutters and downspouts*
- ✓ *Garden drainage*

CLEAN OUT GUTTERS ANNUALLY TO AVOID BLOCKAGE OR SAGGING

Fixing gutters and downspouts

GUTTERS AND DOWNSPOUTS *need to be regularly inspected for debris that could cause blockage or sagging. You'd be amazed how much dirt, leaves, twigs, and just plain debris can accumulate in the space of a year.*

Guarding against blockage

Clean out gutters on a regular basis, having first plugged the drop outlet with a rag to stop debris from entering and blocking the downspout. Afterward, run water into the gutter, and check for leaking joints and sagging sections. If fallen leaves are a particular problem, it may be worth installing a leaf-guard over the gutter. Buy prefab mesh leaf guards at large home centers.

Never place a ladder so that it's weight sits entirely on a gutter.

Either lean the ladder against the house wall below the roof line or – better – bolt on a stabilizer and extend the ladder beyond the roof line so that you have something to hold on to as you work. If you have to replace a long section of gutter, consider renting a scaffold.

FIXING SAGGING GUTTERS

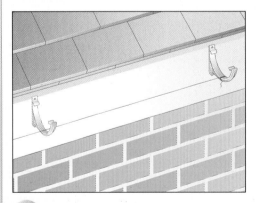

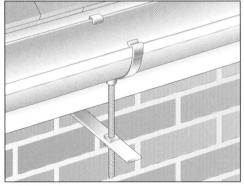

a **Re-align the hanging brackets**

If a large section is sagging, or the brackets are loose, remove the gutters and reposition the brackets using a taut string line as a guide.

b **Install a support bracket**

If the problem is confined to a single joint or bracket, you may be able to correct the sag by installing an adjustable support bracket.

Making repairs

If a gutter or downspout is leaking, first establish the cause. The weak spots on any gutter system are the joints between sections. With galvanized steel or aluminum gutters, the solder or seals on the joint may have failed, or the spike on a spike-and-ferrule may have rusted through. If the gutters are vinyl, it may be that the gasket has failed or dislodged. Vinyl can crack, and metal will corrode if not maintained. All downpipes are vulnerable to cracking during a freeze if partially blocked.

When patching gutters, use a patch of the same material as the gutter. Incompatible metals can rust through electrolytic action. Metal patches shrink and expand at a different rate than vinyl.

REPAIRING LEAKING METAL GUTTERS

a **Seal leaking joints**

Clean and scrub around the leaking joint, and seal with butyl rubber sealant. If this doesn't stop the leak, remove and replace the connector.

b **Patch holes with roofing cement**

Patch small holes with roofing cement. Cut a patch (of the same material as the gutter) and lay on a bed of roofing cement over the hole.

Repair or replace?

Most existing gutter systems are metal, but today vinyl is becoming much more common. Gutters, downspouts, and components such as elbows come in a range of sizes, so replacing a damaged part may mean a long search for a match. Take the section you're replacing with you to your supplier. If push comes to shove, you can have a roofing and gutter contractor create a replacement section on site, something that will save labor but cost a pretty penny. If you have a galvanized steel or aluminum system, your top priority is to keep it in good condition and to treat signs of damage or corrosion as soon as they appear. Metal gutters last for years if properly maintained.

While you're at it, check the integrity of the gutter's hanging brackets, the fascia board to which it's attached, and the soffits underneath. If there's a sign of rot, patch in a new section of board or remove the stretch of gutter and replace the board entirely. Internal gutters on older homes are exceptionally prone to rot, and the rot can quickly spread, so consider replacing them with aluminum or vinyl systems.

Never attempt to install a "seamless gutter" yourself. They are extruded on site with a special machine so you'll need to choose a contractor. Pick one that has references and work site insurance; all one needs to get in the business is the machine!

Replacing gutter and downspout sections

If you can't find the parts, or a section is damaged, you'll find it easier to replace an entire run. Ask your supplier about step-down or step-up pieces for joining new components to existing; the same applies to sections of downspouts. Vinyl gutters are easy to remove, but for metal types, you'll need a helper. The joints between sections are normally joined with cement or soldered, and you may have to saw through the bracket bolts with a hacksaw. Set the brackets for new gutters in place using a taut string line. The run should tilt toward the downspout by about ¼ inch for every 4 feet of length.

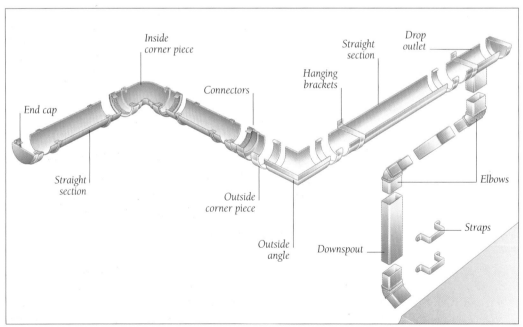

■ **A typical gutter system:** *if you're opting for wholesale replacement, draw a rough sketch of the run and use this diagram to note what components you need.*

Garden drainage

STOPPING RAINWATER from damaging your home is only half the battle. It's just as important to make sure that the water drains away properly – that is to say, neither so slowly that it causes the ground to become waterlogged, nor so fast that it provides no benefits for plants.

Improving the soil

Garden drainage is first and foremost an issue of soil type. In clay soils, for example, water tends to collect on the surface rather than drain down into the subsoil. Excessively sandy soils, by contrast, tend to drain too rapidly, depriving plant roots of much-needed moisture and causing the topsoil to dry out. The remedy is to dig in one or more ammendments over a period of time – anything up to a year – so that you gradually "improve" the soil and change its drainage properties.

■ **Dig in ammendments** *to a depth of around 1 foot and thoroughly mix them with the existing soil. Don't expect instant results: soil improvement is a gradual process.*

If you're unsure how well your soil drains, try this simple test. Dig a hole about 6–8 inches wide by about 1 foot deep and fill it with water. If the hole drains within 10 to 20 minutes, you've got sandy soil that drains quickly; if it takes more than 8 hours to drain, you have a drainage problem.

Consult your local nursery or garden center to find out what ammendments work best in your area and soil type, bearing in mind what you plan to plant. Generally speaking, very heavy clay soils benefit from being mixed with well rotted compost or manure to aerate them and break up the particles. But plants such as lavender or succulents thrive in much faster-draining, sandier soils, in which case the soil might benefit from the addition of fine sand.

Creating an underground drainage system

If your garden is permanently waterlogged, and you haven't either the time or the inclination to improve the soil, consider building raised beds to get your plants above the problem, plant water-loving plants such as those sold for use in ponds or wetlands, or build a deck to avoid the issue altogether. If you opt for a deck, though, make sure that surface water cannot pool around the wood or its supporting structure, or you will leave the deck vulnerable to rot and insect attack.

If all else fails and you still have standing water in your yard or garden, consider excavating and building an undergound drainage system similar to the foundation drain field that keeps basements dry. You can use such a system over a small waterlogged area, or extend it over the entire yard.

There are few hard and fast rules for land drain systems, and most people improvise with whatever materials are available locally. The important thing is to have a central drain tile run through the worst affected area and into a drain cylinder that will disperse the excess water quickly underground. Perforated branch pipes with open joints can extend to either side of the drain tile as necessary.

If you suddenly come across a layer of sand while digging out an underground drainage system, stop! Utility companies use sand to mark the placement of essential services pipes. Call the company and make sure you are not digging into a dangerous area.

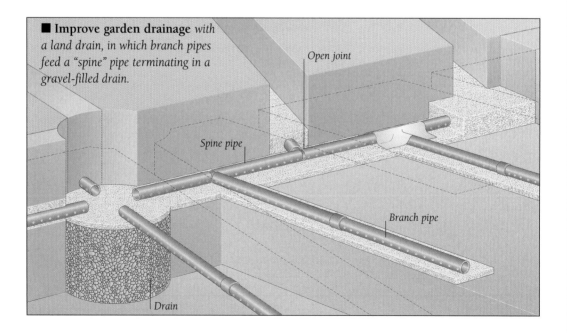

■ **Improve garden drainage** with a land drain, in which branch pipes feed a "spine" pipe terminating in a gravel-filled drain.

Open joint

Spine pipe

Branch pipe

Drain

Mark the pipe runs for the drain on the surface using stakes and string. Remove and store any turf, then dig the trenches. The ideal depth is 2 feet, but stop before this if you reach hardpan. The trenches should slope very gently – about ¼ inch per foot – toward the drain cylinder.

Line the base of each trench with about 2–3 inches of gravel or loose rubble and compact with a heavy wood tamp. Then cut the drain pipe to length with a hacksaw, allowing for open joints wherever they meet a branch pipe. Assemble the branch pipes and lay all the pipes in their trenches. Leave ¼-inch gaps at the joints, then cover the joints with squares of heavy-duty polyethylene sheet. Cover the pipes with a further 2 inches of gravel, taking care not to disturb their positions, and cover with soil to complete the drain.

■ **The spine pipes of a** *land drainage system end in the land drain – a pit filled with gravel and covered with subsoil, topsoil, and turf.*

A simple summary

✓ Inspect your gutter system once a year (preferably fall). Clear out any debris that could cause a blockage and repair any obvious damage or problems.

✓ If you experience difficulty getting parts, or if runs are sagging in more than one place, it may be easier to dismantle the entire system and replace it.

✓ Poor garden drainage is usually remedied by improving the soil. Be aware that soil drainage problems can affect wood structures, in which case they need to be dealt with right away.

✓ In extreme conditions where water is a persistent problem, it may be worth building an underground drainage system.

PART FIVE

Chapter 20
Know Your Plumbing

Chapter 21
Home Plumbing

Chapter 22
Know Your Electrical

Chapter 23
Electrical Jobs

Chapter 20

Know your Plumbing

TIME SPENT GETTING TO KNOW YOUR HOME'S plumbing system won't be wasted, especially if you learn how and where to turn off the water in an emergency. Troubleshooting, too, becomes easier once you know what order to approach things in. But, as with electrical systems, if there is something you don't understand, seek professional advice.

In this chapter...

✔ Where the water comes from

✔ Where the water goes

✔ How water gets heated

✔ Turning the water off

✔ Hot water troubleshooter

JOINTS IN PIPES ARE EASY TO MAKE IF YOU FOLLOW THE RULES

Where the water comes from

UNDERSTANDING HOW WATER is supplied to, and distributed around, the home is the first step toward becoming a confident home plumber.

Municipal or well?

The water supply to your home comes from one of two sources: a municipal water utility, or from a well on your property. Most homes in the US are supplied through water utilities, which route water under pressure through water mains. The water comes into your home through a main water supply line, is routed through the water meter, and then to cold water supply lines and, separately, to the water heater. Well water is pumped out of the well directly into a storage tank inside the home.

Regardless of the source, the water supply inside the home is pressurized, which ensures that it flows at force from faucets and showerheads throughout the home. Given the fact that the pipes in the system bear the stress of this pressure, the challenge is to ensure they don't leak or, if for any reason they do, that they are repaired before the damage becomes extensive.

Increasing contamination of ground water tables throughout the country means that all wells should be regularly tested for contaminants. Contact your local county extension service for testing guidelines and resources.

Water conditioning

Water supplied through municipal utilities is treated and conditioned – "hard" minerals are removed. Municipal water is considered safe to drink, although rare cases of contamination do occur. Once inside the house, the water is routed to a water heater for heating, and to cold water supply lines. From there, the two follow identical pathways through the house.

Water from wells is electrically pumped up into a pressurized holding tank that automatically shuts off the pump when full. The well will either use a durable submersible pump, or an external jet pump. Both can be adjusted for more or less pressure. Well water tends to cause more plumbing problems because it contains a higher concentration of minerals and can erode or clog pipes. It is also more likely to be contaminated, and many wells feed through a filter system. The tank may become waterlogged, in which case the supply valve should be closed and the cold water turned on while the tank refills with air.

MUNICIPAL SYSTEM

One of the first features of a municipal water supply is the main shutoff valve that should be just after the meter. Make sure you know where it is. You'll find it's also helpful to map out the other lines and fixtures of your system.

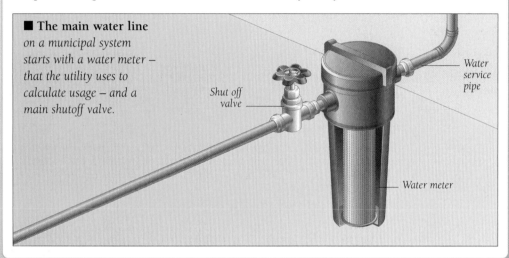

■ **The main water line** *on a municipal system starts with a water meter – that the utility uses to calculate usage – and a main shutoff valve.*

Shut off valve

Water service pipe

Water meter

WELL WATER SYSTEM

If you are plagued by low-pressure in your lines, you'll need to adjust the pump pressure. Always follow manufacturers' recommendations for maximum pressure and check your tank for possible problems at the same time.

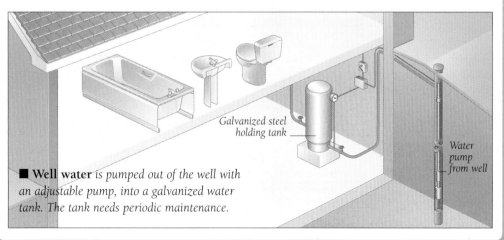

Galvanized steel holding tank

Water pump from well

■ **Well water** *is pumped out of the well with an adjustable pump, into a galvanized water tank. The tank needs periodic maintenance.*

Where the water goes

GETTING WATER OUT OF A HOME *is often trickier than getting it in.*
Most drainage systems rely on gravity to move the waste water and it doesn't
take much to block the flow in a near-horizontal drain or waste pipe.

The DWV system

The drain system in your home works primarily on gravity,
and is called the drain-waste-vent (DWV) system. This is
because all the drains direct waste water and solid wastes
through branch lines to a main *soil stack* that either routes all
waste water to the municipal sewer system, or alternatively to
a septic tank on your property. Positioned physically above the
drain pipes in the system, waste vent pipes and vertical vent
stacks provide an exit for gasses that accumulate in the system,
as well as drawing in fresh air that prevents suction in the
lines, keeping the water flowing freely. A *wet vent* combines draining and venting
functions for different fixtures. The main waste vent stack runs all the way from your
basement up to the roof, where it is topped by a roof vent.

> **DEFINITION**
>
> *The main stack routing waste*
> *from branch lines to the main*
> *sewer line is called the* **soil**
> **stack***. Any pipe that serves as*
> *a drain for one fixture and as*
> *a vent for another fixture is*
> *called a* **wet vent***.*

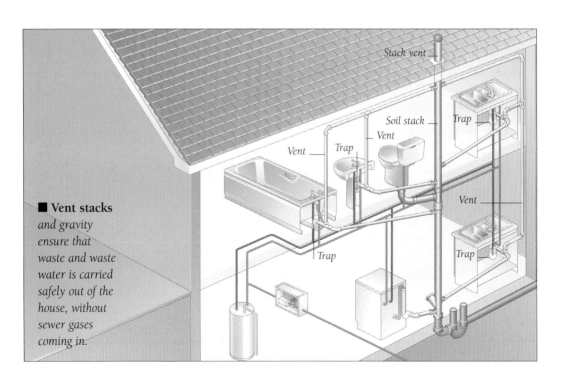

Stack vent

Soil stack

Vent

Trap

Vent

Trap

Vent

Trap

Trap

Trap

■ **Vent stacks**
and gravity
ensure that
waste and waste
water is carried
safely out of the
house, without
sewer gases
coming in.

Any waste drain is equipped with a trap. This U-shaped bend of pipe stops gasses from backing up into the home. The main sewer line leading out of the house includes a cleanout that can be used to clear blockages.

Septic systems

Most DWV systems are connected to a main municipal sewer line that leads to a waste treatment facility. These are relatively trouble-free connections. But homes in rural areas, or those that are not serviced by a water utility, must dispose of waste water in a localized septic system. These systems are relatively simple but must be maintained to function effectively.

The sewer line from the home is routed to a large underground septic tank in a nearby area of the property. Solid wastes settle to the bottom of the tank where microorganisms digest it. The waste water flows out to distribution boxes, and is then slowly released through drain pipes into a "drain field," where it is absorbed and slowly cleansed of any remaining contaminants as it filters through rock and soil layers to the water table. The septic tank must be periodically flushed of the accumulated solids by a professional to continue operating efficiently. If local codes permit it, you can also install a graywater system, which routes wastewater and liquid wastes from areas such as sinks and showers through a more modest treatment system. This is a useful system to consider if your yard is heavily landscaped.

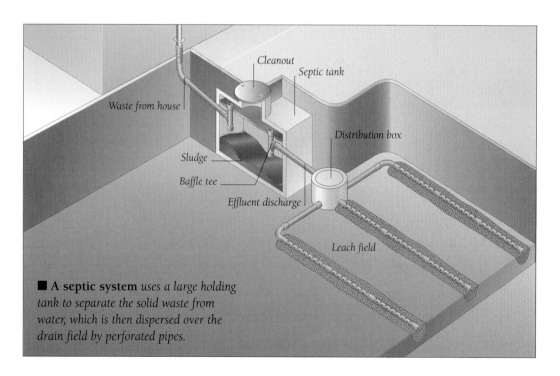

Cleanout

Septic tank

Waste from house

Distribution box

Sludge

Baffle tee

Effluent discharge

Leach field

■ **A septic system** *uses a large holding tank to separate the solid waste from water, which is then dispersed over the drain field by perforated pipes.*

How water gets heated

WATER HEATERS ARE SO INTEGRAL to the way we live, that we hardly notice them until they break down. Whether you have a gas or electric heater, it pays to maintain it, and watch for signs that it needs replacing.

The big two

Although you can choose from among solar-, propane-, or oil-powered water heating units, the vast majority of homes use one of two types: either gas or electric. Generally you replace the unit with the type that the home is currently set up for.

The fuel of choice

Natural gas-powered water heaters account for more than half of those sold. The average gas heater will last 15–20 years with proper maintenance, and is relatively inexpensive to run. Modern gas heaters have options that you might consider depending on the circumstances. If you have hard, scaly water, buy a heater with a self-cleaning feature that prevents lime and mineral build-up. As with other large appliances, look for the most energy efficient model – a rating available from the manufacturer and often listed on the unit. Savings can run to 20 percent per year.

This type of heater uses a gas burner at the base of the unit, so the bottom of the tank needs to be kept clean for the most efficient operation and longest life. Drain and flush the unit once a year, or have a plumber do it. Regularly inspect the drain valve, which should act as a pressure-relief valve in case the pressure builds inside the unit. Also ensure that the flue venting the gas from the flame is never blocked, or a potentially dangerous situation could result. Fix any leaks immediately, before they turn into a flood.

■ **Gas water heaters** *are extremely efficient and economical, but always observe the same safety measures you would with a gas stove.*

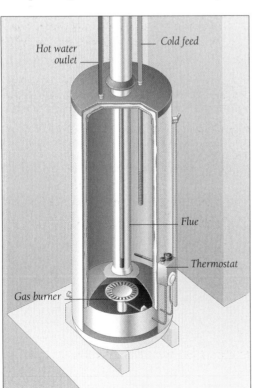

Hot water outlet

Cold feed

Flue

Thermostat

Gas burner

The electric option

Electric heaters are considered somewhat safer than gas types, but are also less efficient and cost more to run. The construction is much like a gas heater, except that instead of a gas burner at the base of the unit, there are electric heating elements in the side of the heater, and there is no need for a vent. They also have a drain valve and should be regularly flushed to remove scale and other mineral buildup. When replacing the element or thermostat, always buy a unit of the same voltage and wattage rating.

Modern water heaters use insulated core and many will operate inefficiently if wrapped with an insulating blanket. Check the manufacturer's recommendations before wrapping your water heater.

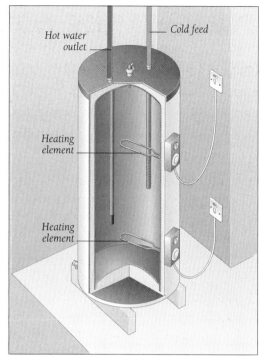

■ **An electric heater** *may be less explosive than a gas type, but it can still be dangerous. Turn off all power before inspecting or repairing the unit.*

Hot water outlet — Cold feed

Heating element

Heating element

ASSESSING YOUR HEATING REQUIREMENTS

Regardless of the type of water heater you use, eventually you will have to replace it. When the time comes, your family may have grown, or your needs changed. Be sure to buy a heater that meets – but doesn't exceed – your needs. Too small a heater means you'll regularly run out of water, too large and you'll waste a lot of energy.

Persons in household	Electric	Gas
1–4	40 gal.	30 gal.
5–7	50 gal.	40 gal.
7 and up	65 gal.	50 gal.
Above 10	80 gal.	65 gal.

Add one "person" for every luxury water appliance you have, including an automatic dishwasher, jacuzzi tub, and multihead shower.

Turning the water off

KNOWING HOW to turn the water off and drain a given pipe or area will take the panic out of plumbing emergencies and save a fortune in plumber's charges. But don't wait until the worst happens: try it now, so that you can be sure that all valves are in good working order.

Going with the flow

In the case of a big emergency, or where you can't find the shutoff valve for a particular fixture, you can use the main shutoff valve that is located right after the water meter, where your main water supply enters the house. It's a good idea to locate this valve so that you know where it is in case of an emergency. The next step that any wise homeowner takes is to map out where the other shutoff valves are for different areas of the house. Write these down and you'll be giving yourself a big shortcut when it comes time to replace a toilet or fix a leak.

1. Be aware that your home may not have been plumbed with shutoff valves for each run of pipe, or each different section of the house. You may have to look farther down the line. If a potential problem area – such as a bathroom – is not covered, consider installing a shutoff valve in the branch lines feeding it.

2. Some jobs won't require shutting down the entire branch supply line. For instance, if you are replacing a faucet, the undersink valves will shut off the water supply so that you can install the new fixture.

3. Older homes often don't have fixture shutoff valves. Take the opportunity when replacing a fixture or repairing a leak to install undersink shutoff valves in both hot and cold lines. Use a compression fitting to splice the valve into the copper supply line, and use new flexible lines to feed the fixture.

4. If running new supply lines or rerouting existing lines, be sure that the shutoff valves are placed where you can easily get at them. This may involve cutting a new access panel in the wall.

Check your main shutoff valve once a year. In older homes, the valve may have corroded and may no longer effectively cut off the supply of water. A plumbing emergency, such as a big basement leak, is not the time to figure out that your main shutoff valve doesn't work!

Steam heating systems

Many older homes are heated by steam heat, or by a hot-water heating system, in which heated water is supplied from a boiler through a system of cast-iron radiators or baseboard heat convectors. The system is fairly effective but needs occasional maintenance to run efficiently. Heat from an individual unit is controlled by opening or closing the inlet valve. A common problem is a knocking known as "hammering" that occurs when air gets trapped in the line. If this happens, bleed the unit with the heating system on: simply open the bleeder valve until water runs out, then close it.

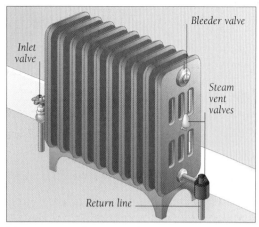

■ **A steam radiator** *is a basic heating structure with tubes surrounded by fins that disperse heat, and air vents that release steam buildup.*

Keeping hose bibs safe

In colder parts of the country, freezing weather will play havoc with the familiar exterior hose bib valves. When winter comes, use the shutoff valve on the inside, which controls the line to the hose bib. Leave the hose bib open to release any remaining water and bring hoses inside to prevent cracking. Special frost-proof sillcocks are available for extreme cold-weather conditions. These have a long stem that reaches inside the house, and are angled back toward the shutoff valve

TYPES OF SHUTOFF VALVE

Common shutoff valves include drain-and-waste (or globe) types; gate valves; and simple cutoff valves servicing a single fixture.

GLOBE VALVE   GATE VALVE   BALL VALVE

Hot water troubleshooter

WHEN THE HOT TAPS *run cold or dry up altogether, try to resist the temptation to panic. There's a good chance that you can sort the problem out without professional help, and even if you can't, you will save money if you can point the plumber in the right direction.*

1) Water flows, but is cold or lukewarm

Assuming that any room thermostats and water heating controls are correctly set, this points to a problem in the water heater.

● **For a gas heater**, consult the manual and check that the pilot light is on. If it has gone out, you will need to relight it. Remove the access panels and light a match. Keep your face and clothing away from the pilot light cavity while you light it, and, with the match in place, press the red reset button on the control box. Keep the reset button pressed for a minute, and then turn the gas flow switch on the control box to on. Check one last time to see that the pilot light is lit and then carefully replace the access panels. If the pilot light keeps going out, either the pilot light unit itself is faulty, or there is a problem in the gas supply itself. In either case, you should call a plumber to evaluate and repair the system.

The problem can also be caused by excess sediment in the tank, in which case you should drain several gallons of water through the tank.

● **For an electric heater**, check the relevant fuse or circuit breaker at the breaker box. Check the power lines to the heater and remove the access panel (with the power off), and check that the wire contacts are secure. If the wires are all connected, press the reset button on the thermostats, replace the access panels, and turn the power back on. If that doesn't work, check the heating elements. Usually, there are two, one top and one bottom. If the water just gets lukewarm, the problem is usually the top element. If it gets hot and then goes cold quickly, it is usually the bottom element. Replacing one or the other element should solve the problem. If none of this works, the thermostat unit is faulty and should be replaced. This is a fairly difficult task, and if you are reluctant to work with electrical elements, leave this to a professional.

If hot water consistently runs out in a large household, the problem may not be a system problem, but may be the result of too many demands being made on your hot water supply. It's important that the water heater is big enough to meet the demands of the number of people in the house. If you bought your home from a couple and you have a family of five, you may be faced with the reality of buying a new, larger water heater if you want an appropriate supply of hot water.

2) Water doesn't flow at all

This suggests that the cold supply to the system has been cut off or there is a major leak in a supply line. Immediately check throughout the system for a leak, and work back to the main supply line to find a blockage or problem.

Occasionally, the municipality may have shut off the water main in order to undertake construction work. Check the drain-and-waste valve nearest where the main water supply pipe enters your home to see if water is flowing. If you are on a well, check that the supply pump is operating correctly, and that there are no blockages in the line from the pump to the house.

3) Water scalding hot

Water that is too hot is dangerous and can cause pipes and taps to scale up in hard water areas. Lower the thermostat setting on your water heater – a good idea anyway to conserve energy. A safe setting is usually about 120°F.

4) Leaking water heater; high pilot flame

A water puddle around the base of the water heater, or a pilot flame that is visibly flaring out around the access panels, are critical signs of water heater failure and a dangerous situation. Replace the water heater immediately.

A simple summary

✓ In most homes, water is supplied by a municipal utility, through a water main in the street. Homes not serviced by municipal sources must get their water from wells.

✓ The wastes in a home are disposed of through a system knows as the drain-waste-vent system (DWV), which uses vertical waste stacks.

✓ Water is heated instantaneously, or indirectly via a hot water storage cylinder.

✓ Practice turning the water off so that you don't get caught in an emergency.

✓ Most hot water problems can be traced by a process of pure logic, and many can be fixed without professional help.

Chapter 21

Home Plumbing

O NCE YOU'RE FAMILIAR with how your system works, you can tackle
anything from simple repairs, to the more substantial alterations
needed to accommodate a new sink, basin, bath, or shower.

In this chapter...

✓ Clearing clogs

✓ Fixing leaks in pipes

✓ Fixing a leaky faucet

✓ Repairing toilets

✓ Replacing faucets

✓ Making alterations

✓ Installing new fixtures

✓ Shower upgrade

A NEW FAUCET CAN BRING AN OLD SINK BACK TO LIFE

Clearing clogs

MOST CLOGS *inside the home can be dealt with using chemicals, a plunger, or a hand auger. You'll probably need a specialist to clear a main drain – don't be fazed by their jargon and high-tech equipment: most clogs are easily cleared.*

Taking the plunge

If you can't reach a clog because it's too far down a pipe, let the water in the pipe do the work for you. Water can't be compressed, so a force that you apply at one end of a water-filled pipe will be transferred to the other. A plunger won't just push on the blockage, but pull on it as well, which makes it more efficient than many so-called high-tech devices. Buy an all-purpose plunger for the sink, bath, and shower, and a double-headed plunger for toilets. Kitchen sink clogs tend to be fat or soap, both of which respond better to chemical cleaners.

Avoid clogs by disposing of cooking grease in the trash, not the sink; likewise rice and pasta. And don't overuse dish soap, which can congeal in the pipe and make clogs worse.

BLOCKAGE CURES

a **Clearing with cloths**

If you don't have any tools on hand, use a couple of cloths to clear a clog. Place one cloth over the sink overflow, then scrunch up the other and pump up and down on the drain.

b **Using a plunger**

Fill the sink with water and block the overflow with a cloth. Smear soap around the plunger to help form an airtight seal, then pump up and down vigorously over the drain.

The next step

If a clog doesn't respond to plunging, dismantle the trap over a bucket and use a hand auger. You should pull the clog out of the line if possible. Some clogs – those made of soap or grease buildup – may be harder to clear. In this case, work the blockage free with an auger, then flush the line with hot water to clear what's left. More persistent clogs can occur in the branch drain lines connected to the main waste vent stack, and in the vertical vent stack itself. Clear branch lines by locating the sanitary fitting and clean out at the end of the line. Open it and use an auger to clear the blockage. For the main waste stack, open the main drain cleanout plug and use an auger or – in cases where that doesn't work – a power auger to clear the drain. You may have to work through the roof vent if the blockage is farther up the vent stack, but use caution on the roof.

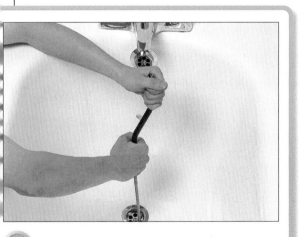

c **Using a wire snake**

Most clogs in sinks and showers are caused by a buildup of hair and soap in the trap, which respond best to a wire snake. Just wind it down through the hole and clear the clog.

WASTE PIPE WISDOM

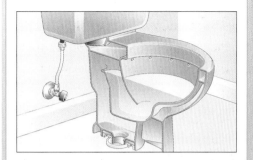

■ **A built-in trap** *is a common source of toilet clogs; try a plunger first, then use a hand auger to clear the clog.*

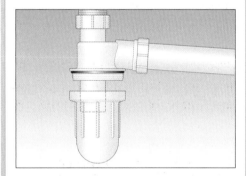

■ **Bottle traps** *are easily blocked and don't meet most codes. It's generally best to replace with a U- or P-trap.*

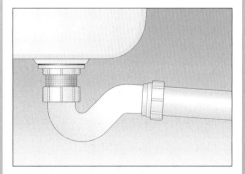

■ **Bath and shower traps** *may be backed up by a waste line that is not vented properly to the vertical waste vent stack.*

Fixing leaks in pipes

CONTAIN SMALL DRIPS with a sponge or in a bowl while you gather the tools and materials needed to make a permanent repair. But if you're faced with a burst pipe, act quickly with appropriate repairs.

Plan your move

Faced with a leak, your first task is to isolate the supply as close as possible to the problem and drain the pipe (see pp. 264–65). If the pipe is accessible, aim to make a permanent repair using a clamp. A burst pipe due to corrosion or damage means that the entire length of pipe will have to be replaced. If the repairs are extensive and involve opening a wall, inspect the entire area including branch pipes, traps, and fixtures, to see if anything else can be done at the same time.

A pinhole leak can be a sign of more significant problems; the cast iron pipes common in older homes are prone to corrosion from the inside out. Once you've fixed the leak on a cast iron pipe, have a plumber check the condition of all similar pipes.

EMERGENCY REPAIRS

The three methods shown here will buy you time to make a proper repair, but only the coupling and pipe clamp will work long-term. In an emergency you may have to use whatever comes to hand – duct tape, car body filler, or even putty.

a **Fit a coupling**

If the leak is accessible, drain the pipe, cut through, and fit a compression repair coupling.

b **Use epoxy putty**

If the leak is partly accessible or is at a joint, patch with quick-drying epoxy putty.

c **Clamp it**

A pipe clamp has the advantage that you don't have to turn the water off first.

Making permanent repairs

You can repair a burst or leaking copper pipe with simple fittings soldered in place. However, soldering takes a certain level of expertise, and a poorly soldered joint is likely to fail. You may also have to fix pipes in areas where soldering is not appropriate, such as in walls with highly flammable surfaces nearby.

A better alternative is often compression repair couplings or flare joints – but only if you cut the pipe ends with a pipe cutter. If you have to use a hacksaw, compression repair couplings are definitely the best option. Compression repair couplings can be bought in different links, for both ½ and ¾ inch pipes. The pipe is simply cut, the nuts and coupling positioned and then tightened in place. This is much simpler than other repairs.

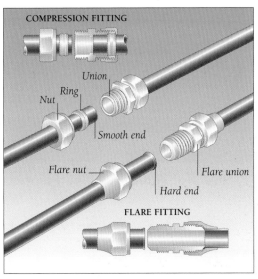

COMPRESSION FITTING

Union

Nut Ring

Smooth end

Flare nut

Flare union

Hard end

FLARE FITTING

■ **Flare fittings** *rely on the pipe ends being absolutely smooth and undamaged. Flare the ends with a flaring tip, screw the flare nuts onto the ends, and tighten with a pair of adjustable wrenches.*

REPAIRING A PIPE

① Cut the pipe

Cut the pipe with a junior hacksaw, or pipe cutter, then smooth the cut pipe end with a file or emery paper.

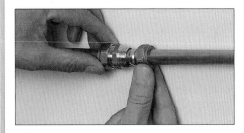

② Sealing the joint

Slide on the nut and ring and place the union between pipe ends. Apply pipe joint compound and screw nuts onto union.

③ Tighten nuts

Use a pair of adjustable wrenches to tighten the compression nut about 1¼ turns past hand-tight. Then turn on the water and test.

Fixing a leaky faucet

A DRIPPING FAUCET won't go away by itself, and if ignored for long enough can cause irreparable damage to porcelain sinks. So fix those niggling faucet problems before they become a major headache.

Many types, easy solutions

There are two basic types of faucets: compression and washerless. Compression faucets have washers or seals, the others have different devices depending on whether they are ball-type, cartridge, or disc faucets. How you repair a faucet depends on the type. Compression faucets are usually double handled and are simple to repair. Washerless faucets are more reliable and can also be repaired easily when they leak.

When replacing worn faucet parts, match the originals. Replacement kits are identified by make and model; but to be sure, always bring the old parts with you to the store.

Regardless of the type of faucet, use care when disassembling and put a rag or the plug in the sink – it's easy to lose the small parts that make the faucet mechanism, and some parts such as small screws are impossible to replace!

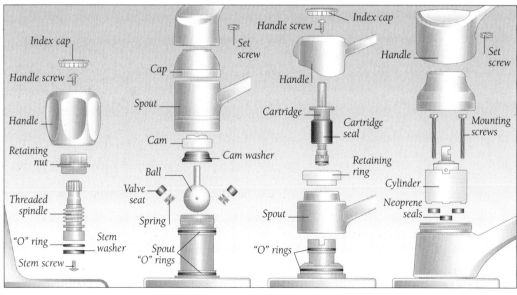

COMPRESSION FAUCET   BALL-TYPE FAUCET   CARTRIDGE FAUCET   DISC FAUCET

REPLACING A FAUCET WASHER

Washers vary in shape and size; some are flat, others are slightly domed. For ease of replacement, buy a universal washer kit.

1 Remove handles

Turn off the water and remove the handle. You may have to use a handle puller if it won't come off easily. Then remove the stem assembly as a whole.

2 Remove old washer

Remove the old washer either by prying it away from its baseplate, or by unscrewing the stem screw or retaining nut that holds it on.

3 Fit and run

Fit the new washer, and replace the retaining screw or nut. Assemble the tap and run it fully open to clear any grit or debris from the washer seating.

FIXING A LEAKING STEM OR SPINDLE

A compression faucet leak can also happen because of problems with the stem seals or seat. If the metal itself is compromised, it's best to buy a new faucet.

1 Remove stem

Remove the stem and check the type. Tophat stems should have their diaphragms replaced. Other types will hold the spindle with a nut or screw.

2 Remove spindle

Tap the spindle head sharply on a piece of wood to free it from the mechanism and reveal the seals. In a reverse-pressure stem, the washer will be inside.

3 Replace seals

Replace the seals and washers and smear with silicone lubricant; then re-assemble the stem. Make sure the nut or screw is tight before replacing.

Repairing toilets

FLOAT VALVES AND THE VARIOUS PARTS *of a tank system do more work than most plumbing components, so it's common for them to fail. Fortunately, they can be repaired with hardly any tools or specialist knowledge.*

Repairing float valves

Toilet flushing is controlled by a *float valve* that has an overflow in case the valve doesn't work. The float valve usually fails because one or more of the parts wear out, but overflows can also occur if the float itself springs a leak and fills with water. Often, simply adjusting the valve will stop it from leaking. Most valves have a screw to adjust the level, but on some older models adjustments are made by simply bending the *float ball* arm.

The common diaphragm *ballcock* float valve is simple and easy to take apart with a screwdriver and a pair of adjustable wrenches. However, newer toilets sometimes use a "float cup"

■ **The tank system of a toilet** *may look complicated and any of the components shown can fail at some time or another. But the assembly is simple. Replacing or repairing parts is not difficult, should the need arise.*

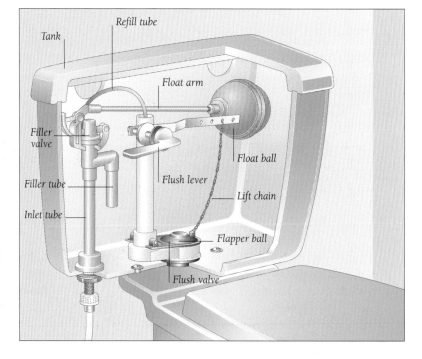

Refill tube

Tank

Float arm

Filler valve

Float ball

Filler tube

Flush lever

Inlet tube

Lift chain

Flapper ball

Flush valve

ballcock, where the ball actually rides up and down the stem of the ballcock, or a "floatless" ballcock. These are also easy to to repair and can both be adjusted with a screwdriver. Replacement kits are available for all three kinds.

Don't bother trying to fix a very old or badly scaled float valve — it's far easier and fairly inexpensive to install a modern plastic replacement, available from any home center or hardware store.

Flushing problems

Aside from float valve problems, the ballcock seal may fail. If water continues to run out around the rim of the ballcock after the tank is full, replace the washer or diaphragm.

- **In a diaphragm ballcock:** unscrew the float arm and cap and replace diaphragm and any other damaged parts. If the assembly is worn, replace the entire ballcock.
- **With a float cup ballcock:** remove the rubber cap, push down on the cap, and rotate counterclockwise to remove. Replace the seals inside, and any other parts you find that are badly worn.
- **With older plunger-valve ballcocks:** release the plunger mechanism and replace the plunger and packing washers, and any other seals.
- **Floatless ballcocks:** you will have to replace the entire mechanism if it fails.

REPLACING A FLAPPER VALVE

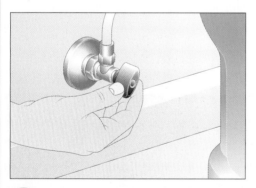

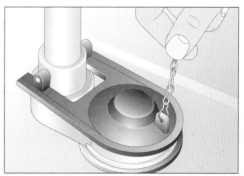

a **Removing the old flapper**

Turn the water off (above) and drain the tank. Unhook the chain from the top of the flapper, and remove it from the mounts on the overflow tube, or slide it up the tube if it's attached that way.

b **Installing a new flapper**

Install the replacement flapper valve and slide or hook it into position. Make sure it closes to form a tight seal and adjust position if it does not. Reattach hook (above) and flush to check.

Replacing faucets

NOTHING BRIGHTENS UP *a bathroom or kitchen quite like new faucets. Modern flexible tap connectors make the job a lot easier than it used to be, and you can use the same techniques when installing brand-new plumbing fixtures.*

Choosing new faucets

Depending on the faucet you're replacing, you will choose from two- or three-post faucets, and from those with or without supply tubes. Although there is a wide range of faucet styles, you have to find one that fits the holes in your sink, or you will be stuck with a major modification job (or the option of replacing your sink to suit the new faucet). Before shopping, measure from the center of one tailpiece (the mounting screw post) to the other tailpiece, and from those two to the center tailpiece. For more flexibility in design, choose from faucets with handles separate from their spigots. Measure twice to be sure and, if possible, bring the old faucet with you to the store to check the alignment of the tailpieces.

Get yourself comfortable for this job. Use a pillow if you're lying down in a bathroom, looking up under a sink. And make sure you have enough light to see the fittings clearly.

REMOVING OLD FAUCETS

This can be tricky because old mounting and coupling nuts can become bonded to the tailpiece with corrosion or accumulated gunk.

a Use a basin wrench

Spray the nuts with penetrating lubricant, let it soak in, then loosen with a basin wrench.

b Saw off the old nuts

If a nut won't budge and there is sufficient access, saw through it with a junior hacksaw.

c Drill and pry off

Otherwise, drill through the nut, first with a small bit, then a larger one, and pry off.

INSTALLING A FAUCET

Although these steps show a kitchen faucet being installed, the procedure is roughly the same for any other faucet, including bathroom faucets.

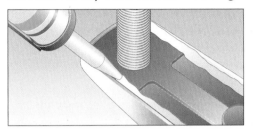

1 A good seal

Clean all traces of old putty off the sink. Seal the base of the faucet with a bead of plumber's putty or silicone caulk (above).

2 Tighten faucet in place

Position and press down the faucet, then fasten from underneath by tightening the mounting nuts over the friction washers on the tailpieces.

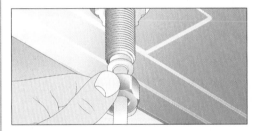

3 Connect supply lines

Connect the hot and cold flexible supply tubes to the tailpieces on either side (above), tighten the coupling nuts with a basin wrench.

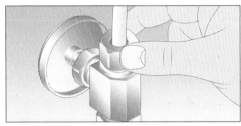

4 Attach at valves

Connect the other ends of the supply tubes to the undersink shutoff valves. Tighten a quarter turn over hand-tight. Restore the water and test.

Making connections

When replacing a faucet, use flexible tubing – either braided steel, vinyl, or chromed copper – even if the original tubes were copper. Measure the distance between the bottom of the tailpiece and the shufoff valve and buy the next longest length of flexible tube. Flexible tubing allows for replacement without having to cut and tap tubing.

Some faucets come with preattached copper supply tubes that run alongside the center tailpiece. Connect these directly to the shutoff valves using compression fittings. The lines are color coded: blue for cold and red for hot. Kitchen sinks often have sprayer hose attachments. These are connected to the center tailpiece of an appropriate faucet in the same way as the supply lines, using a hose nipple fitting.

Making alterations

TEEING INTO OR MODIFYING EXISTING *pipes to take new or replacement fittings is seldom as daunting as it seems, but you may want to call in a plumber if you have to run a brand new vertical waste stack or branch line.*

Arranging hot and cold supplies

Small modifications are best made with flexible copper connectors using compression or flare fittings. For larger alterations, it's quicker to use presoldered joints and elbows, with compression-jointed tee fittings at the source. It's a good idea to sketch the pipe runs and individual fittings before you start, so that you don't get caught without a part.

Hot and cold supplies must always be run horizontally or vertically and shouldn't cross over each other. The easiest way to run them is along a wall, affixed with pipe straps at a minimum of 4-foot intervals, although the more supports, the better. The supply tubes and branch pipes servicing most fixtures except for sillcocks and water heaters should never be less than ½ inch in diameter.

Avoid turning the water off for long periods by installing the pipe runs back toward the source, then tapping into the hot and cold supplies last of all.

TAPPING INTO A SUPPLY PIPE

1 Drain and cut

Turn off and drain supply. Mark the pipe and cleanly cut through it.

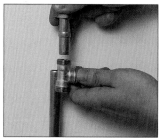

2 Install tee

If you've measured and cut correctly, the compression tee should fit snugly into place.

3 Tighten the nuts

Tighten the nuts on all three sides, making sure you hold the fitting and not the pipe.

SOLDERING NEW CONNECTIONS

People often panic at the mere mention of solder, but where there is sufficient access, it really is very easy. The only other equipment you need is a jar of flux and a propane torch. Two rules. 1: Both pipe and fitting must be absolutely clean; 2: Stuff bread in the end of the pipe to ensure no moisture enters the joint after soldering.

1 Apply flux

Scour the inside of the fitting with a wire brush and clean the pipe end with emery cloth.

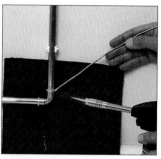

2 Apply heat

Gently heat the joint with a propane torch, protecting any surfaces around the pipe.

3 Solid seal

Heat the joint evenly and apply a uniform bead of solder around joint; clean rough spots.

Modifying cast iron pipe

Many older waste pipes are cast iron and prone to corrosion damage. You can replace a section of cast iron pipe with plastic pipe where regulations allow (some US municipalities don't allow plastic pipes) otherwise you need to replace the whole section. Support the horizontal runs with appropriate strap hangers, and vertical stacks with riser clamps supported on bottom plates, studs, or the floor. Cut the cast iron pipe with a chain snap cutter. Replace it with a section of PVC or ABS plastic pipe about ¼ to ½ inch shorter. Slide neoprene pipe sleeves and banded couplings in place, position the plastic pipe into position. Tighten and run water through the nearest cleanout to test.

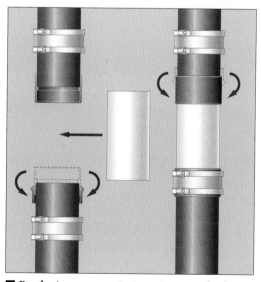

■ **Replacing waste pipe sections** *can be dirty and hard work, so you may prefer to leave the job to a plumber.*

Installing new fixtures

REPLACING A BATHTUB OR SINK isn't as difficult as it seems because there are never more than three connections to be made: hot supply, cold supply, and drain. The only real disruption will be to the surrounding structures.

Changing a sink

Most people these days prefer to have a sink set into the worktop, in which case cutting the hole is by far the hardest part of the job (see p. 189). If a template isn't provided with the new sink, use the sink itself to mark the worktop, then draw a cutting line ¼ inch inside the outline. Put the sink in place and install the faucet and drain fittings. In this case, use flexible vinyl or steel braided lines to make the connections to the shutoff valves, and connect the drain pipe to an approved trap. Finally, install a waste disposer, water filtration unit, or dishwasher connections, if any.

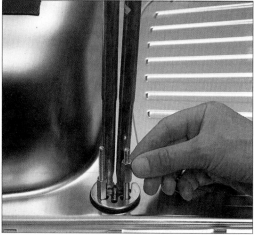

■ **Fitting the faucet**: *before installing the sink, check that the faucet tailpieces fit the holes.*

Changing appliances

Washing machines, dishwashers, and other plumbed-in appliances should have shutoff valves on the hot and cold supply tubes, which makes switching easy. If there aren't, or they don't work, turn off the water, drain the tubes, and install new shutoff valves.

Although you can drain large appliances directly into a sink drain, most codes require a dedicated waste drain. For washing machines, this usually means routing the drain hose into a standpipe drain with a P-trap leading to the vertical waste stack. A dishwasher will require the hose be clamped to a waste-T sink piece plumbed into the sink drain line.

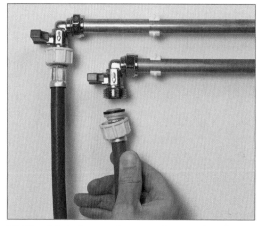

■ **Checking the washers**: *make sure that the appliance supply hoses have rubber washers at both ends for a watertight seal, and don't overtighten the nuts.*

Replace a bathtub

Disconnect the old tub and remove it. Removing an old cast iron tub can be difficult. The simplest way is to smash it up with a sledgehammer (be sure to wear eye protection).

Plumb in new hot and cold water supply handles, and shower supply pipe if necessary, before installing the tub. Ensure the subfloor is properly supported by sound joists and replace any warped or rotted subfloor.

Before putting the bathtub in place, attach the drain waste overflow assembly. This is sold as a kit, complete with pipe and necessary gaskets, drain plug and overflow plate. Before finally installing the tub, it's a good idea to wrap it with insulation to ensure a hot bath stays hot for as long as possible. Slide the tub in place and install the drain tailpiece, attaching it to the drain-overflow assembly at one end, and onto a trap leading into the branch drain. Test the bath and shower faucets and check the drain overflow assembly for any leaks. Finish by retiling around the tub.

Whirlpool bathtubs

Installing a new whirlpool bath is more complicated than replacing a tub with a similar tub. You will need to build a deck structure to support the tub and leave room to wire in the motor. This requires a great deal of carpentry work that must be done precisely for the tub to work correctly. Although it is plumbed in the same way as other tubs, unless your DIY skills are excellent, you should consider hiring a professional to install a whirlpool bathtub.

INSTALLING A TUB

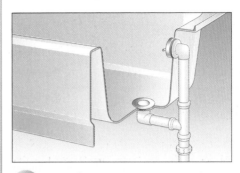

1 **Drain and overflow**

Install the drain waste overflow kit. Test the fit with the tailpiece that will go into the trap leading to the branch line.

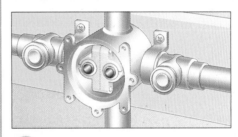

2 **Existing plumbing**

Inspect the existing bath and shower faucets and repair or change as necessary. Add an anti-scald valve (above) if one is not in place.

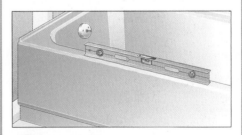

3 **Level the tub**

The bath should be installed level. The required fall to the drain is built into the shape of the bath.

Shower upgrade

IF THE FLOW THROUGH YOUR SHOWER is a trickle rather than a flood, then the time has come to squeeze a bit more performance out of it. Here are some simple tricks of the trade...

A better shower

If your shower is anything but brisk, your household water pressure is rarely to blame. First, try cleaning your showerhead's spray holes with a thin wire, and replace the O-ring washer in the head. If this doesn't help, consider switching to a new model that will also allow you to choose options such as a massaging spray. In addition, take the time to install an anti-scald device required by most building codes and a must-have for your own comfort.

If you don't have a shower in your bath, don't fret! You can add a flexible hose shower adapter with a simple adapter added to your bath faucet. You can find these kits at home centers.

INSTALLING A NEW SHOWERHEAD

Showerheads come in a range of sizes, but most offer different spray settings from regular spray through massaging blasts. However, all are installed easily and quickly, and in roughly the same way.

1 | **Remove the old head**

Wrap the stem with a cloth and use one wrench to hold the stem and one to twist the head off. Be careful not to crimp the stem.

2 | **Install the new head**

Wrap the stem threads with teflon plumber's tape, or use pipe dope, and screw the head onto the stem. Test for leaks.

Installing water filtration

Water filters are more popular than ever, both to remove potential contaminants and improve taste. There are several different types of filtration systems, but most are plumbed in a similar fashion. Install an undersink unit by mounting it below the kitchen sink and tapping the cold water supply with a saddle valve. The valve directs water through a flexible tube, into the filtration unit, and up into a stand-alone faucet that is mounted in a hole in your counter.

Whole-house water filters are plumbed into the cold water main supply, just after the main shutoff valve, with another shutoff valve placed after the filter unit. Attach a jumper wire over the filtration unit and replace the filter according to manufacturer's guidelines.

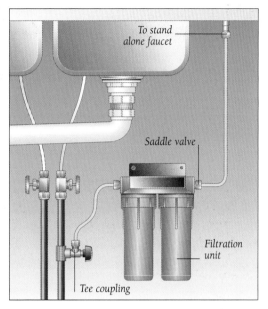

To stand alone faucet

Saddle valve

Filtration unit

Tee coupling

■ **An undersink water filter** *ensures water quality and improves drinking water taste, but must be maintained to work effectively.*

A simple summary

✔ Most clogs can be cleared with chemical cleaners, a plunger or a hand auger.

✔ Mend leaks with temporary solutions, to give you the time to make a lasting repair.

✔ Buy a universal washer kit so that you can fix leaking faucets.

✔ Keep a spare float valve around – a faulty one isn't worth fixing.

✔ When you're replacing an old faucet, be careful not to use excessive force on old fittings; saw through instead.

✔ If in doubt about an alteration, consult an expert.

✔ You can buy couplings to join new fittings to old pipe runs.

✔ Consider upgrading your shower with an anti-scald valve.

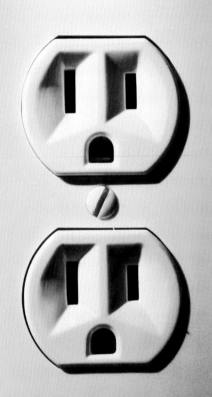

Chapter 22

Know your electrical

FIRST, THE BAD NEWS: don't even think about doing your own electrical work unless you understand how your home's electrical system works. Now the good news: it isn't that complicated. Really. As long as the electricity is completely turned off there is no possibility of getting a shock. So read on, and prepare to be initiated into the not-so-mysterious world of wires, breakers, and circuits.

In this chapter...

✓ Your electrical system

✓ Working with circuits

✓ Outdoor circuits

✓ Troubleshooting

A GROUNDED RECEPTACLE IS ONE OF THE MOST COMMON ELECTRICAL FIXTURES

Your electrical system

ELECTRICITY IS SUPPLIED *throughout your home via wiring that begins at your breaker or fuse box. The different circuits in the system are protected by fuses or breakers that blow or trip in the event of an emergency.*

The power behind the home

Electricity comes into the home via service wires that connect the power lines to your household electrical system. These wires enter through a service head on the roof or exterior wall; old homes generally have one 120 volt line; most modern codes call for two lines. The power is routed through an electric meter to your service box. This is wired with several fuse or breaker panels that each control one circuit, as well as a main supply shutoff.

The key built-in safety measure is the grounding system, in which a grounding wire is run from the breaker box to a cold water metal pipe and to a metal grounding rod buried in the ground. In the event of a fault, excess current is transmitted safely to the ground, reducing the risk of damage to circuit wires or injury to a person touching a faulty component. Breakers and fuses offer protection by tripping or blowing if there is a problem, but may not react fast enough to prevent damage or injury. Consequently, many homeowners now use ground fault circuit interruptor (GFCI) outlets, which shut off the flow of electricity in a fraction of a second. The National Electric Code (NEC) requires GFCI outlets in bathrooms and in kitchens above counters in all new construction and when making replacements.

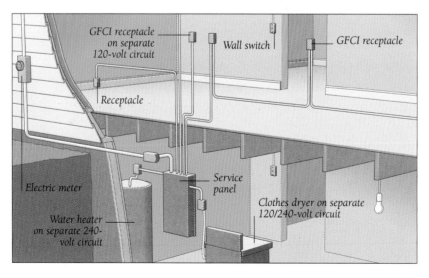

GFCI receptacle on separate 120-volt circuit

Wall switch

GFCI receptacle

Receptacle

Electric meter

Water heater on separate 240-volt circuit

Service panel

Clothes dryer on separate 120/240-volt circuit

■ **Know your circuits:** *power runs through the breaker box via cables to individual circuits that often service multiple fixtures, outlets, and switches.*

TYPES OF WIRE

Electricity is transmitted around the home through different sized wires, which are rated by load capacity according to the American Wire Gauge system. These ratings determine the correct use for any size wire. The wires are wrapped in colored plastic coatings that show their function: red and black are "hot" wires, carrying current under load; white is neutral, returning the current without load back to source; green is a ground; and bare copper is also a ground.

ARMOURED

WIRES

WIRE GAUGE	APPLICATION
#6 (60 amps/240 volts)	Extra-heavy loads, e.g., furnaces, central air conditioning units.
# 8 (40 amps/240 volts)	Heavy loads, e.g., electric ranges.
# 10 (30 amps/240 volts)	Medium-to-heavy loads, e.g., electric washers and dryers.
# 12 (20 amps/120 volts)	Medium loads, e.g., convection ovens and microwave ovens.
# 14 (15 amps/120 volts)	Commonly used for plug outlets and wired-in lighting.
# 16	Mainly confined to extension cords or lamp wiring.
# 18 and up	Very light loads, e.g., thermostats.

TYPES OF CIRCUIT CABLE

Wires are run with others of the same size in circuit cables that are designated by the gauge and number of wires they contain, not counting the ground (e.g., "# 14/2"). There are different types of cable for different circumstances.

- **Armored cable (BX):** wires are run through a coiled metal tube, which also acts as the ground. Used both outside and inside, for example, in basement junction boxes.
- **Non-metallic cable:** older homes may have NM cable covered with a rubber and fabric sleeve, usually without a ground. Modern non-metallic cables enclose a ground, a live, and a neutral wire in a vinyl sleeve.
- **Knob and Tube:** wires are covered in a light sheath of rubber and fabric with porcelain insulating wheel brackets. This type of cable was used for a time around World War II, but is now obsolete and should be replaced.

Working with circuits

ANY GIVEN CIRCUIT IN THE HOME may route power through several different outlet receptacles, switches, and light fixtures. The trick is to identify where the unit falls in the circuit, and what it must do.

Switches and receptacles

Although you may want to wire in features like a doorbell or appliances such as a dishwasher, you'll most commonly be dealing with plug outlet receptacles, switches, and light fixtures. There are different types of outlet receptacles: your home may contain a mixture, depending on how old it is, and on which receptacles have been updated. You may also find a variety of light switches, the most common of which are:

- ●*Single pole:* basic switch for light or power; has two terminals.
- ●*Three-way:* used in pairs to control lights from different locations; has three terminals, one of which is darker than the others.
- ●*Four-way:* used between 3-way switches to control lights from three or more locations; has two brass and two copper terminals.
  - ●**Pilot light:** single pole switch with a built-in light, to indicate location in the dark.
- ●**Double:** controls two fixtures or outlets from the same location.
- ●**Specialty:** includes timer switches and motion sensor switches.

DEFINITION

Single-pole *are the basic switches used to control a light or appliance from one location.* **Three-way** *switches allow control of a light fixture from two locations.* **Four-way** *switches provide control for three or more locations.*

CHOOSING RECEPTACLES

If your house is 15 years or older, you will likely find receptacles with only two slots, missing the third ground hole. These are basic polarized receptacles and are generally no longer used. Chances are, they don't meet code in your area, so consider upgrading your receptacle.

a **Grounded**

Grounded through the rounded third hole; these days, most codes require this type of receptacle as a bare minimum.

b **20-amp**

This is a grounded receptacle with a T-shaped slot for use with larger 20-amp appliances.

Wiring 3-way wall switches

Where two switches control a single light, a pair of 3-way switches are wired into the circuit. These switches may either be wired into the middle of the circuit, or at the end of circuit. Always turn off the main power before wiring in the switches.

■ **In the middle of the circuit**, *connect the black wire from the 2-wire cable to the darker (common) terminal. Connect the black and red wires from the 3-wire cable to the traveler screw terminals. Attach copper grounds to the box and use a wire nut to join the white neutral wires.*

■ **At the end of the circuit**, *the cable entering the box should be a 3-wire plus ground. Connect the black wire to the darker (common) terminal, and connect the red and white wires to the traveler screw terminals. Connect the copper ground wire to the electrical box.*

TESTING CONTINUITY

When a light switch does not operate, the first step is to test the switch. Always test continuity with the main electrical supply turned off. Use a lighted continuity tester, or a more versatile multitester shown here. Start by switching it to the ohm setting.

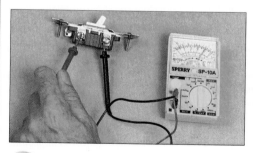

a **Single pole**

Place the probe on one terminal and the clip on the other. The needle should move from infinity to zero (on) if the switch is working.

b **3-way switch**

Put the clip on the darker terminal, the probe on the others, in turn. Flip the switch, and the needle should move as with the single pole.

Outdoor circuits

OUTDOOR LIGHTS AND OUTLETS make any patio, porch, or deck more accessible and usable. Exterior electrical circuits are wired much like internal circuits, but the cabling is different. Regardless of the outdoor wiring project, you should always check local building codes before beginning.

Wiring outdoors

Outlets and fixtures for use outdoors must be weatherproof: never use ones intended for interior use. The wiring also needs to be better protected than interior cable. If an outdoor fixture is wired through the inside of the house, such as a wall cavity, you can use nonmetallic cable. But any cable that runs outdoors above ground must be in either metallic or plastic conduit, and cable that is buried must be approved waterproof conduit, such as underground feeder (UF) or thermoplastic wet (TW).

Cable running underground must be rated for underground use and should be buried at least 18 inches deep. Some existing outdoor systems employ armored cable, which is still acceptable in many building codes.

INSTALLING LOW VOLTAGE LIGHTING

Low-voltage lighting is much easier to install and is often used to light a driveway or path. Low-voltage lights are wired to a transformer plugged directly into an outdoor receptacle. The cables are buried just a few inches under the ground.

1 Position lights

Put stake lights in the ground; post lights should be mounted on decking or wood posts.

2 Bury lines

Lay out the lines. Dig shallow ditches 2–3 inches deep, lay the lines, and cover with soil.

3 Connect source

With the power off, connect the lights to the transformer box. Plug in transformer and test.

A basic outdoor circuit

The circuit below shows a typical outdoor installation, incorporating a GFCI receptacle and floodlights to illuminate a deck..

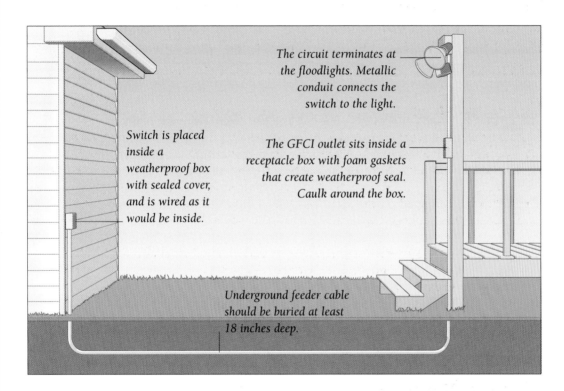

The circuit terminates at the floodlights. Metallic conduit connects the switch to the light.

Switch is placed inside a weatherproof box with sealed cover, and is wired as it would be inside.

The GFCI outlet sits inside a receptacle box with foam gaskets that create weatherproof seal. Caulk around the box.

Underground feeder cable should be buried at least 18 inches deep.

The circuit is created by running a power cable patched into an existing household circuit through a wall to an outdoor GFCI receptacle.

From there, the circuit is routed through approved, weatherproof underground feeder cable to the deck. It is then run through metallic conduit up the side of the deck, through a switch, and on to the security floodlights.

Motion sensor lights and standard floodlights are adjustable. But be a good neighbor and check that the lights don't point at someone else's windows when they're on!

■ **Basic floodlights** *can be operated by a switch or timer (top); motion and heat-sensing lights (bottom) use microwave or infrared detectors.*

Troubleshooting

WHEN AN ELECTRICAL FIXTURE, *outlet, or appliance doesn't work,*
do some detective work before the sparks start flying. Approach the job logically,
and you should be able to pin down the problem in no time. But if the same fuse
blows twice in quick succession, it's time to call an electrician.

What to do when the power goes off

1 **Is the power off everywhere in the house?** If it is, you've probably suffered a power outage. A phone call to your neighbors should confirm this. The next place to check is the main fuse or breaker for the house.

2 **Is the power off on one circuit only?** Confirm this by testing other receptacles or lights on the same circuit. If the answer is "yes," check the fuse or circuit breaker for the circuit in the breaker box. Before you replace/reset, investigate the cause:
- Have you just rewired something? If you have, this is almost certainly the cause of the problem.
- Have you just switched on an appliance with a faulty cord or plug?
  Do you have a multiple-outlet "octopus" plug-in attachment that is overloaded with plugs?
- Are you using a faulty or old appliance?
- Is the light switch, fixture, or receptacle damaged in any way?
- Is there moisture anywhere near the switch or appliance that could have caused the circuit to blow?
- Is there an abnormally heavy load – for example a high-wattage fan-heater?

3 **Is the problem confined to one receptacle?** If so, plug the appliance or lamp into another outlet. If the problem persists, it is with the appliance and is most likely a damaged cord. If the problem is at the receptacle, check that the outlet faceplate isn't cracked or otherwise damaged. If it seems sound, remove the faceplate and check that the cables have not become detached from the terminals.

4 **Is the problem with a single light fixture?** If so, switch off the supply and unscrew the fixture. If the wires are packed too tightly in the electrical box, or within the fixture mounting base itself, they may be short circuiting, or pulling free of the terminals. In older homes, the wire may be crimping or failing due to age and cracking. Do not try a simple fix with electrical tape. If the circuit wires for the fixture are damaged or so old as to be faulty, they can present a dangerous situation if they are not fixed.

Don't take chances!

Safety must be the first consideration in working with any household wiring – inside or out. First and foremost, check that the ground wire for the household system is connected to the cold water main supply, including any jumper wires necessary to jump plastic segments or the water meter. And any time you install or replace switches, receptacles, or fixtures, be sure that the wiring is contained within a proper size electrical box, and that wires are joined with wire nuts rather than electrical tape.

Always wear rubber-soled shoes when doing electrical work, and if you need to use a ladder, make sure it is fiberglass or wood, not metal. Be careful to replace a fuse with the same amperage fuse, or the circuit may overload. And lastly, be sure than any electrical switches, devices, or other components are UL approved.

Trivia...

The author's only experience of an electric shock was a bad one. After removing some kitchen cabinets, I found what looked like an old power cable buried in the wall. I already had a stovetop wired in, so I assumed the old cable was dead; it wasn't, but I could have been!

A simple summary

✓ Always switch off at the main power supply before doing any work on your home's electrical system. All the components that you use should be UL approved, and you should check local codes before tackling any electrical projects.

✓ Don't overload a power circuit with too many receptacles, fixtures or appliances. If you are in any doubt about the proper load for a given circuit, consult an electrician.

✓ Devices such as central air conditioning units often require their own circuits, directly wired from the breaker box.

✓ Use the appropriate receptacle boxes, weatherproof switches, metallic conduit, and feeder cable for all outdoor work.

✓ When you have a problem with a fixture, or outlet, always check the simplest explanation first, such as the fuse or breaker has blown or been tripped.

## Chapter 23

Electrical Jobs

S O NOW THAT YOU KNOW HOW YOUR ELECTRICAL SYSTEM WORKS, it's time to put the theory into practice. Always make sure the main power supply is switched off before you tamper with the wiring in any way.

In this chapter...

✓ Light fixtures and switches

✓ Installing fluorescent lights

✓ Installing track lighting

✓ Adding outlet receptacles

✓ High- and low-voltage jobs

✓ Installing fans

✓ Outdoor wiring

✓ Garage door openers

WIRED-IN LIGHT FIXTURES BRIGHTEN A ROOM IN MORE WAYS THAN ONE

Light fixtures and switches

NEW INCANDESCENT LIGHTING FIXTURES can supply a wealth of light and add a whole new look to a room, but they must be properly wired and supported to prevent any potential problems.

How ceiling lights are supported

A replacement light fitting must be (1) securely fixed to the ceiling by a mounting strap in the electrical box and (2) wired within an approved ceiling box. The trouble with existing light fixture mounting plates is that they are often simply screwed to a plaster ceiling or partly into a joist, neither of which meets code.

When removing a hanging light, mark the fixture wires for live and neutral — the connections are not always clearly coded.

Ideally, the old fixture will be wired through an approved electrical box, with proper supports to nearby joists. If it isn't, you will need to install a new electrical box to meet code. For large chandeliers, you may need to provide support beyond the mounting strap for the electrical box. There are many different support attachments for electrical boxes, including bar hanger brackets that fit joist to joist, boxes with mounting flanges to screw directly to studs or joists, and boxes that screw directly into joists. You may also decide to use a plastic self-supporting box for use in locations without a nearby joist. These are simply pushed up through a hole made in the ceiling, and are supported by tabs on the box body. Regardless of the box you choose, always check local codes for applicability.

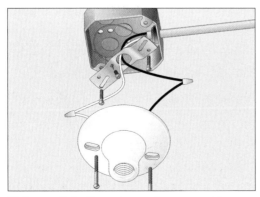

■ **A new light fixture** *must be supported by a mounting strap with a grounding screw.*

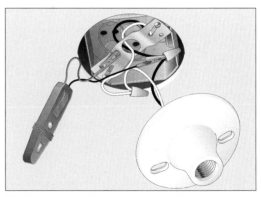

■ **Always test for power** *by touching one tester probe to ground and the other to each wire.*

Installing recessed lighting

Recessed lighting is more problematic than flush fit or hanging lighting, because the light creates a lot of heat inside the canister, creating the potential for melting wiring or causing a fire. Follow code requirements when installing recessed fixtures, and always be sure that they are properly supported. The fixture should be attached to a separate wire connection box connected to the cannister with armored cable. Make sure that insulation batts are cut so that all insulation is at least 3 inches away from the light cannister. The cannister should also be free of any other impediments, ensuring it's not touching any other surface. It's even more important than with other lighting that the bulbs used do not exceed the fixture manufacturer's requirements for maximum wattage.

INTERNET

www.necdirect.com

If you're planning on doing a lot of electrical work, order the National Electrical Code handbook from this site, or check the resources link.

CHANGING A CEILING LIGHT

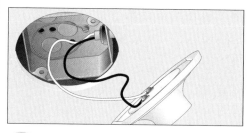

1 **Remove old fixture**

Switch off the main power supply and unscrew the mounting plate of the old fixture. Test for power, then remove wires.

2 **Install new mounting strap**

If the electrical box is missing a mounting strap, install the one that comes with the light fixture, ensuring that the ground wire screw is attached.

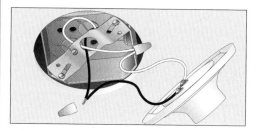

3 **Connect wires**

Use wire nuts to connect white to white and black to black on the fixture. Pigtail the copper ground to the grounding screw.

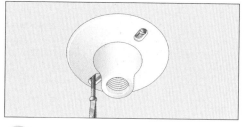

4 **Mount fixture**

Screw the base to the mounting strap and screw in a bulb with a wattage rating no greater than the rating for the fixture. Turn the power on.

Changing light switches

There are many reasons to install a new switch: to make a straight replacement for a damaged or old-fashioned unit, for a change in style, to convert to a dimmer, or even to use a specialized switch. Whatever the reason, if you take care to label all the wires, you can't go far wrong.

Buying considerations

If you are planning to make a straight replacement, just buy a comparable switch, but if you want to replace one switch with another type, you may have to buy a new faceplate to match. Think through your needs carefully before buying.

Is it just a simple single-pole switch you want, or would it make sense to wire in a three-way switch to control a light from two locations? Perhaps you want to be able to control a light from more locations with a four-way switch. Do you need a timer switch? Do you need an illuminated switch to make it easy to find in the dark? There's a switch for almost every need.

If you are going to install a new switch that will require more wiring than that which was in the box before, you may have to replace the electrical box with a larger type.

Never cram wires into a box; they should always have room enough to sit comfortably in the box.

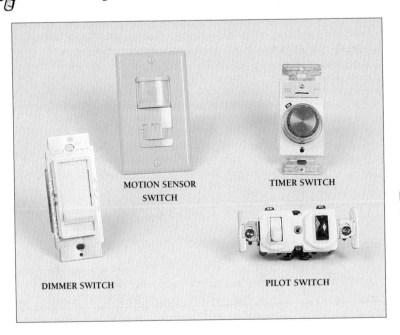

MOTION SENSOR
SWITCH

TIMER SWITCH

DIMMER SWITCH

PILOT SWITCH

■ **Specialty switches** *include motion sensor switches, timer switches, dimmer switches, pilot switches, and programmable switches – a highly effective security device!*

Which switch?

Single-pole switches are the most common, and are therefore the ones that most often need to be replaced. Older mercury switches can last decades, but standard toggle switches wear out much quicker than that. Whenever you need to replace a single-pole switch, consider whether another type of switch would better suit your needs.

Dimmer switches offer more flexibility in controlling lighting and come in a range of styles; some can even be installed as three-way switches. In addition to the standard "button" dimmer, you can buy slide dimmers with backlit faceplates and toggle dimmers that look like standard switches.

Specialized switches are also available. For security, you might want to consider either a timer switch or a programmable switch. Timers activate lights or fixtures at preset intervals, making them useful for outdoor lighting. Programmable switches have more flexibility, and can turn lights on or off on a random basis, making it seem as if someone is always home. Motion sensor switches are another option. They can be set on automatic to turn a light on when a person or pet passes the switch, and can also be used as a manual switch. Automatic switches work in much the same way, allowing you to turn on a light with a wave of your hand. All of these switches are as easy to install as a three- or four-way switch, and can be wired into the middle or end of a circuit.

INSTALLING A DIMMER SWITCH

Installing a dimmer switch is relatively easy. Wiring in a three-way dimmer is slightly more complicated, but is done in the same way as a three-way toggle switch.

1 **Remove old switch**

Turn the power off and remove the old switch, marking wires if they are not color coded.

2 **Wire in dimmer**

Use wire nuts to connect the live and neutral wires to the dimmer wires.

3 **Test and finish**

Test the switch, turn power off again, and attach the switch and faceplate.

Installing fluorescent lights

FLUORESCENT LIGHTING WAS ONCE the illumination of choice for commercial installations, but these days it offers a wealth of possibilities for every room in the house.

Choose by location

Perhaps the most common type of fluorescent light for the home is the "strip" light frequently used for workspaces from the undercabinet kitchen fixture to the hanging garage shop light. But the styles available go far beyond those humble uses. Decorative fluorescent fixtures include framed and shaped styles that are appropriate for a wide range of decors. For tight spaces, use a "circleline" fixture with a circular bulb. Of course, you can still opt for the unobtrusive recessed fixtures for total coverage, such as in the center of a kitchen or den. Regardless of the fixture, you'll benefit from the long life of a fluorescent tube – up to ten times greater than a standard light bulb.

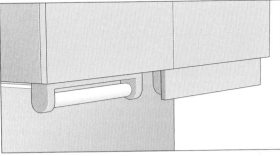

■ **In a kitchen,** *an undercabinet fluorescent fixture may have its own switch and can be wired directly into a junction box.*

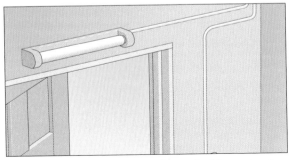

■ **In a walk-in closet,** *it may be preferable to wire the light source through a switch in the circuit.*

Simple construction

Fluorescent fixtures have few components to go wrong, making them some of the most trouble-free lighting fixtures for the home. The tube itself is the most likely part to fail, but this can be easily slid out and replaced. The body of the fixture contains the wiring and ballast, a special transformer that routes power to the sockets at either end. Occasionally, the ballast will fail. This is most apparent if the light flickers constantly and the ballast leaks fluid or hums. Replacing the

Installing an Undercabinet Fixture

1 Wiring

Either run a connection to the closest electrical box or, if you are installing a separate switch, install the switch box near the light.

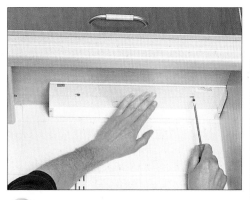

2 Attach the fixture

Run the wiring for the fixture and screw it to the underside of the cabinet, after checking that the bottom of the cabinet will support the light.

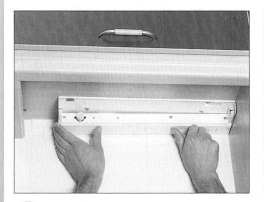

3 Connect and check

Close up the electrical box or switch and install the fluorescent bulb in the fixture. Turn the power on and check that the light works.

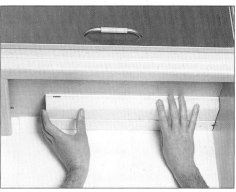

4 Check and finish

Leave the light on for a while and check that it does not hum, and that no flickering occurs. Clip the diffuser into place.

ballast is an option unless the expense would be greater than buying a whole new fixture. Diffuser covers – the glass or plastic that covers the tube – come in a wide range of styles and soften the rather harsh white light of the tube. Some older units may contain a small plug-like device known as a starter. Starters are not expensive, so it makes sense that these should be replaced whenever the bulb is replaced.

Installing track lighting

TRACK LIGHTING is sleek and attractive, with the added benefit of adjustability. Fairly simple to install, this form of incandescent lighting offers you the chance to spotlight whatever you want to in a room.

A flexible alternative

Track lighting is a simple alternative that allows you to focus the light exactly where you want it to go. Directional spotlights snap into electric tracks, and can be swiveled in any direction and slid to any point on the track. This type of lighting is excellent for focusing on one area, such as the art on a living room wall, or for providing work light in areas such as a kitchen. Home centers and lighting stores offer a wide range of styles, from modest beige "cans" to high-tech, black and steel halogen fixtures. The most important consideration, however, is the light you need.

Don't handle low-voltage tungsten halogen bulbs directly with your fingers, or you'll deposit grease which could cause the bulb to blow. Avoid turning low-voltage lights on and off too often, as this, too, can dramatically shorten bulb life.

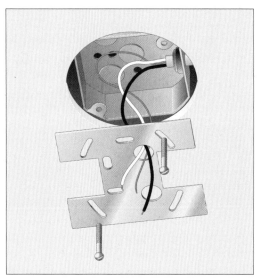

■ **Wire tracks** *into existing junction boxes used by previous light fixtures, or use the same system with a new electrical box.*

No-fuss installation

Installing track lighting takes more time and patience than expertise. The primary track is powered by an adapter that is usually wired into the junction box used by an older light fixture. The track is attached right over the box with a plate, and this is ultimately covered by the track cover. You can run tracks in a variety of layouts – including "L" shapes and crosses – using adapters supplied by the manufacturer. Ends are capped with "dead ends"; be sure to plan and buy all the pieces you'll need at one time. Tracks are screwed into joists whenever possible, or attached to the ceiling with toggle bolts. Be very careful in determining layouts: once installed, you'll find that toggle bolts are nearly impossible to remove.

INSTALLING TRACK LIGHTING

Installing track lighting is relatively easy and provides a flexible lighting solution.

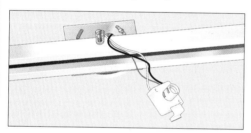

1 Tapping the power

With the power off, remove existing fixture and wire in the adapter. Attach the mounting plate or bracket and screw the primary track to it.

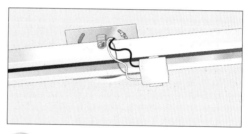

2 Planning layout

Mark the screw holes with a pencil and hold up adjoining pieces of track, if any, to determine the layout and check clearances.

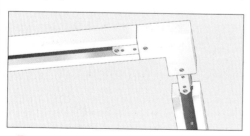

3 Installing track

Drill the holes for the screws or toggle bolts. Attach the first track and connect other tracks with appropriate connectors.

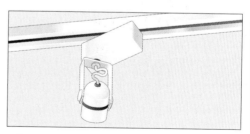

4 Final connection

Insert the adapter into the track, clicking it into place. Attach the cover over the junction box and adapter.

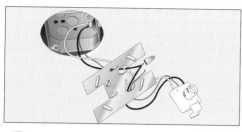

5 Final assembly

Connect the dead ends to the ends of all track runs and snap lights into place, spaced evenly along the tracks.

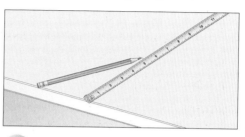

6 Power up and adjust

Install the bulbs if you haven't already done so, turn the main power on, and adjust the lights so they are pointed where you want the light.

Adding outlet receptacles

REPLACING A PLUG RECEPTACLE is a simple procedure regardless of where in the circuit the receptacle falls. Adding a new receptacle is more involved, but the wiring principles are the same.

A simple replacement

You'll need to replace an outlet receptacle for one of two reasons: to update a receptacle that doesn't meet code or isn't safe, or to remedy a problem. Modern codes call for GFCI receptacles in high risk areas such as the kitchen and bathroom, and in older receptacles that have no means of grounding. Older ceramic or unpolarized receptacles should also be replaced to prevent dangerous situations. Replace receptacles with newer units of the same wattage and amperage rating, and replace two-slot unpolarized receptacles with polarized two- or three-slot types.

Be aware that adding a new receptacle – especially when it involves running new cable – may require a building permit. Contact your local zoning board or building department to determine if you need permission before tackling your project.

Wiring receptacles

Receptacles are wired differently if they are at the middle or the end of a run.

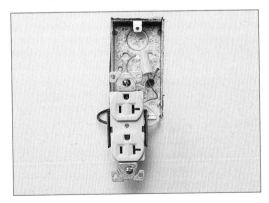

a **End-of-run receptacle**

One cable enters the box with two leads and a ground. Ground is pigtailed to box and receptacle and white wire to silver, black (hot) to brass screw.

b **Middle-of-run receptacle**

Two cables enter the box. Grounding wires are pigtailed together, with box and receptacle grounds, both blacks to brass (hot), and white wires to silver.

INSTALLING A GFCI RECEPTACLE

The most common usage for the GFCI is to protect a single outlet, described below.

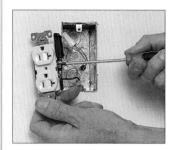

1 **Remove old**

Turn off the power and remove the old receptacle. Pigtail the white neutral wires and connect to terminal marked "white."

2 **Connect power**

Pigtail black hot wires, and connect to terminal marked "hot line." Connect ground to ground terminal.

3 **Replace and test**

Install the GFCI receptacle in the box, turn the power on, and test according to the manufacturer's instructions.

A complicated addition

Adding a new receptacle can be a large project, especially if you need to run cable to the new electrical box, but the convenience of a more accessible plug outlet may be worth the effort. However, if you're not sure where the circuit runs in relation to where you want to put the socket, consult an electrician. It's easiest to wire in an end-of-run receptacle, although you may have to install a middle-of-run box based on where you want the outlet. After running cable, follow the wiring instructions for replacing a receptacle (see opposite).

Running cable

Running cable is not complicated, but it is best done with two people. Decide what source you need for the connection (usually the closest receptacle), then make the opening for the new box. Run the cable from the host by the most direct route. This may mean drilling access holes in bottom plates or studs, and you'll need access to walls and to the basement. Feed the cable through walls and other openings by taping the cable to fish tape and using the fish tape to draw the cable through the opening. Cable run along joists should be secured to the joist with cable staples attached about every 3 feet. If you have to run across joists, drill holes for the cable, rather than stapling to the edges, and attach metal guards to prevent anyone from hammering or drilling into the joist and through the cable. Feed cable to ceiling junction boxes by cutting a pilot hole at the top of the wall, and feeding up through the existing box to the ceiling box.

High- and low-voltage jobs

WIRING HIGH-VOLTAGE APPLIANCES *such as central air-conditioning units and electric ranges is not as simple as other wiring projects, and is potentially more dangerous. Unless you feel well equipped to handle the challenge, leave it to an electrician. Servicing simple fixtures such as doorbells and low-voltage circuits is far less dangerous. These are simple circuits, presenting only moderate risk.*

A case for caution

Although many large appliances such as dishwashers and clothes dryers are wired direct to their own breaker, an outlet for a high-capacity window air conditioner is a good project to tackle.

The codes will be less complex and the wiring itself is less complicated. However, before you start any high-voltage wiring project, consult your local building authority to determine what the relevant codes are and if they require a licensed electrician to perform the work. Always follow the building department's guidelines.

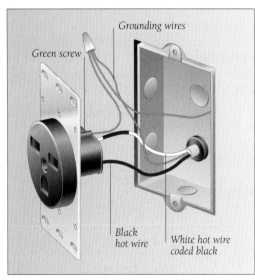

50 AMP RECEPTACLE

30 AMP RECEPTACLE

■ **Wire a 240-volt window air** *conditioner direct to a 240-volt breaker. White and black run from the breaker to the receptacle's traveler terminals; ground is pigtailed to green screw.*

■ **High-voltage receptacle** *prong configurations vary, depending on how many amps they are rated for. From left to right: a 30 amp, and a 50 amp receptacle.*

Different high-voltage appliances use different receptacles, so choose the appropriate receptacle for the unit you're wiring in. The receptacle should come with its own box and must be UL approved. Use the appropriate gauge wire, matching the receptacle rating to the wire number: a #8 for a 40 amp or greater, #10 for a 30 amp, and #12 for 20 amp. Any receptacle rated 30 amps or greater should be wired with a four-wire cable.

Low-voltage electrical fixtures

Low-voltage systems power small but handy features of the home, ranging from the front doorbell, to the heating and cooling thermostats and some modest lighting systems. Any fixture on a low-voltage system is powered by a small transformer that is wired into an electrical box and attached to the side of the box. Transformers sometimes give out, but this is no big deal – they are one of the easier electrical elements to replace. Simply turn the power off, disconnect the low-voltage wires, then the connections in the electrical box, replace with a matching transformer, and rewire.

One of the most common low-voltage upgrades is to replace an older thermostat with a programmable model. Like all low-voltage projects this is a basic task that requires little skill. Start by turning off the power and removing the coverplate of the old thermostat. Disconnect and mark the wires with the labels identifying the screw terminal locations they were taken from. Remove the old unit, screw on the new unit, and reattach the wires to the manufacturer's instructions. All that's left to do is program the unit for the most efficient use of your heating and cooling system.

TROUBLESHOOTING A DOORBELL

There are three main areas where your doorbell is likely to go wrong: the switch, the wires, or the transformer.

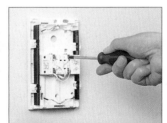

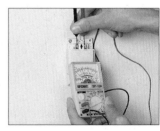

a **Check switch**

Check the switch wire connections, then remove and check continuity.

b **Wire inspection**

Inspect all the wires at the chimes and down to the transformer.

c **Test transformer**

Use a voltmeter to check that the transformer registers within 1 or 2 volts of rating.

Installing fans

WIRED-IN HOUSE FANS *not only provide comfort and convenience, they clear moisture and odors from the living space.*

Many applications

Fans can be installed in many locations around the house, from a bathroom, to the attic, to the fan in a range hood over your stove. Some, like a bathroom vent fan that stops condensation from gathering, are meant for a specific purpose, while others, such as a whole-house fan, provide general benefits.

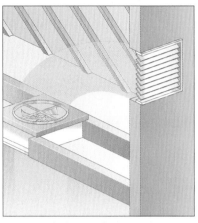

■ **A whole-house fan** *provides comfort on a par with central air conditioning, at a much lower cost.*

A whole-house fan is a great investment that offers all the cooling many houses will ever need. Installed in an attic over a louvered opening in a hall ceiling, the powerful fan draws heat out of the living space into the attic. Some fans require cutting a joist for installation, but many modern fans are designed to sit centered atop a joist, making them easy to install. A whole-house fan should have an automatic cutoff feature in the event it overheats and a fire safety device that closes the louvers and shuts off the fan in the case of fire. Always use a fan-rated, variable speed switch.

INSTALLING A WHOLE-HOUSE FAN

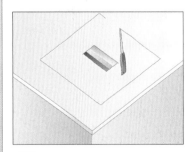

1 **Mark hole**

Mark and cut the hole in a hall ceiling, centered on an attic joist. Use the manufacturer's measurements to size the hole.

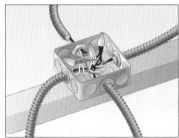

2 **Wiring for fan**

Wire the fan power line into a junction box with the power off. Use armored cable and check that the fan won't overload the circuit.

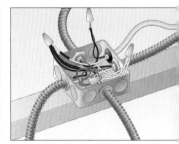

3 **Wire box for switch**

Using two-wire NM cable, wire the switch into the junction following the manufacturer's instructions and safe practices.

Bathroom venting

In small bathrooms or those without windows, a moisture vent is essential to stop excess condensation from causing problems such as mold and mildew growth. Bathrooms are best vented directly through the wall to the outside, but in some cases this is not possible. Alternatively, you can always connect the fan to a roof vent with ducting.

Buy fans that are rated for the space you are looking to vent. An oversize fan may pull air through the space better but it will use more electricity and may also be noisier than a smaller unit!

Ceiling fans

Ducting is also used when you are installing a ceiling fan (some come with lights). Ceiling fans can be vented through a duct to the outside wall or to a roof vent – whichever is most convenient. Choose between a rigid duct, which is best for straight runs, or a flexible duct tube, which is better for snaking through attic and ceiling cavities. Regardless of the type of duct you choose, try to keep the vent as close as possible to the fan. The longer the distance between the two, the weaker the pulling power of the fan. If you must duct over 5 feet, you may need a fan with a higher *cfm (cubic feet per minute) rating* for a larger space.

> **DEFINITION**
>
> *The* **cfm (cubic feet per minute) rating** *is a measure of how much air the fan will move through a space. Follow the manufacturer's recommendations to match square footage and fan cfm.*

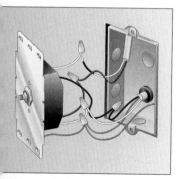

4 **Run cable to switch**

Use fish tape to run the cable down through a hallway wall. Install an electrical box for the switch and run cable into it.

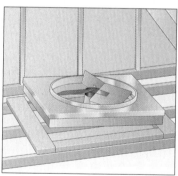

5 **Install fan**

Frame the fan and install on the joists following the supplied instructions. Ensure that it is level and secure.

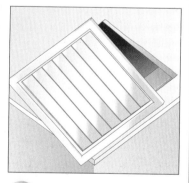

6 **Finish up**

Wire the switch in the new electrical box according to the manufacturer's instructions. Install louvers and test.

Outdoor wiring

WIRING FIXTURES into an outdoor circuit is similar to wiring them inside, except that you must use components specified for exterior use.

Installing outdoor lighting

One of the most basic and useful outdoor wiring projects is installing lighting. Low-voltage "stake" lights are easy to install, with a transformer that plugs into an outdoor receptacle. But for more effective coverage, you can wire in a flood light or security light directly into an exterior circuit. The lights are wired according to manufacturer's directions, much like interior lights. You can wire a motion sensor light on the side of a house using cable routed through metal conduit and wired into a weatherproof junction box or receptacle. A back porch door light can be wired directly into the house with NM cable, running to a switch on the inside. Just be sure the exterior fixture is weatherproof.

■ **A security light** *with motion sensors is a simple yet effective security measure.*

OUTDOOR ELECTRICAL

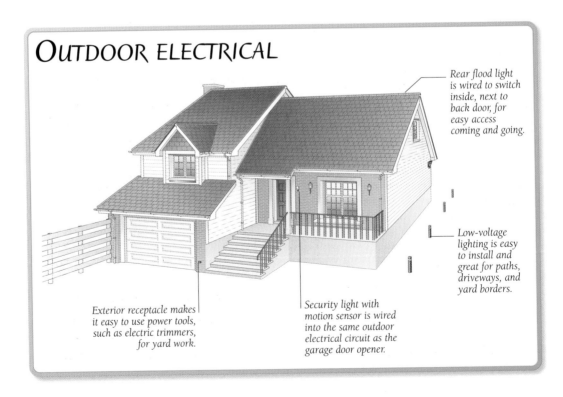

Rear flood light is wired to switch inside, next to back door, for easy access coming and going.

Low-voltage lighting is easy to install and great for paths, driveways, and yard borders.

Exterior receptacle makes it easy to use power tools, such as electric trimmers, for yard work.

Security light with motion sensor is wired into the same outdoor electrical circuit as the garage door opener.

Exterior receptacles

The steps for wiring exterior receptacles aren't much different from those for wiring inside the house. However, most codes do specify that exterior receptacles must be GFCI outlets. And they should always have a cover. If you have an older receptacle without one, update it.

Before running an underground feeder or conduit, check with your local utility about the location of any underground lines in your yard. One call can prevent a disaster!

To run an electrical line out to a deck – to service post lights, for instance – use an extension ring on an existing outdoor receptacle. This fixture allows you to run a conduit extension off the receptacle. As with other projects, it is essential to check the local building codes. Do not assume the pre-existing conduit meets code; codes are regularly updated. For example, in some areas it is acceptable to run underground feeder cable by itself, as long you have dug the tranch deep enough.

Many other localities require that the cable be run inside a weatherproof metal or plastic conduit (a good idea in any case!) The goal is that the conduit be completely watertight – use threaded fittings and seals where necessary. Lastly, if you don't need another outdoor receptacle, consider running the interior service line out through an LB fitting – a simple enclosure installed on the side of the house for routing the cable out through conduit.

WIRING OUTDOOR RECEPTACLES

1 **Inside out**

Turn power off and knock out a hole in the back of interior receptacle. Drill through to the outside. Wire cable for the new receptacle.

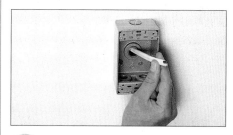

2 **Install exterior electrical box**

Use a keyhole saw to make an opening for box, and install an exterior-rated electrical box. Pull the cable into the box.

3 **Wire and attach faceplate cover**

Wire the exterior GFCI receptacle and install with the gasket in place, and attach the cover if not attached. Turn the power on.

Garage door openers

AN ELECTRIC GARAGE door opener is one of the great conveniences available to the homeowner, and installing one is an excellent weekend do-it-yourself project. The latest kits have compact remote units and can be adapted to fit just about any model of overhead door.

Choosing a system

Garage door opener kits are available for both roll-up and tilt-up doors. Regardless of the type of door, you'll want one with a ½ hp motor – smaller motors have shorter lifespans. Choose from three types of motors: chain driven (the most popular), screw, or belt drive. Chain drive is the fastest and noisiest; screws are smooth and slow, and belt drives are quiet and smooth, but not as fast as chain drive. Laws require that all new openers be sold with two types of a safety devices: an automatic "contact reverse" system, whereby if the door closes on an object it automatically reverses to open; and a set of infrared sensors that detect if anyone is in the path of the door, reversing it immediately. All openers also include manual override features, so that you can disengage the door in case of an emergency, or if the power goes out. Openers are sold with explicit directions that clearly outline installation. It's wise to have a helper for lifting and securing the motor. Brackets and supports are usually predrilled for easy adjustment. The door must clear the garage joists or ceiling by at least 2–3 inches, and the motor and track must be securely mounted to cleats or bracing between joists.

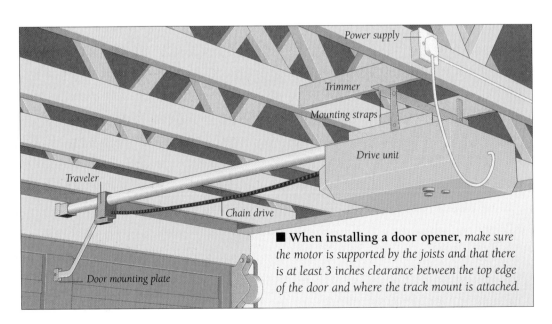

Power supply

Trimmer

Mounting straps

Drive unit

Traveler

Chain drive

Door mounting plate

■ **When installing a door opener,** *make sure the motor is supported by the joists and that there is at least 3 inches clearance between the top edge of the door and where the track mount is attached.*

Wiring the door

Wiring for a garage door opener is fairly basic. Although older opener motors were sometimes wired directly into a junction box, modern units plug into a 120-volt outlet (never into an extension cord). Wires for the inside pushbutton switch and infrared sensors are supplied with the unit, and should be run the most direct route to the terminal connections on the motor unit. Exterior keypads are sometimes wired directly to the opener from their location, although many new models include battery operated keypads. As an option, the opener can be wired to an exterior light, so that the light comes on when the opener operates.

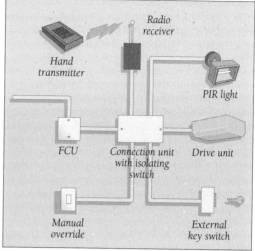

Hand transmitter

Radio receiver

PIR light

FCU

Connection unit with isolating switch

Drive unit

Manual override

External key switch

■ **The wiring layout** *for an automatic opener is relatively simple. All connections except for the keypad run to the motor unit.*

A simple summary

✓ When changing ceiling light fixtures, ensure that the light is connected through an approved box with the correct strap.

✓ When installing a dimmer switch, you may need to replace the existing box if the wires become too cramped.

✓ Undercabinet fluorescent fixtures are easy to install and useful.

✓ Track lighting provides a flexible lighting solution.

✓ In high-risk locations such as bathrooms and kitchens, always use GFCI receptacles.

✓ Low-voltage circuits, such as doorbells, are simple to service.

✓ Wired-in house fans provide comfort and clear moisture.

✓ Weatherproof components must be used for outdoor fixtures.

✓ Garage door openers are simple to wire and install.

More Resources

Professional Organizations

Even for someone with my experience, there are times when I have to call in the professionals. You may get by with finding contractors by word-of-mouth for small jobs, but when you need complex and potentially expensive work undertaken, do yourself a favor and get in touch with the relevant professional association. Many offer guarantees for potential contractors, as well as insurance and up-to-the-minute consumer advice. They may also be able to refer you to a state or local organization.

Air Conditioning Contractors of America
2800 Shirlington Road
Suite 300
Arlington, VA 22206
(703) 575-4477
www.acca.org

American Association of Woodturners
3200 Lexington Avenue
Shoreview, MN 55126
(651) 484-9094
www.rtpnet.org/aaw

American Institute of Architects
1735 New York Avenue NW
Washington, DC 20006
(800) AIA-3837
www.aia.org

American National Standards Institute
1819 L Street NW
Suite 600
Washington, DC 20036
(202) 293-8020
www.ansi.org

American Plastics Council
1300 Wilson Boulevard.
Suite 800
Arlington, VA 22209
(703) 253-0700
www.plastics.org

American Rental Association
1900 19th Street
Moline, IL 61265
(800) 334-2177
www.ararental.org

American Society of Gas Engineers
3223 East Scarborough Road
Cleveland Heights, OH 44118
(216) 932-2442
www.asge-nat.org

American Society of Home Inspectors
932 Lee Street
Suite 101
Des Plaines, IL 60016
(847) 759-2820,
www.ashi.com

American Solar Energy Society
2400 Central Avenue
Suite G-1
Boulder, CO 80301
(303) 443-3130
www.ases.org

American Wood Preservers Institute
2750 Prosperity Avenue
Suite 550
Fairfax, VA 22031
(703) 204-0500
www.preservedwood.com

Finishing Contractors Association
2000 L Street NW
Suite 200
Washington, DC 20036
(202) 530-5200
www.finishingcontractors.org

National Association of Home Builders of the US
1201 15th Street NW
Washington, DC 20005
(202) 822-0200
www.nahb.com

National Association of Waterproofing Contractors
25550 Chagrin Boulevard
Suite 403
Cleveland, OH 44122
(800) 245-NAWC
www.waterproofers.org

National Concrete Masonry Association
2302 Horse Pen Road
Herndon, VA 20171
(703) 713-1900
www.ncma.org

National Consumers League
1701 K Street NW #1200
Washington, DC 20006
(202) 835-3323
www.nclnet.org

National Electrical Contractors Association
3 Bethesda Metro Center
Suite 1100
Bethesda, MD 20814
(301) 657-3110
www.necanet.org

National Glass Association
8200 Greensboro Drive #302
McLean, VA 22102
(703) 442-4890
www.glass.org

National Kitchen and Bath Association
687 Willow Grove Street
Hackettstown, NJ 07840
(877) NKBA-PRO
www.nkba.org

National Roofing Contractors Association
10255 West Higgins Road
Suite 600
Rosemont, IL 60018
(847) 299-9070
www.nrca.net

National Wood Flooring Association
16388 Westwoods Business Park
Ellisville, MO 63021
(314) 391-5161/(800)422-4556
www.woodfloors.org

Painting and Decorating Contractors of America
3913 Old Lee Highway #33B
Fairfax, VA 22030
(703) 359-0826/(800) 332-7322
www.pdca.com

Plumbing Contractors of America
1385 Piccard Drive
Rockville, MD 20850
(301) 869-5800
www.mcaa.org/pca

Plumbing–Heating–Cooling Contractors Association
180 South Washington Street
PO Box 6808
Falls Church, VA 22040
(703)237-8100/(800)533-7694
www.naphcc.org

Security Industry Association
635 Slaters Lane
Suite 110
Alexandria, VA 22314
(703) 683-2075
www.siaonline.org

Internet and Magazines

The internet is now bubbling over with sites and electronic magazines dedicated to home improvements, as well as subscription offers for more established publications. The listings below are some that I have found to be particularly useful and which don't require payment to access their online information.

American Woodworker
Covers every aspect of woodworking, including cutting lists, tool advice and techniques from the experts. Site also includes tips and hints.
Order online or call (800) 491-7504
www.americanwoodworker.com

Better Homes and Gardens
Magazine and large online site with decorating tips and storage ideas for the home. Also covers gardening and entertaining and cookery hints.
Order online or call (800) 867-8628
www.electronichouse.com

DoItYourself.com
A massive site dedicated to all things covering the home. Supplies information on contractors, insurance, and home equity as well as detailed "how-to" info and home repairs advice.
www.doityourself.com

Electronic House
Site covering every aspect of home electronics. Also offers subscriptions to *Electronic House* magazine.
www.electronichouse.com

Family Handyman
Specializing in all areas of do-it-yourself home improvement. Site also includes tips and hints.
Order online or call (800) 491-7504
www.familyhandyman.com

homestore.com
Features hundreds of do-it-yourself projects together with equipment guides, decorating ideas, and real estate info.
homestore.com

ImproveNet
An extensive online guide to home improvements, featuring projects, advice, and free online quotes from contractors.
improvenet.com

Martha Stewart Living
Home lifestyle magazine.
Order online or call (800) 999-6518
www.marthastewart.com

Remodeling Online
Online magazine with ideas, plans, and projects for renovating the home.
One Thomas Circle NW
Suite 600
Washington, DC 20005
(202) 452-0800
www.remodeling.hw.net

Today's Homeowner
Site covering all areas of home improvement. Also includes information for *This Old House* magazine.
Order online or call (800) 898-7237
www.todayshomeowner.com

Books

With books covering every conceivable area of home improvements, the best starting point for the beginner is one of the several excellent general purpose publications. For more specific areas, try logging on to *www.amazon.com*, which provides an up-to-date guide to the latest releases, as well as featuring readers' reviews and comments.

The Big Book of Small Household Repairs: Your Goof-Proof Guide to Fixing Over 200 Annoying Breakdowns
Charles Wing, Rodale Press, 1999

Bob Vila's Complete Guide to Remodeling Your Home: Everything You Need to Know About Home Renovation from the #1 Home Improvement Expert
Bob Vila and Hugh Howard
Avon Books, 1999

Built-In Projects for the Home (Black & Decker Home Improvement Library)
Creative Publishing International, 1993

The Complete Idiot's Guide to Home Security
Tom Davidson et al., Alpha Books, 2001

Designing Your Gardens and Landscapes: 12 Simple Steps for Successful Planning
Janet MacUnovich, Storey Books, 2001

Drywall: Pro Tips for Hanging & Finishing
by John D. Wagner, Creative Homeowner Press, 1999

Easy Style: 300 Decorating Shortcuts
Linda Hallam (Editor), Better Homes & Gardens Books, 1998

Flooring Basics (Basic Series)
Rick Peters, Sterling Publications, 2000

Home & Garden Television's Complete Fix-It
Time Life Books, 2000

Home Lighting
Stacey Berman, Leisure Arts, 1998

Home Renovation Workbook: A Step-By-Step Planner for Creating the Home of Your Dreams
Jain Lemos, Chronicle Books, 2001

Measuring, Marking & Layout: A Builder's Guide
John Carroll, Taunton Press, 1998

Measure Twice, Cut Once: Lessons from a Master Carpenter
Norm Abram, Little Brown & Co., 1996

New Complete Do-It-Yourself Manual
Reader's Digest Adult, 1991

1001 Do-It-Yourself Hints & Tips: Tricks, Shortcuts, How-To's, and Other Great Ideas for Inside, Outside, and All Around Your House
Reader's Digest Adult, 1998

The Original Basement Waterproofing Handbook
Jack Masters, Master Jack Publishers, 1999

Popular Mechanics Home How-To
Albert Jackson et al., Hearst Books, 2000

Reader's Digest Complete DIY Manual
Reader's Digest, 1998

Working Alone: Tips & Techniques for Solo Building
John Carroll, Taunton Press, 1999

A Simple Glossary

ABS Type of plastic pipe used in drain-waste-vent pipes, cheaper and weaker than PVC.

Aerator Water-saving device installed in faucets and showerheads.

Aggregate Coarse stone, gravel, or similar additive used with cement to create concrete.

Ampere (amp) A measurement of the rate at which electricity flows through a circuit.

Alkyd paint The term used for oil-based paints, because most are now alkyd-based.

Anchor bolt Hefty bolt set into concrete to use as an attachment for supporting members or different types of hangers and supports.

Apron The trim piece beneath a window sill.

Armored cable (BX or greenfield) Wires run through a spiral, flexible conduit.

Auger A plumbing tool consisting of a reel and flexible metal cable used to clear stubborn clogs.

Backfill Loose soil, stone, gravel, or a mixture used to fill the space excavated around a foundation wall.

Backsplash A vertical section of tile, board, or other material that borders the rear of a countertop.

Ballcock The valve that controls the water supply for a toilet tank.

Balloon framing A type of construction whereby studs are run from the foundation to the roof, rather than from floor to ceiling.

Baluster A turned piece of wood installed as a support for a staircase handrail.

Balustrade All the pieces that make up the handrail construction on stairs, including the handrail itself, newel post, and balusters.

Batten A thin wood strip used to attach paneling or to cover joints in board siding.

Batter board Flexible wood board attached to stakes, and used as a level guide for strings defining foundations or laid surfaces.

Beam A thick, straight, heavy steel or wood member placed horizontally to help support a building's load.

Blind nailing A method of nailing a board through the edge to hide the nails.

Blocking Boards installed between studs, rafters, or other members to add strength and provide a fire stop.

Blow bag An expandable diaphragm that connects to a hose and is used to clear drains with pressure.

Branch line A pipe that connects fixtures to the central plumbing water supply.

Bridging Reinforcing braces in the shape of an X, placed between joists.

Brush comb A special tool used to remove paint from a brush.

BTU (British Thermal Unit) A measurement of heating power.

Butter To apply mortar to a brick or other masonry surface.

Butt joint The most basic woodworking joint, created by nailing the end of one board to the end edge of another.

Casing The trim around a door or window.

Carriage The notched boards that hold the rises and treads in older staircases, running parallel to the stringer.

Cement board A type of wall board made with cement, and used to finish walls in bathrooms for its water-resistant properties.

Chair rail Decorative wood molding installed horizontally 36 inches up from the floor.

Check valve A plumbing valve that allows the water to flow in only one direction.

Cleanout A large screw-type plug in the end of a drain line that allows for access for clearing clogs.

Closet flange Circular fitting at the top of a toilet drain, used as the base for the toilet.

Coaxial cable A special cable used to connect television jacks.

Collar beam A supporting member that connects two opposing rafters.

Column A vertical supporting member that can be made of wood, concrete or metal.

Composite lumber Wood members created by layering different types of wood or wood particles, or by forming under pressure wood pieces and additives.

Conduit Rigid plastic or metal tubing used to protect wires.

Control joint A scored line in concrete to relieve pressure and limit cracking.

Convectors Pipes with fins that transfer heat from the hot water or steam in the pipes to the air in a room.

Cope To cut a piece of molding to fit against the profile of another piece.

Corner trowel Trowel with an angle to seat joint tape and level compound in corners.

Crazing A problem in concrete where many minute cracks appear across the surface.

Crosscut Sawing across the grain of the wood.

Cripple stud Short vertical stud that is placed between the top plate and header or between a sill and bottom plate.

Dado A groove cut across a board.

Deadman A temporary T brace used to shore up the end of a supporting member while a ceiling panel is positioned.

Dedicated circuit A circuit–usually high voltage–that runs directly to one fixture or wired-in appliance and back to the service panel.

Deglosser Special chemical treatment used on gloss paint to make it appear matte.

Diverter valve The valve that switches water flow from your tub faucets to the showerhead.

Dragging The technique of drawing a brush through a thick coat of wet paint to achieve a decorative look.

Drip edge A piece of metal that is formed over the edge of roof sheathing to guide rain off the roof.

Drip cap A metal water barrier installed over a window to keep water from penetrating the wood frame.

Dry well A pit dug in the ground and filled with fine stone or gravel, used to collect water so that it can seep down through soil and away from structures.

Drywall Wall surfacing, usually made of gypsum, and sold in rigid sheets of varying thicknesses.

DWV (Drain-Waste-Vent) The system for removing waste and water from the home.

Eaves The portion of the roof at the bottom end of the rafters, which juts out beyond the walls of the house to create an overhang.

Efflorescence White residue composed of salts, staining masonry walls.

Escutcheon The metal plate that seals the hole in a wall out of which a pipe is run.

Face-nailing Driving a nail in directly perpendicular to the surface of the wood.

False beam A hollow member created by joining three boards to create a U-shaped channel, then finishing the exterior to make it look like a beam. Used to cover exposed pipe runs across ceilings.

Fascia The board that creates the face in front of a soffit and the end of the eaves.

Felt paper The primary sheathing used as an underlayment for roofing and siding.

Finial A decorative wood piece used to finish the top of a post.

Fire brick Special high-temperature brick used in fireplaces for its ability to withstand heat.

Fireplace insert A self-contained metal unit that sits inside a fireplace firebox, making the fireplace more efficient.

Fish tape A hooked, metal line used to pull electrical wires through walls or other cavities.

Flap sander A drill attachment consisting of a steel wheel with bristles around its edge.

Footing A concrete foundation used to support load-bearing posts or joists.

Frieze The board between the soffit and siding, either overlapping siding, or sealed to it.

Gable The triangular end of a pitched roof.

Galvanized Coated with zinc to prevent oxidation.

Gingerbread Decorative wood trim used on porches and roof edges in older homes.

Gooseneck Curving section of handrail.

Gusset Triangular brace used to reinforce the corner of frames.

Hardboard A panel made of wood products, not suitable for support.

Hawk A steel plate with a handle, used to hold compound when sealing drywall joints or for mortar when working on masonry.

Header A heavy, large beam that provides support over doors, windows, and other framed openings.

Heat gun Tool used to strip paint by blowing, creating intense heat on the surface.

Heating tape Tape with electrical wire embedded, used to warm pipes with an electrical current to keep them from freezing.

Hearth The masonry or stone footing that forms the base of a fireplace.

HEPA (High Efficiency Particulate Air) filter Special filter for removing small airbone contaminants.

House jack Extremely heavy duty jack capable of supporting and raising heavy loads, such as part of a foundation, in small increments of less than an inch.

HVAC (heating, ventilating, and air condition) The complete system for heating and cooling the house.

Isolation joint A layer of rubber, wood, steel, plastic or felt that separates a poured concrete surface from an adjoining surface such as a wall.

Jack post A strong, telescoping steel support post used to temporarily support heavy structures.

Jack rafter A short rafter piece positioned between two normal rafters or between a rafter and top plate.

Jalousie window Window with louvered glass slats that opens and closes with a crank.

Jamb The vertical sides of any building opening.

Joint compound The special puttylike material used to seal the joints between drywall and provide a bed for drywall tape.

Jointer Tool used to shape repointed joints in masonry walls.

Joist A thick horizontal framing member run on edge to support floors or roofs.

Junction box Electrical box used to contain wires where they are connected to each other or a fixture.

Kerf A thin groove cut in a piece of wood.

King stud The full-length stud that runs alongside a jack stud.

Knee wall Short, framed wall positioned between

sloping rafters and a floor.

Laminated veneer lumber (LVL) A special type of thick and durable plywood used for headers, joists, beams, and other supporting members.

Lap joint The joint formed when a notch cut out of one board fits into a recess in another board.

Latex paint The generic term for water-based paints or those that can be cleaned up with water.

Lath Thin wood stripping or metal mesh used as a base for stucco or plaster wall surfaces.

Ledger A wood member positioned horizontally to act as an attachment plate and ledge for other members.

Line level A type of bubble level that is hung on a string between two points to determine level over a significant distance.

Lintel The header over any opening created in masonry, such as a door or fireplace.

Mastic Strong versatile adhesive with the consistency of mud.

Miter The joint cut in two pieces of wood to join them at an angle.

Mortise A recess cut into a piece of wood to accommodate a fixture such as a hinge.

Mortise-and-tenon A wood joint in which one piece is cut with a recess and the other with a tab that fits the recess.

Muntin The framing piece that holds smaller panes of glass in place in a larger window or door frame.

Nail guard Steel plate attached to edge of joists to prevent accidental nailing through electrical cable.

Nail set A simple tool used to drive nail heads below the surface of wood.

Paint mitten Washable fabric mitten used for painting irregularly shaped objects such as radiators.

Particleboard Wall surfacing sheet created by mixing wood particles with resin.

Paver Any brick, concrete, or other formed piece of masonry used to line exterior bedded surfaces.

Penetrating oil Lubricant used to free frozen metal parts.

Pier A formed concrete structure that supports columns, posts, or joists, as with a deck.

Pilot hole A hole drilled to prepare a piece of wood to receive a screw and prevent splitting.

Pipe joint compound Puttylike material used to seal threaded plumbing joints.

Plinth Wood piece forming transition between door molding and baseboard molding; also the decorative wood base piece used with built-in structures such as bookshelves and cabinets.

Plumb Exactly vertical.

Prehung door A door sold in its own frame, ready to be installed in an opening.

Pressure treated lumber Finished wood members that have been impregnated with preservative under extreme pressure.

Putty stick A crayon-like piece of colored wood putty used to disguise scratches in wood.

PVA (polyvinyl acetate) Also known as "white glue," all-purpose adhesive for wood, ceramics, and other simple household repairs.

PVC (polyvinylchloride) A type of plastic used in many modern plumbing pipes.

Rabbit A cutout in the face of a piece of wood, along one edge or in the end.

Raceway An external wiring conduit through which wiring can be run along the outside of a wall.

Rebar Strong, rigid metal bars used to reinforce concrete and concrete block structures or surfaces.

Receptacle The electrical fixture including a plug outlet and box.

Reducer Special fitting that allows pipes of two different sizes to be joined.

Reverse-osmosis filter A type of undersink water filtration system that uses a member to remove impurities.

Ridge The peak that runs along the highest point of a roof.

Rip Sawing with the grain of the wood.

Riser A vertical pipe carrying water upward or the piece of a stair that stands vertical.

R-value The measure of a materials resistance to heat transfer.

Sanitary fitting A coupling that connects waste pipes and allows solid waste to move freely down the system.

Sash The part of the window that moves.

Scarf The joint made by two pieces of wood, with their ends cut at 45° and then slid together.

Scab A piece of wood cut to the profile of an existing or damage structural member, to reinforce and support the repair.

Screed A board used to remove excess concrete and level a laid surface, by drawing it along perpendicular to guide boards.

Service head The weatherproof entry point for electrical service wires coming into the house. Usually located on the roof or upper wall of the house.

Service panel The box where the electrical power enters the house and is divided into separate circuits. Can be fuse type or breakers.

Screw clamp The basic clamp, with two wood block legs connected by two long screw handles.

Shed roof A roof with a modest decline and that slopes in only one direction

Sidelite A thin vertical fixed window positioned alongside a door.

Sillcock A special outdoor faucet used to prevent frost damage.

Sister A matching piece of wood used to reinforce a post, joist, or beam.

Skim coat The final layer of plaster or surface coating on a wall; also the process of applying that coating.

Slab-on-grade A poured concrete foundation that is both the footing for the building and the first floor.

Sleeper Thin strip of wood used to support flooring over a hard surface.

Snake The common name for plumbing augers.

Soil stack The main vertical waste pipe that carries wastes from branch waste lines down to the main sewer connection.

Sole plate The bottom supporting member of a framed wall, nailed horizontally along the floor.

Soffit The board installed underneath the edge of rafters, running lengthwise, facing parallel to the ground.

Soleplate The board used as the base or bottom for a stud wall.

Spalling A flaking on masonry surfaces that is a sign of deterioration.

Splash block A cement channel used under the downspout of a gutter system to lead water away from the foundation of the home.

Stile The vertical piece of wood in a door or window sash.

Stool The thin shelf butted against a windowsill.

Story pole A long board marked with regular measurements to check height of framing, siding or other surface treatments.

Strainer The metal or plastic drain pocket below the drain hole of sink, feeding into the drain line.

Strand board A composite panel created by random wafers of thinly sliced wood sandwiched together.

Stringer The diagonal boards along the sides of stairs, that support the treads and risers. Can be open–showing the sides of the stairs–or closed.

Stub out A plumbing connection that sticks out through a wall and connects to a fixture.

Stud A vertical two by four used to frame a wall.

Subfloor Rough plywood surface used as a base for hardwood floors.

Swale A concave channel running across a slope, used to direct water running down the slope toward a foundation to another area.

Sweat soldering The process of soldering a joint by heating the metal, then melting the solder on the heated surface.

Sweep A conduit corner piece that forms a gradual, curved 90° corner, allowing wire to be pulled more easily through the conduit.

Tack cloth Sticky cloth used to remove fine dust.

Tail The lower end of a rafter.

Tailpiece The mounting post through which supply lines are run on a faucet.

Tamp A thick board or specially designed tool used to compact earth or other surfaces.

Tankless heater A type of water heater that heats water as it flows through supply pipes, not efficient for high-demand households.

Tie A separate wood or metal piece used to reinforce the joint between two members.

Toenail Nail in at an angle through one board into another board.

Top plate The top, horizontal member of a framed wall.

Torpedo level A short bubble level with a magnetic base.

Transformer The electrical device that changes the voltage in a circuit.

Trap A curved section of plumbing pipe designed to stop foul gas from entering the house.

Tripwaste A bathtub drain plug controlled by a lever in the overflow opening.

Truss plate A metal reinforcing plate attached to the corners of wooden frames and overlapping the bottom chord.

Tubing bender A coiled spring that is slipped over flexible tubing to bend it without kinking.

Underlayment A plywood or particleboard surface applied over subflooring to provide a smooth base for laying ceramic tile, resilient flooring and other sheet flooring.

UV filter A water filter installed in the main water supply line, that destroys bacteria and certain impurities with UV light.

Valley The runoff channel between two sloped roof sections.

Veneer A thin layer of wood used as decorative surfacing on other wood.

Voltage The measure of electricity under pressure.

Wainscotting Wood paneling installed on the bottom third of a wall and capped with a special molding.

Wall cap Venting fixture for the outside end of duct work run through a wall.

Water hammer A knocking in plumbing pipes.

Wattage The measure of electricity used.

Weep hole A hole drilled in a wall to allow water to seep through, such as in a basement.

Wet wall A wall constructed to contain and cover a run of plumbing pipes.

Whetstone A flat, abrasive stone used–with either water or oil–to sharpen tool edges.

Wire nut The connector used to join two wires. Rated by the size of wire they should connect.

Index

A

air conditioners 314
algae 235
angle grinders 41
asbestos 218
asphalt 235, 236

B

ballcocks 282, 283
band saws 41
baseboards
installing 205
painting 92
repairing 205
basements 209
basics
know your limitations
18
timing 18, 19
using contractors
20–1, 258
bathrooms
bathtubs 289
ceramic tiling 116,
118–19
cleaning 28, 29
facelifts 28–9
flooring 28, 138, 139
grouting 28
lighting 29
paints 215
paneling 29
selling your home 34
shower curtains 28
showers 290
splashbacks 29,
118–19
storage 29, 30
venting 317
walls 61
whirlpool bathtubs
289
windows 29
see also faucets;
plumbing
brickwork
fastening to 57
repairing and

repointing 248
building permits 18
burglar alarms 33

C

cabinets
building-in 190–1
changing doors 26,
186–7
installing 188–9
carpets
binder bars 141, 143
carpet pads 140, 143
cutting 142
foam-backed 140–1
froth foam rebond pads
140
tackless strips 142,
143
tufted carpet 142–3
wood subfloors 176
see also floors and
flooring
caulk 116
ceilings
ceiling medallions
(moldings) 202
cornices 203, 206–7
coving 206–7
paint 66
plaster moldings
202–3
see also painting walls
and ceilings
cement 60
ceramic tiling 111–25
access panels 116
around baseboards 116
around windows 125
borders 119
boxing in 116
buying tiles 112
caulking 116, 119, 124
cove base tiles 123
cutting tiles 120–1,
123
drilling 55
edging 124
estimating quantities
112

floors 116, 117, 122–3
glazed or unglazed 112
grout and grouting
115, 123, 124
methods 117
quarry tiles 123
sizes and thickness
112
splashbacks 26–7, 29,
118–19
surface preparation
116
tiling small areas
118–19
tools and materials
114–15
walls 117, 125
chair rails 205
chemicals 44
chop saws 51
circular saws 41, 50, 51
clapboard 250, 251
closets
building-in 192–3
lighting 308
clothing, protective 44,
75, 131, 132
color schemes 24, 26, 67
colorwashing 79
concrete 236
cracked edges 235
finishing the surface
241
laying 240–1
mixing 60, 240
paint 67
paths 240–1
pouring 241
stains and algae 235
surface repairs 83, 234
concrete backerboard 61
condensation 71, 214–15
contractors 20–1, 258
cornices
installing 206–7
repairing 203
coving 206–7
curtains
bathrooms 29
poles, rods, and tracks
58

D

decks
building 242–3
maintenance 230–1
dehumidifiers 215
doorbells 315
doors
casings 204
creating doorways
198–9
front doors 32, 163
hanging a new door
160–1
hardware 162
hinges 152, 161
locks 32, 162–3
painting 93
patching frames 159
patio doors 155
peephole viewers 163
planing down 153
rot 158
rotten threshold
moldings 159
security 32, 94, 162,
163
sliding doors 32,
192–3
sticking 152–3, 155
stripping 130
warping 153
weatherproofing 166
downspouts see gutters
and downspouts
drainage
DWV system 266
gardens 259–61
gutters and
downspouts 256–8
septic systems 267
soil stacks 266
vent stacks 266
wet vents 266
see also plumbing
drill sets 55
drilling 54–5, 57
drills 40
driveways
choosing a surface 236
paving 239

drop cloths 19
drywall
  cutting 63
  fastening to 57
  hanging 62–3
  joining at corners 63
  patching holes 71
  tiling over 117
  types 61

E

electricity 293–321
circuit cables 295, 298, 313
  doorbells 315
  fans 215, 316, 317
  four-way switches 296
  garage door openers 320–1
  GFCI receptacles 294, 313
  grounding system 294, 296
  high-voltage jobs 314–15
  lighting 298, 304–6, 307, 308–11, 318–19
  low-voltage jobs 315
  outdoor circuits 298–9, 318–19
  power outtages 300
  receptacles 296, 312–13, 314, 319
  running cable 313
  safety 19, 45, 68, 107, 301
  single-pole switches 296
  switches 296–7, 306–7
  testing continuity 297
  thermostats 315
  three-way switches 296, 297
  troubleshooting 300–1
  wire types 295
estimates 20

F

fans
  bathroom venting 317
  ceiling 317
  cfm (cubic feet per minute) 317
  exhaust 215
  whole-house 316–17
faucets
  ball-type faucets 280
  bathtubs 289
  cartridge faucets 280
  choosing 284
  compression faucets 280, 281
  disc faucets 280
  installing 285
  leaks 280–1
  removing old faucets 284
  types 280
  washerless 280
  washers 280, 281
  see also plumbing
fencing 224–9
  building 226–7
  disguising 25
  painting 83
  preparing the site 224
  repairing 228–9
  rot 228, 229
  setting the posts 225
  styles 224
  see also gates
filling
  cracks and holes 70–1
  woodwork 52, 91
fireplaces
  dampers 219
  fireboxes 219
  flues 216, 217, 219
  gas fireplaces 214, 216, 217, 219
  open fireplaces 216, 217
  renovating 217, 218–19
  replacing fireplace borders 220–1
  smoke detectors 33

wood-burning stoves 216, 217
  wood fireplaces 214
flashings 208, 253
floors and flooring 137–49
  bathrooms 28, 138, 139
  ceramic tiles 116, 117, 122–3
  floating wood floors 144–5
  foam underlayment 144
  installing a wood subfloor 176–7
  kitchens 26, 138
  paint 67
  parquet flooring 146–7
  sanding 132–3
  sealing 133
  self-leveling subfloors 178–9
  sheet vinyl 28, 138–9
  staining 128
  underfloor ventilation 176
  vinyl floor tiles 28, 148–9
  wood floor repairs 174–5
  see also carpets
flues 216, 217, 219
French windows 32, 93

G

garage door openers 320–1
gardens
  drainage 259–61
  furniture 25
  lighting 25, 298, 299, 318
  mirrors 25
  plant containers 25
  security 33
  selling your home 34–5
  soakaways 261
  soil improvement 259

window boxes 25
  see also decks; fencing; gates; paths; patios
gas
  fireplaces 214, 216, 217, 219
  safety 19, 27, 216
  water heaters 268, 269
gates
  making and hanging 227
  repairing 229
glues and gluing 52
gravel 60, 236
greenboard 61
grout and grouting 28, 115, 123, 124
gutters and downspouts
  access 256
  blockages 256
  repairing and replacing 257–8
  sagging gutters 256

H

heating
  steam heating systems 271
  water heaters 268–9, 272, 273
  see also fireplaces; insulation; ventilation
hinges
  cabinets 186–7
  doors 152, 161

I

insulation 212–13

J

jigsaws 41

K

kitchens appliances 26,

27, 288, 314
cabinet doors 26,
186–7
cabinets 186–9
color scheme 26
countertops 26, 189,
288
facelifts 26–7
flooring 26, 138
lighting 27, 308–9
shelving 27
sinks 288
smoke detectors 33
splashbacks 26–7,
118–19
storage 30
see also faucets;
plumbing

L

ladders and platforms
safety 45, 80–1,
246–7
security 33
stairwells 80
leaks 278–81
lighting
bathrooms 29
ceiling lights 304,
305
circuits 296–7
dimmer switches 306,
307
for DIY 45, 68
floodlights 299
fluorescent lights
308–9
indoor 24
kitchens 27, 308–9
low-voltage 298
outdoor 25, 298, 299,
318–19
recessed 305
security 32, 33, 318
switches 297, 306
three-way switches
297
track lighting 310–11
lining paper 70, 98–9
locks

doors 32, 162–3
windows 32, 164–5

M

maintenance
4-year cycle 82
decks 230–1
masonry 248
drilling 55, 57
painting 83
repointing 83, 248
repairing 248–9
masonry bolts 57
measuring and marking
39, 48–9
metalwork 83
mirrors 25, 34, 59
miter boxes 51
moisture 214
water seepage 209
wicking 208–9
see also condensation
mold and mildew 71, 83,
88, 134
moldings *see* cornices;
plaster moldings;
polyurethane
molding; wooden
molding
mortar 60, 83

N

nails and nailing 54, 56,
61

O

oiling wood 86, 129

P

paint
bathrooms 215
ceiling paint 66
climate-specific paints
66

colors 24, 67
concrete paint 67
estimating quantities
66
exterior 67
floor paint 67
indoor 66
latex 66
lead paint 131
oil-based 86
porch paint 67
primers 66, 90
rust-preventative paint
67
stucco paint 67
surface technique
paints 66
textured paints 24,
66, 76
water-based 86
painting equipment 86–7
brushes 86, 87
paint pads 74, 86
rollers 72–3
painting walls and
ceilings 24, 65–83
colorwashing 79
cutting in 73, 86
lighting during DIY
68
lining paper 70
masking fittings 68
masonry 83
paint pads 74, 86
preparation 68–71
preparing surfaces 69,
70
rag-rolling 78
repairing cracks and
holes 70–1
rolling 72–3
sponging 78–9
spray painting 75
stains and cleaning
71
stenciling 77
stripping wallpaper
69
texture painting 76
ventilation during DIY
68
painting woodwork

85–95
bare wood 88, 90–1
baseboards and
molding 92
cutting in 86
doors 93
equipment 86–7
exterior 82
fencing 83
finishes 86
knots 88, 90
preparation 88–91
priming 90
stripping wood 130–1
windows 94–5
paneling walls 29, 196–7
particleboard 61
paths
asphalt 235
concrete 240–1
see also paved areas
patios
choosing hard surface
236
decorating 25
excavating 237
outlining 236
planning 236–7
see also paved areas
paved areas
cracked edges 235
laying pavers 238–9
leveling the
foundation 237
planning 237
replacing slabs 234
stains and algae 235
see also asphalt;
concrete; patios
picture rails 205
pictures, hanging 59
pipes
boxing in 196–7
insulating 213
leaks 278–9
soldering 287
see also gutters and
downspouts;
plumbing
plaster moldings 202–3
plaster walls, tiling over
117

platforms 80
plumbing 263–91
   ballcocks 282, 283
   bathtubs 289
   clogs 276–7
   compression joints 279
   flapper valves 283
   flare fittings 279
   float valves 282–3
   hose bib valves 271
   hot water troubleshooting 272–3
   kitchen appliances 288
   leaking faucets 280–1
   leaks in pipes 278–9
   pipe alterations 285, 286–7
   replacing faucets 284–5
   showers 290
   shutoff valves 265, 270, 271
   sinks 288
   soldering 287
   steam heating systems 271
   toilets 282–3
   turning off the water 270
   waste pipes 277, 287, 289
   water filters 291
   water heaters 268–9, 272, 273
   water sources 264–5
   see also drainage; faucets
pointing 248
polyurethane molding 203
power planers 41
preserving outdoor woodwork 83, 86, 134–5
primer 90
propane torches 131

Q
quarry tiles 123
quotes 20

R
rag-rolling 78
rolling 72–3
roofs
   access 246–7, 256
   patching blisters 252
   repairing flashings 253
   repairing flat roofs 252–3
   repairing shingles 251
   working on 247
   see also gutters and downspouts
rot 158, 159, 228, 229
routers 41

S
safety 18
   chemicals 44
   drilling and screwing 55, 57
   electricity 19, 45, 68, 107, 301
   fatigue 42
   gas 19, 27, 216
   heat strippers 131
   ladders and platforms 45, 80–1, 246–7
   lead paint 131
   power tools 40, 44, 45
   propane torches 131
   protective clothing 44, 75, 131, 132
   sanding 132, 133
   scaffold towers 246, 247
   ventilation 42, 44, 68, 75
   water supply 270

sand 60
sanders 41, 132, 133
sanding floors 132–3
sawing timber 50–1
saws 39, 40, 41, 50, 51
scaffolding 81, 246, 247
screwing 54–5
screws 55, 56, 61
sealing floors 133
security 21, 32–3
   burglar alarms 33
   doors 32, 94, 162, 163
   ladders and tools 21, 33
   lighting 32, 33, 318
   smoke detectors 33
   windows 32, 94, 154, 164–5
self-leveling compound 178, 179
selling your home 34–5
sheet paneling 197
sheetrock 61
shellac 86, 129
shelving
   adjustable 182–3
   built-in 184–5
   disguising 31
   kitchens 27
shingles 250, 251
showers
   curtains 28
   improving performance 290
   installing shower heads 290
   walls 61
siding 250–1
smoke detectors 33
soakaways 261
soldering pipes 287
spackle 70
splashbacks 26–7, 29, 118–19
sponging 78–9
spray guns 75, 135
staining and varnishing 127–35
   drawers 128
   oiling and waxing wood 86, 129

preparation 91, 128
sanding floors 132–3
sealing floors 133
staining floors 128
stripping wood 130–1
   testing the stain 128
   varnishing 91, 129, 133
stains and cleaning 28, 29, 71, 235
staircase repairs
   balusters (spindles) 172, 173
   banisters 172–3
   creaking 170
   handrails 172, 173
   newel posts 173
stairs 170–1
stairwells, access to 80
stenciling 77
storage 29, 30–1, 181
   DIY tools and materials 42–3
   see also cabinets; closets; shelving
stripping guns 131
stucco 248
   paint 67
   repairing 83, 249

T
tiles
   quarry 123
   vinyl floor 28, 148–9
   see also ceramic tiling
toilets, repairing 282–3
tools and materials 37–45
   do's and don'ts 38, 40
   hand tools 38–9
   painting equipment 72–3, 74, 86–7
   power tools 40–1, 44, 45, 131, 295
   renting 18, 40, 41, 114, 132
   safety 40, 44–5, 55, 57, 128, 131, 133
   sanders 41, 132, 133
   security 33

storage 42–3
strippers 130–1
tiling equipment
114–15
wallpapering
equipment 102–3
see also clothing,
protective; ladders
and platforms
TSP cleaners 71, 235

V

varnishes 86, 128
polyurethane 86, 129,
133
shellac 86, 129
spar 129
varnishing
applying 129, 133
preparation 91
stripping wood 130–1
ventilation and
condensation 214–15
bathrooms 317
during DIY 42, 68, 75
fans 215, 316–17
fireplaces 214,
216–17
underfloor 176
windows 166, 214
vinyl
sheet vinyl 28, 138–9
siding 250
vinyl floor tiles 28,
148–9

W

wall anchors 56, 57
wallpapering 97–109
adhesive 101
arches 106
around radiators 106
around switches and
fittings 107
around windows 106,
107
borders 108–9
buying wallpaper

100, 101
cornering 105
equipment 102–3
estimating 100, 101
hanging 104–5
lining walls 98–9
order of work 101
paste 101
pasting and folding
104
preparation 98
problem areas 106–7
stripping paper 69,
98
types of paper 99,
100
walls (exterior)
access 81, 246–7
fastening to 56–7
repointing 83, 248
repairing masonry
248–9
siding 250–1
walls (interior)
building partition
walls 200–1
ceramic tiles 117, 125
creating doorways
198–9
drywall 61
fastening to 56–9,
182–3
lining paper 70, 98–9
loadbearing 198
moldings 202
paneling 29, 196–7
removing partition
walls 198
repairing cracks and
holes 70–1
stains and cleaning
71
surface preparation
69, 70
uneven walls 24
see also painting walls
and ceilings;
wallpapering
water
conditioning 264
filters 291
leaks 278–81

municipal system
264, 265
pressure 264
shutoff valves 265,
270, 271
turning off 270
wells 264, 265
see also drainage;
faucets; plumbing;
water heaters
water heaters
assessing
requirements 269,
272
electric 269, 272
gas 268, 269, 272,
273
troubleshooting
272–3
waterproofers 134
waxing wood 129
weatherproofing 166–7
windows
bathrooms 29
casement windows
94, 95, 154, 165
double-hung windows
32, 94, 95, 156–7, 165
French windows 32,
93
hardware 164
locks 32, 164–5
painting 94–5
planing down 153
reglazing 89
repairs 154–9
replacing glass 155
rot 158
sash cords 156
security 32, 94, 154,
164–5
sills 158–9
sliding windows 155
sticking 152–3, 154,
155
ventilation 166, 214
warping 153, 154
weatherproofing 166,
167
wood filler 90, 91
wood shakes 250
wood stain 86, 128, 134

wood toners 134
wooden molding
installing 204, 205
mitering 51
painting 92
repairing 204–5
woodwork
cutting 50–1
drilling 54–5
exterior 82, 83, 86,
91, 134–5, 158
filling 52, 91
finishes 86
gluing 52
joints 53
knots 88, 90
measuring and
marking 48–9
mitering 51
nailing 54
oiling 86, 129
preservation 134–5
rot 158–9, 228, 229
sawing 50–1
screwing 54–5
sealing 83
squaring up 48–9
stripping 130–1
waxing 129
see also fencing;
painting woodwork;
staining and
varnishing
workbenches 42

Acknowledgments

Author's acknowledgments

I would like to thank Mike Trier, Edward Horton, Chris Peterson, Christine Heilman, Nich Hills, and Judy Forvargue for their sterling support, my wife Kate for holding the children at bay during my long hours in front of the computer, and Nicki Gault and Jerry Udall for their invaluable help during the completion of the project.

Publisher's Acknowledgments

Dorling Kindersley would like to thank the following people for their contribution to this project: Neal Cobourne for jacket design, Beth Apple for jacket text, and Melanie Simmonds for picture library research.

Packager's Acknowledgments

M-Press would like to thank Mike Trier for planning and commisioning, Edward Horton for project management, Jerry Udall and Robert Bennet for design, Nicki Gault and Ieva Augustaityte for picture research, Ed Herridge, Nich Hills, David Preston, Harriet Williams, and Judy Forvargue for editiorial assistance and to Chris Peterson of Blue Steel Communications NYC for his expert consultancy. A big thank you also to Jeff Carroll and Darius Valaitis in our photographic studio, to our illustrators – Andy Green, Patrick Mulray, Peter Bull, Rob Garrard, Steve Cross, Ian Palmer, and Robert Farnworth – and to Caroline Hunt and Heather McCarry at DK.

Photo Library; 178r: DIY Photo Library; 179l: DIY Photo Library; 179r: DIY Photo Library; 180: Elizabeth Whiting; 182: DIY Photo Library; 192tl: DIY Photo Library; 192tc: DIY Photo Library; 192tr: DIY Photo Library; 192bl: DIY Photo Library; 192bc: DIY Photo Library; 192br: DIY Photo Library; 194: Houses & Interiors; 210: Elizabeth Whiting; 215tl: DIY Photo Library; 215cl: DIY Photo Library; 215r: DIY Photo Library; 215bl: ArtechUK Ltd.; 216: Houses & Interiors; 218: Houses & Interiors; 219l: Houses & Interiors; 219c: Houses & Interiors; 219r: Houses & Interiors; 220l: DIY Photo Library; 220c: DIY Photo Library; 220r: DIY Photo Library; 221: DIY Photo Library; 222: Stone; 225l: DIY Photo Library; 225c: DIY Photo Library; 225r: DIY Photo Library; 226l: DIY Photo Library; 226c: DIY Photo Library; 226r: DIY Photo Library; 227tl: DIY Photo Library; 227tc: DIY Photo Library; 227tr: DIY Photo Library; 232: DIY Photo Library; 239tl: DIY Photo Library; 239tr: DIY Photo Library; 239cl: DIY Photo Library; 239cr: DIY Photo Library; 239bl: DIY Photo Library; 239br: DIY Photo Library; 242: Timber Decking Association: 243: Timber Decking Association; 244: DIY Photo Library; 246: DIY Photo Library; 262t: Stone; 262b: Adobe; 274: Houses & Interiors; 292: Stone; 299: Elizabeth Whiting; 302: Elizabeth Whiting; 317: Houses & Interiors; 318: DIY Photo Library

All other images and illustrations © Dorling Kindersley

For further information see: www.dkimages.com